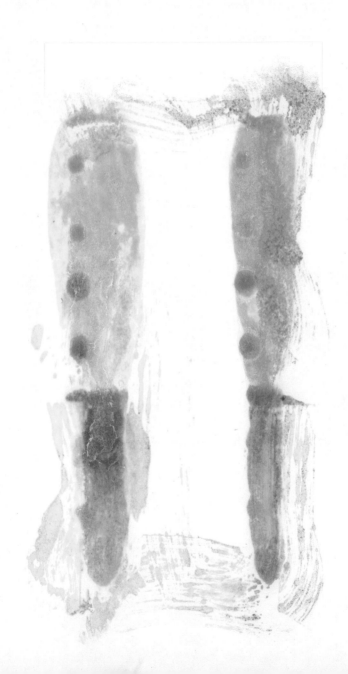

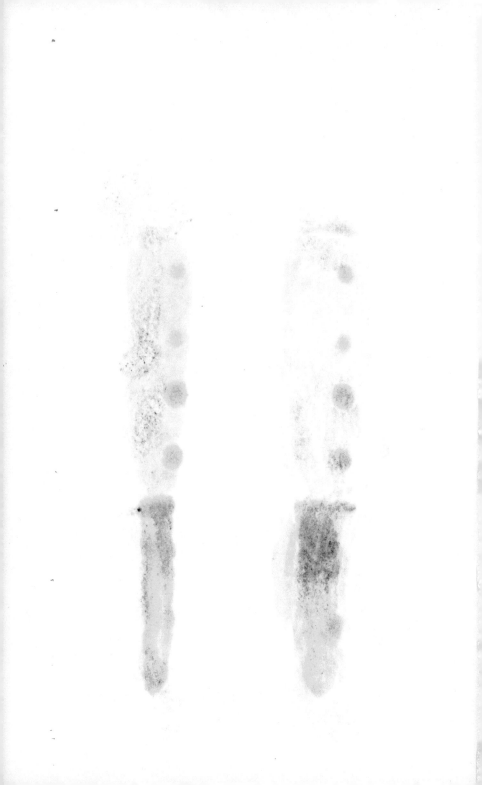

HOSTAGE
COP

HOSTAGE COP

The Story of the
New York City Police
Hostage Negotiating Team
and the Man Who
Leads It

By
Captain Frank Bolz
and
Edward Hershey

Rawson, Wade Publishers, Inc. New York

Copyright © 1979 by Francis A. Bolz and Edward Hershey
All rights reserved
Published simultaneously in Canada by McClelland and
Stewart, Ltd.
Composition by Dix Typesetting Co. Inc.,
Syracuse, New York
Printed and bound by R.R. Donnelley & Sons Co.,
Crawfordsville, Indiana
Designed by Gene Siegel
Sketches by Frank Bolz
First Edition

Library of Congress Cataloging in Publication Data

Bolz, Frank, 1930–
  Hostage cop.

  1. Bolz, Frank, 1930–   2. Police—New York (City)—
Biography. 3. New York (City). Police Dept. Hostage
Negotiating Team. I. Hershey, Edward, joint author.
II. Title.
HV7911.B64A34 1979   363.2'32   79-64199
ISBN 0-89256-102-5

For Ruth and Victoria.

The wives of most police officers and reporters wait at home and worry. While this book was written, they waited a good deal more.

Acknowledgments

The authors want to thank some of the many people who have made the New York City Police Hostage Negotiating Program as well as this book possible:

Dr. Manfred Schreiber, Police President of the Munich Police (now the Bavarian Police), for his assistance and frankness in recounting the Munich Incident, which helped in the formulation of the NYPD plan.

Assistant Chief Inspector Simon Eisdorfer, NYPD, Retired, who conceived the New York City Police Department's hostage program.

Dr. Harvey Schlossberg, Ph.D., NYPD, Retired, who put his new psychological career on the line when he and Bolz developed the negotiating techniques that are used around the world today.

Deputy Inspector Arthur Freeman, NYPD, Retired, who brought the people together and introduced Bolz to Schlossberg.

Lillian Hessian and the women at the Claddagh, for their concern and understanding.

Deputy Inspector Daniel St. John, Lieutenant Stanley Carris, Police Officer Frank Gallagher, and all of the men and women of the Emergency Service Unit, whose teamwork, knowledge, restraint, and discipline make the hostage recovery program work.

Dr. Robert Kupperman, Ph.D., Chief Scientist, U.S. State Department, for his assistance in the anti-terrorist operations.

Dr. Frank Ochberg, M.D., U.S. Mental Health Services, for his assistance on Victimology.

Chief of Detectives John Keenan, NYPD, Retired, who, contrary to tradition, kept Lieutenant Bolz in the Detective Bureau when he became Captain Bolz.

Sergeants Kenneth Bowen, John Byron, Robert Louden, and Larry Mullins, who back up and direct the team in the absence of Frank Bolz.

Freya Manston, who brought the authors together.

F. Dana Winslow, a counselor and friend.

Howard Schneider of *Newsday*, who learned to live with a bleary-eyed criminal justice reporter.

Bruce DeBoar, a courageous young man.

Contents

PART ONE

Talk Now, Shoot Later

CHAPTER ONE

A Very Special Cop

It is a master sergeant's face, the one they see from behind their own personal barricades, plain yet strong, with eyes that can be compassionately reassuring or steely firm, depending on the circumstances. It is a face that tells no lies, though at times it allows its beholder to read from it what he wishes.

Frank Bolz brought the face to the job, but twenty-four years with the New York City Police Department have done their share to temper it, just as they have helped mold the man.

If the department's computer were programmed to sift the experience and attributes of all its 24,000 officers, it probably could not produce anyone better qualified to lead the Hostage Negotiating Team than Frank Bolz: intelligent, patient, outgoing, firm, disciplined, adept.

But no machine picked Frank Bolz for the job. Things do not happen that way in the NYPD. At the end of eighteen years on the force, it was still another of Bolz's qualities that put him there, perhaps that most important attribute a New York cop with ambition can possess: timing.

In recent years, the City of New York has owned up to the fact that it is not so much one large melting pot as it is a multifaceted ethnic conglomerate, a collection of largely homogenous neighborhoods.

Straddling the city's Brooklyn–Queens border, Ridgewood was such a neighborhood when Frank Bolz was born into it in 1930, and in great measure it still remains so. Row after row of clean, modest houses, like the six-family dwelling

3

in which Frank was raised (and where his mother still rents an apartment), testify to the neat, if austere, lives of the generations of German immigrants who have inhabited Ridgewood for most of this century.

Neighborhoods like Ridgewood and nearby Maspeth and Glendale have withstood the onslaughts of urban decay much more successfully than any number of other once-fashionable places which were characterized by taller buildings with shallow roots. Some of those places "turned" almost overnight.

Ridgewood's demise will be slower and of natural causes —primarily the aspirations of its children for more and better. A visitor does not notice many youngsters on the streets these days. That is just the reverse of the way it was when Frank Bolz was growing up in the forties, when the neighborhood's large groups of teen-agers were considered a public nuisance.

They would gather on Onderdonk Avenue, just boys and girls trying to hang out. When the police came to clear the street, the kids would scatter and regroup a few minutes later on Woodward. If the cops went there, it was back to Onderdonk, a kind of mindless game that Frank and his friends suddenly tired of one afternoon. They marched to the local stationhouse where Frank Bolz, a negotiator at age fourteen, demanded that the cops find the kids a place to congregate.

If that sounds like a scene from a cornball Mickey Rooney movie, it is nonetheless true that large parts of New York were like that in those days. In Frank's youth, a couple of policemen named Eddie Dreitlein and Joe Mahoney talked to some local merchants who owned a building nearby and in a few weeks Ridgewood had its own chapter of the Police Athletic League, which met every Friday night in the donated quarters (over a pool hall, of all things). The cops and the kids played ball, ran dances, went on field trips, and produced fund-raising talent shows at the largest movie theater in Ridgewood, where Frank Bolz, the sassy kid who wasn't afraid to demand help from the police, was also poised enough to become a master of ceremonies in front of as many as four thousand people.

In many respects, Ridgewood was Middle American then. In one important respect it was not. Ridgewood was still just a five-cent train ride from Times Square, crossroads of the world. It did not offer youngsters like Frank Bolz very many luxuries, but it did provide them with a promising tandem in which to make their way—the security of a small town and the opportunity of the big city.

The son of a textiles salesman, Frank had always liked to draw, so when it came time for high school, he parted company with friends who went to nearby Grover Cleveland High. Instead, he rode the Myrtle Avenue El across Brooklyn to Brooklyn Technical High School, a prestigious all-male school that had sophisticated courses in drafting and engineering and admitted only select pupils. But Frank found it was not his sort of artwork and he transferred still farther away, to the High School of Industrial Arts on East 51st Street in Manhattan, a school which offered a commercial art curriculum to a wide variety of students. The school occupied a rundown old building that had served as a Union Army hospital almost a century earlier during the Civil War. Some students came to school in chauffeur-driven limousines. Others, like Frank, took three subway trains for a nickel, hoping they were also taking a shortcut to success on Madison Avenue.

Extracurricular activities at Industrial Arts High were somewhat limited. Frank did join the glee club, where he exhibited a sense of pitch that far outdistanced his other vocal qualities. "Stand near Bolz," the director would order any of his better singers who had a tendency to wander about the scale. "He'll keep you on the note."

At sixteen, Frank applied for working papers and landed the ultimate after-school job, jerking sodas at Wilkinson's Ice Cream Parlor on Fresh Pond Road, a street in Ridgewood that had long since outlived the body of water for which it had been named. Wilkinson's was a popular local hangout where one of the few non-Germans in the neighborhood, an Italian kid with the unlikely name of Julius, would drive the owner crazy by mounting a table and singing a cappella for as long as anyone would listen. His last name was La Rosa, and a few years later the whole country was listening to him on the Arthur Godfrey Show.

Between school and work, Frank Bolz still found time to

stick with the Police Athletic League, now a community fixture, and he especially began to notice a pretty, long-legged Ridgewood girl named Ruthie Dude who attended most of the meetings, possibly because she had noticed Frank as well. They were married after a five-year courtship.

Reality set in three months after graduation. Frank Bolz decided he was going nowhere, marching up and down Madison Avenue with his portfolio of artwork. He took a job delivering heating oil, then went to work at a dye plant that belonged to the textiles firm which employed Frank Sr. as a salesman. The plant was in Brooklyn, the parent company across the East River in Manhattan's famed garment center along Seventh Avenue. After the firm was convinced that Frank Jr. knew the business firsthand, it promoted him to the other side of the river. Like his father, Frank was a salesman, peddling velvet and velveteen to the trade.

Bolz *père et fils* were popular in the firm as well as something of a curiosity—the only two Gentiles employed there. But after three years, Frank Jr. gave it up. The major problem with his work was that he could not lie. And this was a business in which you had to lie.

"My order!" the customer would scream into the phone. "You promised it yesterday and I'm going broke waiting."

"The end of the day, tomorrow latest," the salesman would intone, knowing full well that the material would not be available for at least a week and that tomorrow would only produce another false assurance. Bolz had trouble lying, even professionally.

By 1951 Frank and Ruthie were married and he traded his order forms for a hard hat, signing on with the New York Telephone Company as a splicer's helper. It was a low-echelon job, but in a matter of months, the supervisor assured Frank, a young man like him would move right up the line.

The splicer's helper essentially stood watch, exposed to the elements and traffic on the city's streets, while the splicer worked in the relatively stable, secure climate underground. Frank stood watch through cold winters and hot summers and waited. And waited. After more than three years, he was still a splicer's helper, getting cold and hot and wet, making some side money in Ridgewood either back behind the fountain at Wilkinson's or selling gas-conversion units. He earned seven dollars for each unit he sold to the old German coal-stove holdouts of Ridgewood.

Bolz knew he had more to offer the world than ice cream, gas conversion, and splicer's help. He still found time to work with PAL in Ridgewood, and more than once the officers there had asked him, "Frank, why don't you take the test?"

"Listen," Frank told Ruthie one winter night in 1954, "I was standing out there in the cold and watching the traffic cops. They do one hour out, one hour in. Maybe it's not such a bad idea. At least I'll only be half as cold." Ruthie, who had resisted previous suggestions of a law enforcement career for her man, acquiesced this time. Frank enrolled in a civil service course, passed his exam and waited. On December 29, 1954, Susan Bolz was born. Two days later, her father started at the Police Academy. He had waited a long time for the chance. Frank Bolz graduated second in his class, winning the Police Commissioner's Trophy. The fellow who was No. 1 had the highest score registered at the Academy in twenty-seven years.

Bolz and four other rookies were assigned to the 109th Precinct in Flushing and from the very first night he began seeing some of the favoritism that is legendary on the force. Three of the others assigned there had Italian surnames, while the last man was obviously of Irish extraction, as was the sergeant making the assignments. Bolz and the three Italians arrived first and were assigned to foot patrol. Obviously the young man with the Irish name was to start his police career this frigid night in the comfort of a warm squad car.

Then the rookie with the Irish name showed up. He was a black man. The sergeant quickly readjusted his lineup—Bolz in the patrol car, the other four on foot. Maybe the NYPD was no worse than the society it was sworn to protect, but in some respects it was also clearly no better.

Frank's first permanent assignment was in Brooklyn's 80th Precinct. Along with the adjoining 79th, it covered the black ghetto of Bedford-Stuyvesant.

After a few nights on the job, Frank was told by a seasoned cop, "C'mon, kid, we'll break your cherry." The young cop was about to issue his first summons. The two men did not have to look far—a car was parked flush against a fire hydrant and Patrolman Bolz dutifully wrote the ticket. His summons book was barely back in his pocket when he heard the first siren. Down the block, smoke was pouring from a building. A sergeant just on the scene sent Frank to the corner to divert traffic. It was 10:00 p.m.

Frank was still there four hours later when a squad car pulled up. "Are you Bolz?" the cop behind the wheel demanded. "They've been looking all over for you. They thought you got mugged. What the hell are you doing out here. Your shift was up two hours ago."

"Nobody relieved me," the young patrolman explained sheepishly. The other cop shook his head. "Rookies," he muttered, making the one word sound like a dissertation.

On the way back to the stationhouse, the young cop glanced at the car he had ticketed four hours before and smiled. The summons would be the least of its owner's troubles. Firemen fighting the blaze down the street had rammed in one side and out the other to reach the hydrant.

Frank walked a beat in the 80th Precinct for a year, then was assigned a squad car and a partner, a veteran named Joe Coelln, who was a dozen years his senior. If cops consider their steady partner as second wives, then the Bolz–Coelln marriage was made in heaven, at least from Frank's standpoint.

For one thing, Joe had just come from a command shaken by a departmental probe of tow-car payoffs. He had not been involved directly, but he was close enough to those who were to walk away "with religion," as they say. In those days, there was hardly a cop in town who paid for a meal while he was wearing his uniform, but that was viewed as a minor courtesy back then. Beyond an occasional hamburger, Joe Coelln made it clear to his new, young partner they would play it very straight. It was not in the new man's character to do it any other way, but that was beside the point. Almost no cop starts out a cheater, but peer pressure can extract a large price, and more than one bad cop has traced his troubles to an early partner's assurance that "this is the way things are done here."

Joe Coelln had another trait to offer Frank Bolz—lack of ambition. A few nights into their partnership, Bolz and Coelln were patrolling their seven-block sector when they spotted a young man in an alleyway behind a grocery. When they reached him, the man had two cans of soup and one can of tomatoes. He wasn't exactly Willie Sutton, but it was an arrest, their first as a team.

"Can I take the collar?" Frank asked with some hesitation.

"Kid," Joe answered with a laugh, "you want to be a detective? You can have every collar. I'm perfectly happy doing what I'm doing out here on the street."

Nowadays, police are paid overtime in New York City when their presence at bookings, arraignments, or court hearings takes them past their normal duty hours. Then, the officer who officially took credit for the arrest and shepherded his detainee through the early stages of the judicial process did so on his own time, his only reward a "collar" credited to his record for future promotional consideration.

So Frank accompanied the young perpetrator he and Joe had caught red-handed, winding up in court the following morning. By then, he was feeling some compassion for the hapless detainee and was not upset to hear a Legal Aid Society lawyer advise the young man: "Look, just tell the judge you were hungry, that's why you took the food."

"It was all I could fit through the window," the young man answered, exhibiting a shard of truth at a very ill-timed moment.

"Sixty days," the judge said, and Frank Bolz walked into the sunlight outside Brooklyn Criminal Court, his first collar behind him, shaking his head.

The partners made seventy arrests during the next thirty months, and Joe Coelln proved true to his word. Bolz got credit for sixty-nine of them. The exception came after a fracas in a local social club. Susan was scheduled for eye surgery the next morning so Frank asked Joe to take that one collar. What neither could know then was that Joe would still be taking it years later—sued for a total of $205,000 on false arrest charges.

The plaintiffs finally "won" a three-dollar award, but Coelln never quite forgave Bolz for all the lost time in court, and from that day until his death recently, Frank never missed a chance to tell his old partner, "We made seventy collars in two-and-a-half years, and that was the one you took."

Ultimately, the two men would share credit for their seventy-first arrest, in September, 1958, and it would change their lives.

It was something of a strange sight to start with: a street fight at 4:00 A.M. at the intersection of Vanderbilt Avenue and St. Mark's Place among white youths in an overwhelmingly black neighborhood. But it was not the racial composition of the combatants that was most striking about this particular fight. It was the sheer, gruesome brutality of the scene.

One young man was standing over another, battering down again and again on his head with a trash can. A second was carving his victim up with a broken bottle. With the help of two officers who arrived at the corner at about the same time they had, Bolz and Coelln rounded up the fight's three winners. One of the victims was dead, another dying.

The city's daily newspapers (there were seven of them then) played the story big. Joe and Frank were whisked off to court, where they spent the next several days, first at booking, then arraignment, then before the grand jury where the DA was pressing for a rapid indictment, and finally back in court after it was voted.

Whenever any extraordinary arrest is made, the precinct files an "unusual" report and sends it downtown. Frank has seen plenty of them, but he will die before he forgets what was scrawled across the "unusual" that followed that particular arrest. It said, "Warrants DD . . . SPK." DD stood for Detective Division. SPK were the initials of Stephen P. Kennedy, the Police Commissioner of the City of New York. Bolz had made it and so had Coelln, who—it turned out—had exaggerated his lack of ambition after all.

"Just one thing's bothering us," a supervisor at headquarters told Coelln as he finalized the two partners' transfer to the department's elite corps. "In more than two years, how come he has sixty-nine collars and you have only one?"

A majority of the 25,000 men and women in the NYPD are police officers (or as they were called in the days before the elimination of sexist terms, patrolmen). They start that way and twenty or more years later they finish that way. Some score well on civil service exams, perform proficiently, stay out of jams, and rise to sergeant, lieutenant, even captain, and still never move into the coveted Detective Division.

Officers pass no exam to gain entrance to the division. They are chosen. And if such a blatantly arbitrary system falls victim at times to favoritism, prejudice, and caprice, it also produces at least one positive result—a sense of pride and esprit that is probably unmatched in any armed unit this side of the Green Berets. The department recognizes this phenomenon and cultivates it. Police officers carry silver-colored shields. Detectives are issued gold ones.

Once in the division, bearers of the gold shield are confronted by a whole new pecking order—first come homicide detectives, followed by specialists in other areas such as robbery, followed by those with more mundane tasks, such as laboratory analysis.

Once, after he had started to wonder whether anyone would ever notice his work on the streets of Bedford-Stuyvesant, Frank Bolz had taken a course in fingerprint technology and he had done so well with it that a detective inspector invited him to interview for a spot in the Police Laboratory.

"Are you nuts?" a lieutenant in the 80th Precinct had asked Bolz after he proudly recounted this impending opportunity. "Do you want to spend the rest of your life running around town with an eyeglass? Give it some time, you'll make it. But that's no way to get into the division. Not for you."

Frank thought it over and came to agree. Then he panicked. The interview had already been scheduled. Was it too late to say no? He made some calls.

"You want out?" a friend at Borough Command advised him. "That's easy. Inspector Cashman hates swearing. When you go for the interview, work in as many four-letter words as you can."

"Inspector," Frank found himself saying earnestly to the man behind the desk later that week, "I don't know if I can handle this shit. I mean, what the fuck, I like it out there in the fucking street, you know what I mean?"

"Son," the inspector said after a few minutes of conversation, "you belong in the street."

But now Bolz would have the gold shield on his terms. First, however, he had to finish among the top 50 percent of his group of newly made detectives at the Police Academy. That was the ticket to immediate placement in one of the precinct squads.

School had never been the most important aspect of Frank's life, but it also had never been a problem. He passed easily and gained assignment to the 81st Squad in the Bushwick section of Brooklyn, not far from the 80th. It was no coincidence. "Once you've worked in Brooklyn and survived," a superviser explained at the time, "that's just about where you can expect to be put."

A modest salary increase came with the promotion, bringing Frank close to $7,000 a year, hardly an exalted figure even back in 1958. But it was enough to send Ruthie house-hunting. She found a $13,000 palace in Queens Village, a community near the Nassau County border that will never be mistaken for a haven of luxury but did represent a step up and away from the cold-water flats of Ridgewood. "You just can't afford this house," the lawyer advised Frank and Ruth. "Look at your income and then look at the carrying charges. It just won't add up."

But Mrs. Bolz had her own form of mathematics. It included a fifty-dollar used car instead of a new model with fancy tailfins and it meant lentil soup, meat loaf, and fried kidneys for dinner, not steak or ham.

Just when the family had grown to accept such austerity, Frank, Ruthie, and the two kids arrived home one night to discover a young man waiting on their stoop. "Are you Mrs. Frank Bolz?" he asked.

"Yes," she said, somewhat concerned.

"I need your signature here and some proof of identity," he said. She had just hit the *Long Island Press* "Moneyword" game for $3,400, half a year's pay. To the Bolzes, it seemed like a million dollars.

Why not? Life in the NYPD had always seemed an awful lot like a Monopoly game anyway. You could almost reduce the opportunities and pitfalls to stops on the board: "Score well on test, advance to sergeant . . . Face departmental charges for being 'off post,' get transferred to foot patrol . . . Arrest major drug dealer, make detective . . . Your supervisor hates you, transfer to Harlem." And so forth. The pressures, politics, and pure chance of the job buffet those who aspire to climb the ladder in the department, as the tide, wind, and luck play upon a lone sailor. But, as Frank Bolz was beginning to understand, a man could always try to be a better sailor, too.

One day, in Brooklyn, Frank got a call from a detective who specialized in wiretapping for the Central Investigation Bureau in Manhattan. The fellow had "a contract" for appointment to the Brooklyn North burglary squad. But first he had to find his way into Brooklyn North. He had done his homework and discovered Frank had the telephone company experience that would qualify him for the CIB work. Would he make the switch?

Frank neither loathed nor feared the ghetto streets of Brooklyn the way some cops did, but the offer appealed to him because it would bring new contacts and add another dimension to his experience on the force. He agreed to go to the CIB, and he spent the next two years tapping people's telephones.

Rightly or wrongly, the Nixon White House, as well as some elements of the FBI, have given wiretapping a very bad name in recent years. It can be abused, of course, but then so can the service revolver in every cop's holster. Wiretapping is a tool of law enforcement made especially necessary by the criminal statutes of New York State, which demand corroborative evidence for conviction in certain kinds of arrests (such as racketeering or bribery cases) where it is usually tough enough to find one cooperative witness, let alone two. In these instances, tapes become an irrefutable witness.

The men and women who place and monitor phone taps are technicians, not swashbuckling spies, although occasionally the job does present its own kind of intrigue. Take the case of the hoodlum who had called several of his best underworld contacts to his home in the Ozone Park section of Queens for a "meet" one afternoon.

Bolz and another CIB tapper were assigned to turn the man's telephone receiver into a transmitter that could broadcast the proceedings to police stationed not far away. First they put a "trouble" on the man's line and tapped in, waiting for him to complain to Ma Bell. As soon as their target called for assistance, Frank put in a call asking the company's technicians to disregard the request. Then he and his partner appeared at the man's door, produced their New York Telephone employee identification cards, and went to work.

It was a complicated job, requiring the conversion of a two-wire receiver into a three-wire transmitter. By 4:15 P.M., with two "phone men" in his house and a group of hoodlums due there in less than an hour, the homeowner was in a state of near-frenzy.

"How long do you think it's going to take?" he would ask every few minutes. The men assured their "customer" that they were working as rapidly as possible. They finished bugging his phone with about fifteen minutes to spare and he thanked them effusively for their diligence—and tipped each man with a crisp, new ten-dollar bill.

Many of Frank's wiretapping jobs were related to the department's continuing role in the hunt for purveyors of abortion, which was illegal at that time. It was a job most CIB men ducked when they could. Much of the work was done by female detectives whom the department employed as abortion-hunters because they were considered more likely than their male counterparts to be capable of establishing a good rapport with the patients, often petrified young girls, who were needed as witnesses.

The problem for the tappers was that these female detectives usually demanded such luxuries as toilet facilities within secure reach of their listening posts, making them harder to find. You'll probably never see this on *Police Story* or *Kojak*, but most male detectives, cramped in a basement monitoring conversations, think nothing, under the circumstances, of relieving themselves on the coal pile in the far corner of the room. However, Bolz willingly accepted the jobs with women, despite their added demands, for the same reason he did a lot of other things in the NYPD: one way to move up was to do what others would not.

It was the same logic that, back in the early days with Joe Coelln in Bedford-Stuyvesant, led him to take one last turn around the sector even if it meant arriving a few seconds late at the stationhouse for the change of shifts. The street hustlers know when the shifts change and that, like everyone else, a cop is likely to want to end his tour as early as possible. More than once, Bolz and Coelln had parlayed this assumption into an arrest.

There *was* one thing Frank decided early in his career that he wanted no part of—spying on other cops. Certainly he understood it was a chore that had to fall to somebody. But the "shoeflies" of the NYPD's Internal Affairs Division made Frank flinch. Not that he was naive. The failings and foibles of the men and women who worked around him were at times painfully obvious. But these were his teammates and there was something about the mission of the IAD that ran contrary to the notion of mutual trust and interdependency, so important if cops were to survive on the streets of New York. Somebody else could go ducking for bad apples.

Thus, when two men from IAD appeared with a request for help one evening in 1964, Frank tried to evade the work. It was an installation in an apartment on Riverside Drive in Manhattan which the department suspected was to be the scene that evening of an illicit rendezvous between a cop and a narcotics peddler. "You don't need us," Bolz told the visitors. "You have your own wiretappers."

But the IAD men insisted, and Bolz and his partner, Bob Jensen, were ordered to go with them. The bug itself was relatively simple. After it was installed, the IAD men took them to dinner, and it began to dawn on the pair from CIB that, in effect, they were under house arrest—to be held in custody by their associates until the anticipated interlude of corruption on Riverside Drive had been consummated. The IAD trusted nobody.

At the table, Frank was quiet but Jensen mentioned that Bolz was near the top of the sergeant's list and was expecting an appointment imminently, which would probably entail his temporary departure from the Detective Division.

"You know, we could use a man like you in our office," one of the shoeflies told Frank. "We could arrange it."

Bolz tore off a piece of bread and stared across the table. "Before I'd work for Sidney Cooper [the head of IAD], I'd rather swing a bat in the 79th," he snapped.

A strange thing happened the next week. Frank Bolz made sergeant—and he was assigned to the 79th Precinct. He'll never know if the conversation and the assignment were mere coincidence.

Life in the 79th, the heart of Bedford-Stuyvesant, could be dangerous for a cop, but more often it was depressing and sometimes even shocking. There was the night two brothers took turns slashing at each other with the same linoleum knife —87 stitches to close the wounds of one, 149 for the other— and then they refused to press charges. And the time a man staggered into the stationhouse, screaming, "She cut my prick off!" He put his sex organ on the desk and dropped to the floor, dead, a moment before his attacker ran in after him. And then there was the time a German shepherd raped a three-year-old girl. At the hospital that night, her grandfather looked at Sergeant Frank Bolz and said with sincerity: "That dog cost me a lot of money. I ain't going to shoot that dog."

But for all the gore and potential danger, Brooklyn at least proved to be an interesting place as well. And Bolz was progressing. Rated No. 1 among the precinct's sergeants, he was put in charge of plainclothesmen and officer training, an obvious boost to his hopes of landing a spot as a supervisor back in the Detective Division. Then, suddenly one day in 1965, he was transferred to the 111th Precinct in Bayside.

The 111th is rated among the prized places to work in the city because it is relatively crime-free and provides the vast number of Queens and Long Island residents on the force with a short ride to work each day. In fact, Frank and Ruthie had just moved to Roslyn, Long Island, not fifteen minutes from the 111th.

Still, the assignment was upsetting. The Police Commissioner, Vincent Broderick, had just announced an experimental program involving the deployment of one-man patrol cars in quiet areas of the city. Frank was a guinea pig. Every night, he would drive the suburb-like streets of eastern Queens, logging 120 miles or more a night. Little more, nothing less, just drive, drive, drive. Five months later, he had talked his way back to Brooklyn, filled with a new appreciation for it. The urban blight never looked more beautiful to anybody.

In November, 1967, Sergeant Bolz became Detective Sergeant Bolz. By then, Frank had already scored well on the test for lieutenant, a position he attained thirteen months later. That meant more money and responsibility as well as another return to the uniformed force. After five months of nondescript missions in various precincts in Manhattan, there was a call from headquarters. Assistant Chief Inspector Harry Taylor wanted to see him the following day.

That evening, Ruthie took a strange call at home. "Before Frank goes for the interview," the man at the other end said, "tell him to meet me at Center and Broome Streets. And tell him not to call me back."

It was a restless night. Why all the secrecy? Was some kind of investigation underway? Frank met his caller the next morning and his relief was instant. All his friend wanted to do was tip him to the offer that awaited him at headquarters: the opportunity to direct the new Stakeout Squad. His informant explained the position and told Frank he had been selected very carefully. "Take it," he advised.

What followed a few minutes later was one of the shortest interviews Frank could have imagined.

"Do you know why you're here?" Taylor asked.

"I have a little bit of an idea," his visitor responded.

"Do you want the job," Taylor snapped.

"Yes," Frank said.

"Sit down," Taylor replied.

The idea was to organize a cadre of ice-veined cops who would don bulletproof vests and sit in the rear of selected stores, a shotgun trained on the front counter. The locations were likely stick-up targets. Day after day, the man on the stakeout would be expected to sit, poised and silent, waiting for a robbery. If it happened, he was to identify himself and order the intruder to disarm. Any response but immediate capitulation would be met with a shotgun blast.

Frank established the squad and was rewarded, after five months of its operation, with another gold shield as head of a special undercover unit in the Detective Division. Ultimately, he was more than grateful that he had moved on. The Stakeout Squad was disbanded after three controversial years, attacked by its detractors as a de facto version of capital punishment without a trial. It did not help the squad's image that, in an era rife with racial tension on the city's streets, every one of the twenty-four presumed bandits killed by stakeout cops was either black or Hispanic.

Not that Bolz's new mission lacked some unnerving features of its own. He was asked to recruit a dozen young, streetwise cops to infiltrate the netherworld of New York, the fringes of the mob, the prostitution industry, narcotics trafficking, and street crime. What the NYPD envisioned for this group were marginal members of the force, perhaps men who had barely passed the background investigation and could be plucked out of the Police Academy after only a few days there. It was most important for their own safety that they not respond as a police officer would in any given situation.

Wherever Detective Lieutenant Frank Bolz went during the ensuing thirty months, on duty or off, his mind was preoccupied with his crew of undercover agents. For security's sake, he and his sergeant, Jim Kelly, were their sole link to the force. He would cash and deposit their paychecks, meet them at predetermined locations for debriefings, and try to check on the whereabouts of any man who failed to call in at the appointed time.

For the men in his unit, the assignment meant total immersion. One of them turned to an avocation of his youth—he became a pool shark, by all reports as successful a hustler as New York's poolrooms have ever known. Another sat on street corners day after day hawking bogus perfume in mislabeled bottles. Another, somewhat of a dilettante to start with, had joined the force on a lark and had eased nicely into the role of a jet-setter. He went to the right parties and fed the

NYPD a continuous flow of information about the sleazy side of the Beautiful (if unsuspecting) People. That particular operative was also providing the city's taxpayers with quite a bargain, spending sums far in excess of his police officer's salary as he flitted about on the job just for the fun of it.

Of course, most of the undercover action was concentrated at the other end of the city's economic spectrum. And not all of it always developed exactly as planned. There was the time, for example, when Frank arranged to have one of his troops committed to the Queens House of Detention in the hope that he could elicit information about a case of suspected arson from another inmate there.

Aside from Frank and his superiors, the only person who knew the "inmate" to be an impostor was the jail warden. The undercover agent had been carefully fitted with an alleged crime that would place him near his target on a tier of cells reserved for serious felony cases. He met the man and wormed his way into the target's good graces before finally broaching the subject—offering to trade legal opinions on the charges facing each of them.

But a third man was listening to the conversation. "Listen," he advised the pigeon, "never discuss your case with nobody—not him, not me, nobody. You never know who's a cop!"

The advisor was Willie Sutton. Yes, *the* Willie Sutton, transported to the jail from an upstate prison shortly before his eventual parole on a writ application he had filed. Whether Sutton had sized up the undercover cop, had been tipped somehow, or was merely offering the sage counsel of a veteran jailhouse lawyer, the incident had certainly short-circuited the mission.

Bolz decided to pull his man out. But it was not that simple. When he notified the warden that the agent could be freed, the warden responded sheepishly that the man could not be found anywhere in the facility. For an anxious twenty-four hours, the labyrinthian New York City Corrections Department searched for him, while Frank grew increasingly despondent over the likelihood that the cop had been "made" and done away with.

Then came the good news. He had merely been "misplaced, lost in the system'' and inadvertently transferred to Rikers Island with a group of other inmates. ''It happens all the time,'' the warden said, not so reassuringly.

The following morning, with an assistant district attorney and a defense lawyer friend of Frank's named Walter Crowley playing their roles, the undercover cop was to be released. The defense would move for dismissal in Queens Criminal Court and the prosecutor would concur.

But it was not over yet. ''Wait a minute,'' said the judge, who was not in on the deal. ''What's going on here?''

Rumors of case-fixing were rife and, before his very eyes, a city judge was watching both sides agree to drop serious felony charges against a defendant. He ordered the ersatz inmate back to jail and summoned both sides to his chambers for questioning.

''Who are *you?*'' the judge demanded when Frank joined the group. When he was told, the judge exploded. Why hadn't he been informed of the ruse? Bolz tried diplomacy. ''Your Honor,'' he said, ''we always operate on the theory that the fewer people who know the better.'' Finally, the undercover man was returned to court and released.

For more than two years, Bolz shepherded his flock into and out of such escapades, losing nary a one and helping to develop the kind of information that led to a number of quality arrests. Then, as it so often does in the NYPD, departmental politics intervened. As part of an overall reorganization, spurred by a personal rivalry between two high commanders, the Central Intelligence Bureau of the Detective Division was merged into the separate Intelligence Division. Bolz was unceremoniously ''flopped'' into the Fourth Robbery Squad in Manhattan.

Almost immediately, he was dispatched for one, then another special assignment. The first was the investigation of one of a series of ambush attacks on city police in the early seventies, all as pointless as they were brazen, this one the gunning down of a pair of cops named Curry and Binetti.

For six months, working twelve hours on, twelve off, Bolz helped direct an investigation that led to arrests. In the interim, he managed to achieve another milestone, the culmination of a thirteen-year off-hours effort: a bachelor's degree in police science from the John Jay College of the City University of New York. He had come a long way from scooping vanilla ice cream and peddling gas stove converters.

After the Curry–Binetti case, Bolz spent another six months on the frustrating and ultimately fruitless probe of a Broadway producer's murder. The police came to believe they knew the culprit's identity. Perhaps someday they'll be able to prove it. After that, he returned to Brooklyn, this time in the 90th Precinct, which offered its share of mean streets and something else, Williamsburg, home of many of the city's Orthodox Jewish sects.

A German-American lieutenant amid the bearded, fur-hatted Hassidim of Williamsburg?

Some years earlier, Bolz had been one of the founders of the Steuben Association, a social and cultural organization intended for police officers of German parentage and named for the German general who helped the colonies fight the Revolution. At the first meeting, several of the organizers stressed to other charter members the importance of demonstrating to the rest of the force that this was not some sort of neo-Nazi Bund group.

"That's all well and good," one cop said from the floor, "but by the same token, we better be sure we don't end up with any Hebes in here."

There was a hush and then Frank Bolz stood to respond. Anyone, he said, including any officer of Jewish descent, would be welcomed proudly, he declared, as long as he was interested in pursuing his Germanic heritage.

The anti-Semite's stand gathered no support and he stalked from the room. It was only then that a man named Licht, a full inspector whose rank was the highest in the room, stood to speak. "I am proud to be a German," Inspector Licht said. "And I am proud to be a Jew." Every other mouth in the hall dropped open. Nobody had known. Ironically, the inspector did ultimately take some heat for his enthusiastic participation in the Steuben group—from Shomrim, the Jewish officers' organization.

In Williamsburg, Frank tried to work with leaders from

all the diverse cultures within the 90th Precinct—Jews, blacks, and Hispanics as well as Irish and Italo-Americans.

He was taken aback just once; after the arrest of a Hassidic woman following a probe that included close cooperation with the local Orthodox leaders, a rabbi thanked Bolz and added: "You know, of course, that after she is through with your system of justice, we are going to have to stone her to death." Frank assumed, somewhat uneasily, that he was being teased.

Early in 1972, Bolz was made training officer for the Brooklyn North area detectives. Then, in still another of the seemingly ceaseless series of shakeups within the division, the squad system was sacked, replaced by areawide specialists assigned to pursue specific kinds of crimes.

Mayor John Lindsay's Police Commissioner, Pat Murphy, said the specialization would breed expertise and the larger jurisdictions would eliminate the opportunity for graft, the burning issue in the city because of the headlined revelations of widespread police corruption emanating from testimony by Frank Serpico and others before the Knapp Commission. The idea was to lessen the likelihood that a local detective could press storekeepers, street pushers, or pimps in his immediate area to pay him off.

In Brooklyn North, the commanders assigned to lead the various specialty squads met one day to draw personnel from a common pool—a sort of sports-style draft of talent. The next day, Frank was called into area headquarters and asked to temporarily head up the Brooklyn North Robbery Squad. There *was* one catch. The commander was in the hospital and nobody had "drafted" any detectives for the squad the day before. Bolz would have to make do with those who were not chosen by the others.

Almost immediately, Bolz's crew picked up a likely nickname—"The Dirty Dozen." For the next five months, the squad of detectives nobody wanted roared through the streets of Bedford–Stuyvesant, Brownsville, Bushwick, Williamsburg, Greenpoint, and the like, hunting armed robbers and often reduced to confronting the enemy on his own terms. Before a major operation was undertaken, Frank would be certain that he checked a NYPD-issue shotgun out of area headquarters. Every one of his men already had a shotgun, and lots of other pieces of street artillery that were as necessary as they were unauthorized in an area when a .38-caliber sidearm could do a man only so much good. The official shotgun would "cover" any man forced to employ more than his service revolver in an exchange of fire.

When the permanent squad commander returned to duty, Bolz was sent to Brooklyn Borough Command to organize training, an assignment that promised to provide him a well-deserved respite after a spring and summer on the streets. But something that was happening thousands of miles across the Atlantic would intervene.

Barely a year after inmates at an upstate prison called Attica had seized thirty-nine hostages, a band of Palestinian terrorists captured a dozen Israeli athletes at the Munich Olympics. Both sieges had ended in bloody police assaults that left captors and victims alike dead. Pat Murphy let out the word: New York's Finest needed a hostage program. Murphy's special operations chief, Simon Eisdorfer, asked various commands to provide personnel for such a project. Nobody from the Chief of Detectives' own "palace guard" stationed at police headquarters was interested in trekking all the way to Brooklyn. And in Brooklyn itself, nobody expressed much interest until Detective Lieutenant Frank Bolz, ever the one to seize an opportunity, volunteered.

At the meeting, Bolz met one of the most unusual men on the force, a licensed clinical psychologist named Harvey Schlossberg. The two of them, along with several men from the Emergency Service Division, were asked to devise a training program for hostage negotiations. As usual in the days of the Lindsay administration, the event had already been announced in a press release.

They worked for two weeks, researching material and outlining strategy, and then began to disseminate what they had assimilated to groups of ranking officers who had been transported to an old hangar at Floyd Bennett Field on Brooklyn's ocean shore. By Christmas, the future of the effort was in some doubt. In theory, the newly trained officers were to return to their commands to impart what they had learned to subcommanders, and so the short course in hostage situations would eventually trickle down through the force. Like so many other good ideas pigeonholed for lack of time, money, or resolve, the notion of a specially trained team of officers on hand to deal with desperate hostage-holders seemed to fade faster than the ink on the press releases that had ballyhooed the program just four months before.

Then, at dusk on January 19, 1973, four gunmen entered John and Al's Sporting Goods Shop on Broadway in Williamsburg and announced a holdup. One of the store's proprietors pressed a silent alarm and police responded. Inside, the quartet of thugs was trapped but in possession of enough firearms and ammunition from the store's own stock to hold off a small army. Within minutes, one police officer, Steve Gilroy, was lying on Broadway, dead, and two others were wounded.

The siege at John and Al's would last forty-seven hours. During most of that time, Frank Bolz and Harvey Schlossberg would watch, somewhat helplessly, explaining to one department official after another that there *was* no crack team of trained hostage negotiators, just the outline of a four-week short course on the subject.

And when the siege finally ended, a new chapter in the history of the NYPD had begun. The force *would* have such a crack team, and Detective Lieutenant Frank Bolz, Jr., who had been preparing for his new role effectively if inadvertently for eighteen years, would command it.

CHAPTER TWO

Thirty-Three Hours to Freedom

From the start of the program in the fall of 1972, Harvey Schlossberg and Frank Bolz had helped develop a guide for handling hostage situations and had lectured to inspectors, captains, lower superior officers in command of patrol units, and all members of the Emergency Services Division—the cops responsible for containing sieges as well as ending them, with deadly force if necessary. Bolz, Schlossberg, and Captain Arthur Freeman, the initial hostage training coordinator, agreed that the idea was to establish procedures and familiarize key personnel with them.

The more they researched, debated, and lectured on the techniques of hostage negotiation, the more certain Bolz and Schlossberg became that the mission would require more than a series of lectures. A special unit had to be created to respond to terrorism. But they also understood that certain philosophical and political realities made the chartering of such a group unlikely. Philosophically, the NYPD operated on the theory that each of its 26,000 members should have the ability and training to handle difficult situations. Specialization existed but was discouraged. Politically, any new unit within the department's hierarchy would be viewed as a plum—a sinecure of power, prestige, security—and those in any bureaucracy who are already enjoying the benefits of such a position are traditionally loathe to share the wealth. Indeed, Schlossberg's growing reputation as the psychologist/cop had made him something of a pariah. And Bolz had not been exactly handpicked for the job either.

But Bolz and Schlossberg never had to lobby for a special unit. The John and Al's case did it for them.

John and Al's Sporting Goods Store was located under an elevated train line on New York City's other Broadway—a commercial street in a decaying section of Williamsburg in Brooklyn. Like the legendary Lower East Side across the East River in Manhattan, Williamsburg was an early twentieth-century stepping-stone neighborhood for immigrants. And, also like the Lower East Side, Williamsburg never quite made it out of the Depression.

The owners of the store were not exactly blind to the hazards of doing business in such an atmosphere. When four armed men entered the store at 5:30 on a Friday evening in January, 1973, Samuel Rosenblum, an owner, pushed a silent alarm. It took only three minutes for the first radio patrol car to respond, but the officers were spotted from inside. One of the thugs ordered Rosenblum to lock the door and to motion to officers Henry Lik and John Brady that the store was closed.

Lik and Brady knew their terrain too well to buy that. John and Al's never closed until 7:00 P.M. They backed away and awaited reinforcements. Within minutes, the street was filled with police and the four holdup men were trapped. But so, in turn, were customers and employees of the store. At 7:55, the gunmen made a move, emerging from a side door with Rosenblum in front of them as a shield. The cops stood their ground. Suddenly there was the flash of gunfire. Officer Jose Adorno fell, wounded in the arm; the gunmen retreated back in the store, one of them wounded, and Rosenblum ran to safety.

Flak-vested cops from the Emergency Service Division arrived and began to set up a containment perimeter. Then at 8:10, gunfire erupted again. Officer Stephen Gilroy, who had been crouched behind a train stanchion, was struck in the head. When another officer, Frank Carpenter, tried to drive his squad car between the store and Gilroy's motionless body, he, too, was hit, in the leg.

Commanders at the scene suddenly found themselves in a war zone. Several cops were pinned down in the street, and now both Gilroy and Carpenter were lying in the line of fire. The police opened a barrage, distracting the gunmen and sending them for cover long enough to allow several courageous cops to race in and carry the two wounded officers away. For Gilroy, it was already too late. He had been killed.

With Rosenblum out of the store, nine men and three women customers, an employee, and the other owner remained as hostages. Assistant Chief Inspector Michael Lonergan and Deputy Chief Inspector Simon Eisdorfer were on the scene now and they decided that there was no need for any sudden moves. They ordered all police to cease firing, set up police barriers to eliminate street traffic, ordered nonessential police away from the immediate area, ordered extra police for crowd control, arranged for power to be shut off and trains routed away from the overhead train tracks, and called for the department's armored personnel carrier.

A field headquarters was established at a real estate office down the block from John and Al's. The gunmen had ripped the phones out, hindering any communication. Shortly after the siege began, in response to an invitation from police via bullhorn, a twenty-year-old woman was released to act as go-between. "We mean business," she quoted the gunmen as saying, "and we'll kill all the hostages unless we're allowed to escape." She also told police that the wounded gunman was lying on the floor, apparently in distress. That was confirmed an hour later, when one of the gunmen shouted for police to send a doctor into the store. The police replied, by bullhorn, that medical care would follow any surrender.

The armored car arrived at 9:05 and was employed to rescue six officers and sixteen civilians who would otherwise have had to escape through the line of fire. And was there ever fire! The three ambulatory gunmen had an almost limitless supply of weapons and ammunition from the store's stock. Infuriated by the presence of the bulletproofed vehicle, they tested it with round after round. Each shell missed or bounced harmlessly away, and the Emergency Service police maintained their discipline, discharging not a single shot.

Bolz and Schlossberg had gone to the scene on their own and were doing their best to advise those in command. But their involvement was limited because the negotiation program had been a paper operation, a school for hostage situations out at Floyd Bennett Field. They had nothing in the way of practical aid to offer except their opinions. And they advised police to do what was being done—talk, if possible, and wait. Police had numbers and positions. As the hours flew by and no one was hurt, the odds shifted slowly but inexorably in their favor.

At 4:00 A.M. Saturday, a Baptist minister arrived and asked if he could enter the store with police permission. He was not admitted. But after three Muslim ministers came, at police invitation, one *was* allowed inside. Five minutes later, he returned. The gunmen had been unswayed by his exhortations, he told police. "They said they were willing to die for Allah."

The ministers had been able to tell police what they already suspected—that these were no ordinary stick-up artists, but rather a group of militaristic Muslims who had entered John and Al's seeking neither money nor weapons for future jobs, but rather a revolutionary arsenal of firepower. This would make the police mission that much harder. Seasoned criminals might recognize a lost cause and begin bargaining for something. But religious zealots? Who knew what was on these men's minds?

It had been a long, cold night, and as dawn broke, police confronted another problem. The gunmen were black. Most of the assault force was white. The neighborhood, generally hostile to police in any event, might rise up against the police. To offset such a possibility, black and Hispanic officers were brought in from various commands to handle the crowd, squelching rumors, explaining police strategy, stressing that the four men would not be hurt and that, despite the fact that one of their own had already died, police were seeking a peaceful solution. Muslim ministers, including the man who had appealed in person for a surrender, also tried to calm the neighborhood.

In late morning, first a bullhorn and then a walkie-talkie were placed in front of the store, where they were picked up by hostages. But eventually, each was tossed back outside. Two attorneys with ties to radical defendants arrived and were briefed and then driven up to the store in the armored car, where they shouted for the gunmen to accept the walkie-talkie so communications could begin. Shortly after 3:00 P.M., a gunman agreed to speak over the radio. He demanded food and medical supplies for his fallen comrade.

Police promised to send in food and cigarettes, but any medical aid would be held back for use as leverage in furthering bargaining. At 4:00 P.M., a black activist physician, Thomas Matthew, arrived and volunteered to go inside the store. The three gunmen were told that Matthew was at the scene and they were again urged to surrender. They said no, but that they would release one hostage and guarantee safe conduct for Matthew if the doctor would come inside.

Matthew entered at 5:00 P.M., stayed forty minutes, then left and returned at 8:00 P.M., bringing medical supplies, milk, and juice. His nurse was turned away at that time, but she was admitted at 9:40 and police sent a field telephone inside with her. The batteries on the walkie-talkies had begun to run down. It was 11:00 P.M. when Matthew finally emerged. The wounded man had regained consciousness, he said, but was dehydrated.

There was a second long, cold night for Emergency Service police; and at 7:30 Sunday morning, as if to bid the police good morning, the gunmen began firing from the store, striking a parked patrol car and some store windows across Broadway. Police brass and political leaders held a long morning session at the nearby 90th Precinct, debating whether to storm the sporting goods store. They discussed and discarded a variety of plans of attack.

The resultant loss of life was too predictable for any frontal assault, but the police thought they might be able to tunnel through the wall of an adjoining furniture store and catch the gunmen by surprise. Personnel were dispatched to survey the options available in such a plan.

What police could not know was that one of the hostages, store co-owner Jerry Riccio, was developing an inside-out version of the same plan at the same time. Riccio persuaded the three gunmen to allow him and the other remaining hostages to congregate in the corner of a second-floor balcony, where they would be out of the immediate line of fire in any possible shootout with police.

Riccio remembered that one of the walls of the balcony was actually a thin plasterboard covering a sealed staircase that had once led three flights to the roof of the building. Riccio bided his time, whispering to the others that there might be a way out. Then the moment came. Police surveying a possible entree to the furniture store were too noisy and the gunmen heard them. Fearing an immediate police assault, they raced for sniper positions to the third floor, leaving the hostages temporarily unguarded.

Riccio kicked through the plasterboard (thankful, for once, that walls are not made the way they used to be) and led the hostages up the staircase to a wall ladder and, finally, through a broken skylight. On the roof, Emergency Service officers heard the scramble up the ladder, then aimed, waited —and held fire. They had no way of knowing that it was not the gunmen who were crashing through the roof, and their discipline saved lives. Seconds later, they pulled the last of the hostages to safety and backed off—as the frustrated gunmen, realizing they had lost their hostages, fired wildly through the skylight.

It had been forty-three hours since the start of the siege. Four hours later, following the intervention of several members of the barricaded gunmen's families, the four surrendered —first one, then two others carrying the fourth man on a stretcher.

Mayor John Lindsay, Police Commissioner Patrick Murphy, and all other city and department officials were effusive in their praise of police restraint. His fellow officers had honored the memory of Stephen Gilroy in the best possible way —with a show of classic professionalism. From the time volleys were fired to give police protective cover to recover Gilroy's body Friday night until the surrender Sunday evening, police had been shot at hundreds of times and had not returned a single shot.

The special hostage training program was given its share of credit for the results. Donald Cawley, the Chief of Patrol and soon to be Police Commissioner, praised the program's attention to "criminal psychology, control of firepower, deployment of personnel, clearing areas of civilians, and transportation of hostages—much of it presented as part of simulated siege exercises."

In actuality, Cawley and the others understood they were also lucky. There had been a great deal of outstanding work during the forty-seven hours on Broadway. But much of the Williamsburg operation had simply fallen into place. They recognized as a result of what they had seen at John and Al's that the department's anti-terrorist program would be more effective when the men and women in charge of teaching the techniques were also responsible for putting them into operation. By mid-year, a full-fledged negotiating team would be recruited from the Detective Bureau, trained in negotiation and then put on notice to drop everything and report, like Minutemen, when a hostage call came.

The criminal justice system is designed to balance the rights of the accused with the safety of the innocent. If well-intentioned souls, from United States Supreme Court Justices down, have been known to disagree from time to time on the nature of the balance, at least the abstract notion is clear enough.

The mental health system, on the other hand, is considerably murkier. There, it is possible not only for someone to be adjudged a danger to himself as well as to society and locked up for his own good in the name of medical treatment, but it is also possible for someone to be released, ill-equipped to cope with life, in the name of balancing next year's state budget.

When, as so often happens, the two systems—criminal justice and mental health—come together in a single matter, the results rarely satisfy anyone.

Consider the case of Floyd Steele.

Steele was born in North Carolina in 1918 and by his eighteenth birthday he had begun to amass a criminal record —assault, vagrancy, possession of bootleg whiskey, and the like. In 1950, when he was thirty-two, he got drunk, had a fight with his wife, and beat her to death. "I hit her a little too hard and it caused the blood to rush out of her head,'' was the way he remembered it. He did time for that, and after his release in 1955 he drifted to New York and found work as a porter with the New York City Housing Authority.

Steele was always a bit slow and he drank a lot, which made him a comfortable mark for any number of people, including a variety of lady friends.

One day, in 1963, he woke up to find that one of them, a woman named Louella Moore, had spent his entire savings. He ditched her then, but she wouldn't take no for an answer and trailed him to the home of his brother-in-law. Someone had told Floyd that Louella had a gun. He didn't wait to find out. He walked into his brother-in-law's garage, picked up a rifle that was mounted there, and blew out Louella Moore's brains.

Steele was sent to Kings County Hospital for mental tests and a judge then declared him mentally incompetent to stand trial—unable to understand the nature of the charges against him or to assist in his own defense. He was shipped off to Mattewan State Hospital for the Criminally Insane and spent the next nine years there, technically a patient rather than a convict, but securely locked away in any event.

Then, in 1972, psychiatrists at Mattewan said that Floyd Steele was fit to stand trial.

It was nine years after the fact, and the Queens County District Attorney was only too happy to accept a plea of guilty to first-degree manslaughter—a charge that might well have been entirely appropriate in view of Steele's state of mind at the time he killed Miss Moore. He was sent back upstate, to the maximum-security state prison at Green Haven, ostensibly for a ten- to fifteen-year term.

But under state law, the time he spent at Mattewan had to be included in his sentence. Thus, a year later, when Steele applied for a conditional release (figured on the basis of one day's ''good time'' off for every two days served without incident) the state had no choice but to grant him one. On July 13, 1973, one month short of his fifty-sixth birthday, having spent roughly thirty-two of the previous thirty-seven years of his life in jails, prisons, and mental hospitals, Floyd Steele became a free man. His release was conditioned only on the premise that he break no more laws. There was not even a requirement that he report to a parole officer, counselor, or physician, or that he enroll in any program designed to help him readjust.

He went first to Brooklyn, where he found work as an elevator operator, and then out to Hollis, Queens, to stay with a stepniece, Peggy Dalton Kinsler, her husband, Fred, and Peggy's five-year-old daughter, Avril Letticia Kinsler, in a city housing project. Floyd was to pay twenty dollars a week toward the rent (although as time passed, Steele would claim he had paid somewhat more than that in loans to Mrs. Kinsler). He and the little girl took to each other immediately. He called her "Tisha" and, although there was no blood relationship between them, she called him "Uncle Fly."

He had a touch of diabetes and some other physical ailments and he still drank too much, but Steele's biggest potential problem was less discernible. Under the law, he had been adjudged competent to stand trial—he could perceive the charges and help in his own defense—but such a ruling was relevant merely to the *criminal justice* system. In the eyes of the *mental health* system, Floyd Steele was not much different than he had been the day he shot Louella Moore. He suffered, as he had for years, from schizophrenia.

The trouble began on a very warm June day. The way Steele would explain it later, he had been ambling down the street, thinking about going to the apartment to get out of the first heat wave of summer. There were paper bags flying at the base of the hedges, the winos' bequest to the landscape, and he idly kicked at one. When the bag didn't move, he thought that perhaps a full bottle of wine had been inadvertently discarded and bent down for a closer look. There was no bottle in the bag. There was a .357 Magnum. "Oh, my God," Steele remembered saying to himself, "somebody musta did somethin'."

Steele said he had barely turned the corner when a young man overtook him and asked, in a West Indian accent, "Didn't you pick something up a few minutes ago?"

"I picked it out of the garbage," Steele protested.

"It was mine," the man responded, "and you've got to pay for it. It will cost you sixty dollars." They settled at fifty dollars and Steele took his Magnum back to the apartment, put it in a drawer, and lay down.

It was about 4:30 in the afternoon. At dinnertime, with Fred Kinsler home from work, Steele began to ask Peggy about the money she owed him. Later, she would tell police that Floyd Steele had suggested she would work off the debt with some kindnesses toward him, although he would steadfastly deny he had any such carnal intentions. All he wanted, Steele insisted, was his money.

In any event, Fred Kinsler found the revelation that his wife had borrowed money from "Uncle Floyd" disturbing, and the couple exchanged words.

"You're so smart," she said to Steele. "You couldn't wait until you got in front of him to talk about the money!"

"I'm going to bed," Steele said.

But Fred Kinsler was starting to get the drift. "There's a lotta damn shit going on around here!" he told Steele. He accused Steele of making advances toward Peggy.

"Oh, no, nothing like that," Steele protested. "You're damn right there's a lotta shit goin' on, but it ain't my shit. She's your wife, not mine. If she runs around and cuts out on you, don't get mad at me. I seen what's going on here, but it's not my place to go tellin' anybody. I'm goin' to bed."

Those aspersions hardly cooled things. The argument continued long into the night; and, finally, sometime after midnight, the two men started grappling. Then Steele broke free, ran to his room, and came back with his newly purchased gun.

Peggy Kinsler worked as a counselor at Creedmoor State Hospital, a large mental institution nearby. She knew how to leave places in a hurry. She edged into her bedroom, quickly tied several bed sheets together, tossed them from the window, and climbed down as far as the sheets took her, then jumped, spraining her ankle. Peggy Kinsler hobbled to a phone and called the police.

Upstairs, Fred Kinsler and Floyd Steele were in the back room when the police knocked. Steele refused to open the door and Kinsler decided to make his move. He tackled Steele.

There were two shots. Kinsler, struck by the powerful weapon in the side and the neck at contact range, fell to the floor.

His five-year-old daughter wandered into the room. "What's the matter with Daddy, Uncle Fly," she asked.

"Nothin'," Steele told her. "He's just sleepin'."

The officers who first responded to the call found the door to Apartment 3B locked. Then they heard the shots.

Bolz got his call at 3:10 A.M. Calls to four other negotiators, a wake-up/good-bye kiss for Ruthie, and a glass of milk and he was out of the house in ten minutes and on his way to the Highway Unit garage on the Grand Central Parkway in Queens. Eventually, the department would reclassify Bolz and allow him to have a department car parked at his home in surburban East Meadow, Long Island, so he could speed directly to the scene of hostage situations. This was June, 1974, however, and the hostage negotiators, born out of Attica and Munich and saved by the siege of John and Al's, were still not on the map. Not for another thirty hours, at least.

Summer seemed to have beaten itself by ten days. There was no bite to the pre-dawn air, just a dewy warmth. The job was at a public housing development called the South Jamaica Houses in Hollis, one of a number of southeastern Queens communities with extensive minority populations. Some were as middle class and mobile as their suburban neighbors to the east on Long Island; others were as poor and jobless as their inner-city cousins. They had been plunked into the gaps created when the whites left faster than the blacks arrived.

The year before, a ten-year-old black child named Clifford Glover had been slain as he walked on these streets with his stepfather by a white police officer named Thomas Shea, who swore he thought the boy had turned on him with a gun. Tom Shea had been indicted for murder, but there were inconsistencies in the stepfather's account of his activities that night, and the trial had not gone well for the prosecution.

The case had gone to the jury on the evening of June 10th. There had been riots on the streets of southeastern Queens shortly after the original incident and now, early on the morning of June 11th, tension was running high. Some

black youths had attacked whites, broken store windows, and
started fires in scattered incidents. Anticipating the acquittal
of Shea, police were girding for more trouble.

When Bolz arrived at the housing project, a crowd had
gathered in the street despite the fact that it was 3:50 A.M.
Inside, up on the third floor, New York City Housing Authority Police had produced a pass key to the apartment. Two
adjoining apartments had been evacuated. Bolz and Emergency Service Division officer Reggie Toomey went up one
flight and woke up the tenants of Apartment 4B so they could
see the exact layout of the apartment below. The front door
opened into a long, narrow corridor, which in turn led to a
front room just to the left of the door; a kitchen faced the door,
with a bathroom to the right, then a bedroom adjacent to that,
from which Peggy Kinsler had escaped. The corridor ended at
the entrance to a second bedroom.

Other police interrogated Mrs. Kinsler and neighbors to
try to assemble as much information as possible. Shortly after
five o'clock, the police decided to try to open the door, first to
ascertain exactly where Steele was, whether Fred Kinsler and
his daughter, Avril, were wounded, and if communications
with the gunman could be established.

Quietly, a rope was attached to the doorknob, so the
door, which opened inward, could be slammed shut from the
hall in case of danger. Toomey inserted the key and began to
turn the lock.

"Wait a minute," Bolz whispered. "If he's anywhere
near the door, we'll be sitting ducks out here. Let's knock out
the hall lights first." The apartment itself was totally dark.

From behind him, an officer took his nightstick and
smashed the naked bulb.

"No!" Bolz counseled. "You might want to turn them
on again. Just unscrew them."

The other bulbs were unscrewed and Toomey returned
to the door. He turned the key and the door opened. Toomey
went on his hands and knees and crawled inside. Because of
the residual light from the street, Bolz could barely make out
his shadow on the floor.

Then Toomey moved to his left, down the corridor and

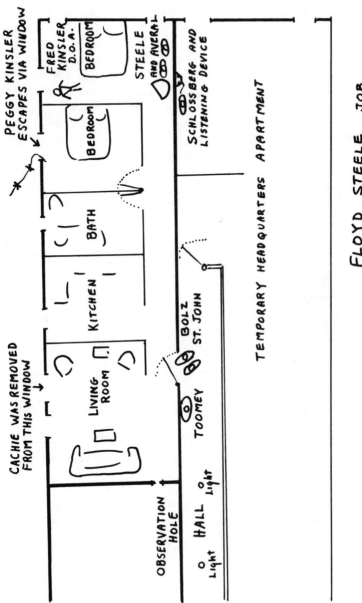

PEGGY KINSLER ESCAPES VIA WINDOW

FRED KINSLER D.O.A.

BEDROOM

STEELE

AND AVERAL

SCHLOSSBERG AND LISTENING DEVICE

BEDROOM

BATH

KITCHEN

CACHIE WAS REMOVED FROM THIS WINDOW

LIVING ROOM

TOOMEY

BOLZ ST. JOHN

TEMPORARY HEADQUARTERS APARTMENT

OBSERVATION HOLE

HALL

Light

Light

FLOYD STEELE JOB

into the kitchen. He turned around and began crawling out of the kitchen when a shot rang out—a terrible blue-white flash and a thunderous noise.

Toomey scrambled back into the hallway and Bolz slammed the door shut. Sitting in the rear bedroom at the end of the corridor, Steele had spotted movement and fired. Toomey was uninjured, but his wristwatch had been shattered. It was a thousand-to-one shot. The bullet had slammed against the face of the watch and ricocheted into the base of the door. Police looked at the one-inch by two-inch hole it left there and shook their heads. Reggie Toomey was lucky to be alive.

The police began to anticipate a lengthy vigil. They established a field headquarters in the apartment next to the Kinslers (a bit too close to the trouble, actually) and set up barricades outside the building to control the crowds and keep them out of the line of fire.

The key was still in the door, and after almost an hour Bolz nudged it open. Some months before, a friend named Gene Bree had given Bolz a couple of toy periscopes, mail order premiums Bree had discovered behind some old packing crates. Something had clicked in Bolz's mind. "For all the thousands of dollars in equipment we have," he said to himself, "I'll bet this thing will come in handy on a job." He got twenty-four of them and presented them as "graduation" presents to his first class of negotiator trainees, who used them while they were working with the department's emergency rescue vehicle, the NYPD's tank. They had renamed Bolz "Rommel" after that.

Now, edging the door open an inch or two, he inserted the periscope and, for the first time, in the light of dawn, saw Floyd Steele, sitting in the rear bedroom with five-year-old Tisha on his lap and a .357 Magnum in his hand. Just out of view, on the floor, lay the motionless body of Fred Kinsler.

Mike Lonergan, the chief of operations, was in command at the scene and, concerned that the circuslike atmosphere might turn ugly in view of the tension over the Shea trial, he told Bolz that he appreciated the containment and negotiation approach. Chief of Detectives Louis Cottell was also on the scene and somewhat less pleased. From the outset of the program, Cottell had been uncomfortable with the idea of responding to violence with conservatism and he muttered his disapproval when Bolz began his approach to Steele by addressing the gunman as "Sir."

Steele had one response for all the approaches. "Close the door!" he called out again and again, raising his Magnum into firing position each time. "Close the door." The police had replaced Bolz's periscope with a large mirror they placed in the corridor and thus they could see Steele's moves now without worrying about entering his line of fire. Yet each time Steele raised his gun, the cops watching the mirror instinctively pulled away, sometimes actually scrambling several feet from the door.

Bolz was having no success coaxing Steele into a conversation when he received word that a couple of black Housing Authority police officers had arrived who said they knew Steele and wanted to try talking to him. As it turned out, neither really knew the man. Were they seeking glory? Not exactly. Time after time, in hostage situations, Bolz would meet cops, neighbors, co-workers, even relatives, who would invent or inflate relationships with the perpetrator of a siege, more out of a desire to do some good than from any hopes of personal reward. Detective Harvey Schlossberg, the psychologist guru of the program, would identify this as still another predictable "syndrome" the hostage negotiators could expect to encounter on mission after mission.

The Housing cop advanced to the door and called out to Steele once and then a dozen times and a dozen times more, naming himself and others whom both presumably knew. But all his efforts earned him was a combat stance from Steele and the now familiar rejoinder: "Close the door!" Throughout the remainder of the ordeal, a succession of volunteers—neighbors, friends, a minister—would assure the police of their ties to Steele and try their luck at prodding him into conversation, all without success.

By noon Tuesday, with no communication from Steele and only muted, barely audible conversation picked up by the bug, the police decided to chance another approach. From the adjacent apartment, the Emergency Service Division drilled a hole in the wall at the end of the corridor, facing Steele. By sheer luck, they came out just above a bookcase with a perfect sight line into the bedroom.

What they saw through the peephole was that Steele would periodically allow Avril to wander about the room, giving them a clear shot at him. There was no question in their minds that they could take him out. He was fifty-five years old with a record of fourteen arrests, two for homicide, and he had just attempted to kill a police officer and almost certainly had killed poor Fred Kinsler. Now he was holding an innocent five-year-old child with a gun. There was every justification to shoot him down.

Outside, the crowd was thickening. An ice cream truck had pulled to a stop down the block and was doing a booming business. Neighborhood youngsters were setting off cherry bombs and other small explosives, scaring the cops, who hoped that Steele would not mistake them for police fire. And not two miles away, a jury was still deliberating the likely acquittal of Officer Thomas Shea. Lonergan himself made the decision. Word of the shooting of Floyd Steele, no matter how justifiable in any legal sense, could spread through the streets of Queens with only one message: the cops have just blown away a poor, crazy old black man. There was no way he would authorize such an act, at least not yet. Attempts to negotiate with Steele had to proceed.

From the size of the hole in the door as well as the total lack of motion from his prone shape, police assumed that Fred Kinsler was dead. They could not be 100 percent certain. Once, during a siege in the office of the Philippine ambassador in Washington, a wounded Filipino hostage lying directly in the line of fire had feigned death and signaled to police in the doorway by moving two fingers on one hand periodically over a three-hour period before the perpetrator gave up. Over the open phone line, police could hear Steele tell Avril, "Daddy's asleep, honey." They could only assume, correctly as it turned out, that Daddy would never wake up.

The police could hear voices from the back room, but they were not clear enough. Someone said that the City Department of Water Supply had just begun using a highly sensitive listening device in an effort to detect blockages and leaks in pipes. The device—two huge suitcases full of electrical gear, actually—was sent up and put in place. The flushing of a toilet two floors away sounded like a tornado followed by the sounds of sheets of toilet paper falling, one by one, down the pipe. But the voices of Steele and Avril were still blurred. The gadget had been designed for plumbers, not eavesdroppers, and after a few minutes it was abandoned.

Bolz shrugged. He picked up a glass, wet it, and placed it against the wall in the apartment police had commandeered as headquarters. From there, he heard Steele and the girl almost perfectly. The ability to improvise was clearly becoming a major asset in such situations, with toy periscopes and drinking glasses sometimes more applicable than television cameras and sonar machines.

"Tisha, we're playing a game," Bolz heard Steele say at one point. "We're playing cops and robbers with those policemen out there. Your daddy's asleep. But when he gets up later, he's going to want some cigarettes." Later on, as police negotiated to send beer and cigarettes into Steele, he would ask "for some cigarettes for Freddy, too," and Harvey Schlossberg cautioned Bolz and the others not to dismiss the request merely as play-acting for little Tisha's sake.

"It's displacement," Schlossberg explained. "He's pushed the fact that Freddy's dead completely out of his mind and he's convinced himself that Freddy's only asleep."

It was late afternoon when Steele finally accepted his first gift from police, a can of beer.

"See if he gives the kid any," Chief Harold Schryver of the Special Operations Division told the negotiators.

They rolled a can of beer not far down the corridor and also threw a handful of lollipops into the apartment. The girl walked down the corridor, picked up the beer, and returned with it to Uncle Fly. Then she went back to pick up the lollipops and Toomey made his move, grabbing her.

Avril Letticia Kinsler literally jumped out of her little sneakers, racing out of Toomey's grasp and down the hall into Steele's arms. She was afraid of the police in the hall, not her Uncle Fly. And he was incensed, for the moment, at their efforts to rescue her.

"We're just playing a game," he told her. And then, for

a long time, every time the police opened the door, he would pull the girl up by the hair on her head, point the Magnum at her and yell, "Close that door! Don't make me do anything I don't want to do! Close that door!"

Slowly, the police tried to regain his confidence. They rolled another can of beer down the hall, this time closer to Steele. This time, they sent some Kool-Aid in for the girl and again, they noted, Steele did not give her any of his beer. What they didn't know is that Schryver had arranged with a local hospital to doctor a six-pack of bottled Miller High-Life with a suppressant in the hopes of inducing drowsiness in Steele.

The hostage negotiators had discussed the possible use of drugs in food and had pretty much discarded the idea as an unpredictable, ineffective tool. Usually, drugs such as Valium must be built up over a period of time. A one-shot dosage, unless it was extremely heavy, would have no predictable effect, according to medical experts. And a dosage heavy enough to zonk the average person might become lethal for some people with a lower tolerance (not to mention a child or the unborn fetus of a pregnant woman) and might lead to severe injury or death for the very hostage police are attempting to liberate.

"Let's say you have fifteen people and you're willing to drug everybody to put the perpetrator to sleep," one physician said. "How are we going to send in an unmonitored dosage when we have no knowledge of the physical condition of anybody inside? Anesthesiologists work one-on-one and they lose patients." Nonetheless, Schryver was in command and if he ordered the beer sent in, it would be sent in.

At 8:30 P.M., Lonergan told Bolz and Schlossberg to go home for the night. Bolz had been in the building for more than seventeen hours now. About the only headway they were certain of after all that time was that the door to Apartment 3B was permanently, if barely, ajar now, with no more calls from Steele for police to shut it. "The door's broken, Floyd, it won't stay shut," Bolz had told him at one point. "We'll keep it just like this, okay?" And Steele had accepted the explanation.

Bolz drove home to East Meadow, downed a Rob Roy, and went to bed, setting his alarm for 4:00 A.M. He awoke at

3:00, after four hours sleep. He was back in Hollis at 4:00 A.M. The scene had not changed too much, although there had been one major accoustical advance and one outrageous rescue as he slept.

During the night, negotiators Al Cachie and Louis Hernandez had tried calling Steele on the phone, but he just picked up the receiver and slammed it back down. Finally, after a number of calls, he merely left the phone off the hook. That became an opening for police, who attached a sensitive amplifier to *their* phone, thus in effect bugging the apartment and giving police an opportunity to hear all the dialogue between Steele and the girl as well as between Steele and the negotiators.

There were also a couple of war stories for the police to recount. First, there was the moment when a female neighbor of Steele's was at the door, trying to engage him in discussion. Cachie, an earnest, likable black detective, prone to adventure, was backing her up. Suddenly the woman said, "Now!" and spun him around into the apartment. He wound up in the front room, to the left of the door.

Why had the woman spun Cachie inside? She thought that Steele had been distracted and that Cachie could work his way from room to room and eventually effect a capture. Oh. But did Cachie have a plan? No. Half-startled by her command to move, he had moved. In fact, Steele had observed his entrance and immediately expressed anger. Cachie was trapped inside. It took a police detail equipped with Morrissey safety belts to rescue Cachie, who crawled out of a window four floors above street level and was then lowered, foot by foot, to the street.

Then there was the matter of the doctored beer. Schryver had gone out and retrieved the beer he had arranged to have spiked with a suppressant. He walked into the apartment commandeered as a headquarters, put the six-pack in the refrigerator, and told one of the cops on duty, "Hey, you, watch that beer! Don't let anybody take it."

Several others, of lower rank, observed the scene and one said, "Just like brass, the cheap bastard. Goes out and brings back one six-pack."

Some time later, the cop guarding the refrigerator went

to the bathroom. A moment later, Reggie Toomey and two other officers, coming off a tour of duty in the hot, darkened hallway, their bulletproof vests making the humid night even more uncomfortable, entered the headquarters apartment. Toomey opened the refrigerator door and could not believe his good fortune. Faster than you could say, "the champagne of bottled beer," he and the other two each downed a bottle of Miller's.

Schryver came in just as they finished and began screaming.

Cheap bastard, one of them remembered thinking. What's he so excited about a goddamned bottle of beer.

"You idiots," the chief snarled. "That beer has stupefying drugs in it! Go home! You're no good to me here now."

So Toomey, who had begun his efforts twenty-four hours earlier by taking a .357 Magnum shell in his wristwatch and had never left, was now driven home from duty. The postscript to the incident was that none of the three reported even an iota of drowsiness, although two said later they believed the doctored beer might well have had the effect of an aphrodisiac on them.

For a good portion of the previous day, Bolz had not negotiated personally with Steele. For one thing, he had been unable to establish a dialogue early on, and Cottell—impatient for an end to the stalemate—had suggested, rather directly, that it might be better to try other negotiators.

Shortly after his return, Deputy Inspector Charles Henry, the top ranking black officer on the scene, walked in and said, "Let me talk to him, I'll get him out of there." Henry donned a black raincoat, went to the door, and tried his best street language approach. "Hey, you muthufucka, you get outta there or I'm goin' ta kick yo' ass!" A few seconds of that and Steele, who had spent a fairly calm night with the exception of Al Cachie's escapade, was shouting back, threatening the girl's life.

Bolz shuddered. "I don't think it's working," he told Henry, who would joke later, "I turned that thing around, Frank. *I* got him to like *you*."

Now Bolz was back at the front door, with Captain Danny St. John of Emergency Services backing him up.

Bolz was leaning in a bit now, trying to maintain some eye contact with Steele—both for intelligence reasons and to help nurture any possible buildup of trust between them. Bolz would check the corridor with his periscope and then, if Steele seemed calm, poke his head in and start talking. St. John would lean in behind him, one hand on Bolz's belt, ready to jerk him away in case of trouble.

The idea was to maintain conversation. Any conversation. First, to lull Steele into a sense of security. And, second, to convince the little girl that the police were not her enemy, so that she would not resist a rescue attempt, as she had done the day before.

"You from the South, Floyd?" Bolz asked.

"Oh, yeah," Steele said, "North Carolina."

"What'd you do for a living down there?"

"A lot of things," Steele said. "I worked the railroads mostly."

"Oh, a gandy dancer, huh?"

"Nah, I didn't do much track work."

"They were just building the railroads when you were born, huh, Floyd?"

"Oh, yeah," Steele said. "I remember seeing them set out for the West in covered wagons when I was a kid, you know?"

"Just think how far we've come in your lifetime, Floyd," Bolz said. "Can you imagine how much Tisha's going to see in *her* lifetime? The way we go to California, now, these kids'll be going to the moon and back."

And on it went. Once, a cockroach crawled up the wall, within an inch of Bolz's nose, and he made no move, fearful that any sudden gesture could unnerve Steele. He spotted a plant in the room. A geranium. And for twenty-five minutes, as Avril Letticia Kinsler completed her twenty-seventh hour on Steele's lap within inches of the .357 Magnum, Steele and Bolz went around and around on the care and feeding of geraniums.

"We ain't going to blow this guy away," Detective Louis

Hernandez said from his perch downstairs, monitoring the conversation. "We're going to bore him to death."

Steele had been up almost forty-eight hours by police calculation. He had consumed a quantity of beer. He was fifty-five years old. How long could he stay up? Harvey Schlossberg could provide an intelligent guess, based on the man's demeanor. But where was Harvey? He wasn't back yet.

A few minutes later, Schlossberg sauntered down the hall. "Where you been?" Bolz asked.

"You won't believe it," Schlossberg said. "I've been downstairs for an hour. The cop on the door said he had orders not to let anybody up." In his own mind, Bolz believed that the local police had exacted their own pint of blood. The evening before, he and Schlossberg, under orders, had held a series of press briefings on the sidewalk in front of the building. They had been on television. And they had obviously touched a jealous chord. He could almost hear it now: "Who do they think *they* are."

It was Wednesday morning. Throughout the rest of the building, and even down the hall from the siege, residents of 109–10 169th Street were awakening. And, quite by accident, one of them helped matters considerably by starting to cook breakfast. The aroma of bacon permeated the hallway, making the police hungry. Why not, they thought. Emergency Service Lieutenant Tony Ferrar got some bacon and eggs and went to work in the headquarters apartment. Then he placed the prepared food near the doorway and, as Bolz and St. John stood at the door, he tried to waft the odor toward Steele and the girl by fanning it with a slab of cardboard.

"Hey, Floyd," Bolz said, "how about something to eat?"

"Naw," Steele said. "I ain't hungry."

"Well, how about the kid? Is she hungry?"

Yes, Avril decided, she would like some breakfast.

"Okay, we'll get some up here," Bolz said. "Maybe you want a cup of coffee, Floyd?"

Yes, Steele said. That would be fine. Bolz placed the plate of bacon and eggs on the floor just inside the apartment door and pushed it a couple of feet up the corridor with a stick.

"You can bring it here," Steele called.

Screw you, Bolz thought to himself. You killed one guy and shot at a cop. I'm not walking in there. Then he told Steele: "No, Floyd, my boss won't let me. Why don't I try to push it farther down. Then I'll step away from the door and you can come get it."

There was a distance of perhaps thirty feet separating Steele from Bolz. After Bolz had shoved the food about ten feet down the corridor, Steele told Avril to pick up the plate and bring it back.

"Get away from the door!" he barked at Bolz as she walked toward the plate, raising the gun as he spoke. "Stay away!"

After Avril had returned to the back room with the bacon and eggs, Bolz repeated the process with the coffee, but Steele did not begin to drink it. He and Bolz continued to talk. By the time Steele remembered the coffee, it was cold.

"Come on," Bolz said, "send her down with it and we'll warm it up."

Again, Steele raised himself into a combat position, covering Avril as she walked down the corridor with the cold coffee. Bolz was poised on the door, gauging his options. "Be ready," he whispered to St. John, who tightened his grip on Bolz's belt.

The little girl handed the coffee to Bolz—and stepped back.

"My God!" Bolz told St. John. "I blew it. We could've had her, and I blew it!"

If we don't get an opportunity like that again, Bolz thought to himself, and this job goes down badly, then I'll always wonder if I could have pulled her out. He tried to put it out of his mind. He and Schlossberg had talked about this kind of thing. It was part of the discipline of the negotiator's role, to press on without being distracted by what might have been, by any sense of guilt. Suddenly, Bolz smiled to himself. Who knows about it? he thought. I do, and Danny does; and, if he doesn't say anything, I won't.

A few minutes later, the hot coffee was ready and Bolz resumed the ritual, edging it down the corridor with a stick, waiting for Avril to retrieve it for her Uncle Fly. She looked up at Bolz after picking up the coffee and asked, "Can I have some more Kool-Aid?"

Avril brought the cup down the hallway for a refill. She had made any number of trips up and back by now, and over the last few Steele had gone through the motions, but was not raising his gun very high any more. Bolz pulled his own arm back a bit. He could feel St. John tightening the grip on the rear of his belt.

"Come a little bit closer, honey," Bolz said. Down the corridor, he could see Steele taking a sip of his coffee. As Bolz accepted the cup, finally, with his left hand, he reached out and locked his right hand around the little girl's wrist and quickly spun around, shielding her with his body. From behind him, St. John yanked hard on the belt, pulling Bolz and the girl into the hallway, out of the line of fire.

Avril Letticia Kinsler was safe.

St. John and Bolz decided that with the girl out of the way, it was time to take the offensive. They entered the corridor, armed with shotguns, and softly but firmly ordered Steele to surrender. And in a few moments, Steele agreed. Thirty-three hours after Avril's mother had escaped from the window and called police, the siege was over.

Frank Bolz walked into the headquarters apartment. He was so emotionally up that he was hyperventilating from sheer excitement. He didn't know whether to laugh or cry. Lonergan walked over. "Get yourself together," he said, "and we'll go out and hold a press conference."

The Shea jury was still out and the Police Department was going to milk this victory to counteract any reverberations from an acquittal. The Deputy Commissioner for Press Relations, Frank McLaughlin, sent for a pretty, white female police officer to bring little Avril out, to prolonged cheers from neighborhood residents. When word reached the street that Fred Kinsler was dead, his wife, Peggy, broke down. That, too, had an effect. The police had spent thirty-three hours talking down a killer.

Bolz called Ruthie, downed a couple of glasses of water, and went downstairs. The press conference was staged in the community room of the housing project. Police Commissioner Mike Codd stood at their side, beaming, as Bolz, Schlossberg, and St. John answered questions and described the evolution of the Hostage Negotiating Team and how it had been trained for missions such as this one.

"Take the rest of the day off," Lonergan told them after it was over. "I'll see you tomorrow." It was 10:00 A.M. They repaired to a bar on Hillside Avenue to sit back and wind down, ordering large breakfasts and giant Bloody Marys. They played the jukebox and the bowling machine and kept talking about the job—a sort of therapy session, really, that would eventually be standard procedure for the team. It was too much to ask of a cop, after all the hours of tension, to just walk away cold, without giving him a chance to wind down emotionally.

After a while, Bolz decided to call in. He was asked to go to the 103rd Precinct stationhouse for some more television interviews. Then he went home to sleep.

The next day's *New York Times* put the story on its front page under the headline: "Siege Ends as Girl Is Pulled to Safety; Stepfather Is Dead." In the very next column was another headline: "Jury Clears Shea in Killing of Boy."

There had been no riots in Queens following the verdict. The negotiating team had rescued the girl and, far from exacerbating tensions, had given the NYPD a much-needed dose of credibility in the area.

"It is quite likely that little Avril owes her life to the coolly patient professionalism of New York's Finest," the *Daily News* declared in an editorial, "and particularly to a special unit created to deal with just such situations." A photo of Bolz, in his now-familiar "uniform" of windbreaker and baseball cap, ran next to it. *Newsweek* told the nation about the team later that week in a two-page spread.

"Lieutenant Francis Bolz Jr., a husky forty-three-year-old detective who commands the hostage unit, began to play all the tricks he knew," the magazine reported. " 'Our main goal,' Bolz says, 'is to save lives—of hostages, of policemen, of bystanders. Our approach is to buy time, until the perpetrator makes a mistake or we wear him down.' "

Avril Kinsler seemed none the worse for wear. At the

hospital, she proudly told doctors that she had dressed herself for the first time in her life.

Her ''Uncle Fly'' was declared mentally fit for trial and then sent to jail. He remained there, awaiting trial, until February, 1976, when he died of a heart attack.

Children are maimed and killed every year in New York City by parental neglect and abuse. And, sometimes, they are held hostage—pawns sacrificed to the fear, desperation, hatred, or lunacy of some trusted adult.

Perhaps Avril Kinsler has suffered no psychological damage from her thirty-three hours with Floyd Steele. Perhaps, years from now, it will take a psychiatrist many visits to ferret it from the recesses of her mind. For the police negotiators, she would be just one of a number of child hostages. And each would retain a special place in the memories of the police called upon to help save a youngster's life.

Often, family quarrels were at the root of the problem. In March, 1976, in Harlem, a man named Melvin Davis, anguished that the courts had ordered his three-and-a-half-year-old daughter turned over to his estranged wife, took the girl onto a fourth-floor fire escape and threatened to jump. After a harrowing half hour of talk, the police managed to distract Davis long enough to grab him and the girl.

Then, late one night in June, 1976, on 168th Street in Jamaica, Queens, not far from the site of the Floyd Steele siege, a twenty-nine-year-old man named James Barker started shouting at his wife Janice to get off the telephone. Then he walked over, pulled the receiver out of her hand, slammed it down and began hitting her.

At that moment, Janice Barker's nineteen-year-old brother, Kenneth Jones, and Jones's girlfriend, Shirley Gilpin, walked into the house and rushed to separate the couple. Barker turned his attention from his wife to his brother-in-law. Push came to shove and shove to stab. Barker pulled a folding knife from his pocket and stabbed Jones three times. Jones staggered into the street and collapsed.

Barker, fearing he had murdered the younger man, lunged for his wife, but she ran off. He grabbed Jones's girlfriend and his own four-year-old stepson, Tony Ferguson, and dragged them into the basement of his house. Officers from the 103rd Precinct arrived, arranged for an ambulance for Jones, and called for more help. At 1:00 A.M., Frank Bolz arrived, entered the house, and proceeded to the top of the stairwell leading to the basement, where Detective Larry Gallagher had already started talking with Barker.

He had a shotgun, Barker said, as well as a knife. From discussions with Mrs. Barker, the police believed there was no shotgun in the house. But they could not overlook the possibility that Barker had one that his wife never knew about. They had to take the man at his word.

The entrance to the basement was near the side door. There was a three-step drop inside to a linoleum-covered landing lighted by a dim red bulb, and then a staircase down. Barker had the young woman and the boy down behind the staircase where police could not see them in the darkness. Bolz crouched on the landing and then went down on his stomach.

"Hey, Jim," he said, "how're you doing?"

"I'm doing fine, man," Barker said. "I had this figured out pretty good. There's no windows down here, no way you can get to me except where you are."

There was no need for phones or a bullhorn, at least. Bolz could talk directly to Barker; they chatted about everything from the high price of defense lawyers to the relative merits of various kinds of grain spirits. A friend volunteered to try to talk him out, but Barker resisted the efforts and stayed in the basement, barricaded with his hostages, through the night. Barker's mother was brought out from Brooklyn. Bolz did not let her shout more than hello, fearing the emotional hazards of a mother–son dialogue, but at least the man knew she was there.

"Hey," Barker said at one point, "I can sure use a drink." And Bolz had the police upstairs send down a bottle of vodka. The two men decided to split the bottle. First Bolz would take a swig, recap the bottle, lean down and roll it across the top of a chest of drawers. Then Barker would edge forward, pick it up, take a drink, and send the bottle back in the other direction.

As the two men talked and drank, they gradually established a rapport. Shortly before 5:00 A.M., Barker said yes, he was about to give himself up. But first he had a few things to do.

"Here," he told Bolz, "take these keys and give them to my mama. I'll be in jail and I want her to be able to get into the house."

"Okay," Bolz said, retrieving the keys from the chest top. "Tell him you've got the keys, Mama!" and the woman called down her acknowledgment.

"And take my money, too," Barker said. "I ain't going to need that in jail."

"First you count it," Bolz cautioned. "We don't want to short-change you."

He had the woman count the money as well and shouted down the total. Now, Barker said, he wanted to fix himself up a bit. It was, Bolz whispered confidently to Gallagher, the classic "surrender ritual."

Actually, he would learn in a few moments, it was something altogether different.

At 5:05, four-year-old Tony Ferguson mounted the stairs, holding the knife out to Bolz. "My daddy said he had to do something in there," Tony said, pointing to the back of the basement.

It was pitch dark and then, suddenly, there was a blazing blue flash. Bolz and Gallagher leaned forward, and then there was a second flash and a thud.

"Christ!" Bolz shouted, "let's go!"

It had not been the surrender ritual Barker had performed, but the suicide ritual. He had dismantled a lamp, plugged the cord into an outlet and touched the live wires, attempting to electrocute himself. He was unconscious when Bolz and Gallagher reached him, and they lifted him up the stairs and into the first floor.

Emergency Service Assault cops, who waited, moments before, ready to blow James Barker away on command, now tore off their flak vests and began trying to save his life. They applied various techniques and finally one said, "He's alive."

"How do you know?" another asked.

"I pulled his balls and he went 'Unnnhh!' " the first cop

said. Seconds later an ambulance was rushing Barker to Mary Immaculate Hospital, where his brother-in-law had been taken five hours earlier.

Both men lived. And then there was Shirley Gilpin. She stumbled out of the basement after Barker had been carried out. Hurt? No, she had fallen asleep in the darkness on a basement couch.

Family disputes are the bane of a cop's existence. Often one spouse who feels the other poses a danger will call the police, only to tearfully retract all expressions of concern after the officers arrive. On other occasions, family members will set aside their own differences long enough to turn, in unison, on the poor cop who has been summoned to break up the ruckus. And, on occasion, police have responded to family quarrels and been shot for their trouble. Understandably, police are reluctant to involve themselves in family disputes. But there are times when they are legally required by the Family Court to enter the fray.

One hot August morning in Brooklyn, two months after the James Barker job in South Jamaica, two officers went to 30 Martense Street to serve a court order on Darnell Oliver. The officers, Edward Adams and Robert Taylor, accompanied Consuela Oliver to the apartment in the hopes of regaining the custody of her two children—Darnell Jr., seven, and Clarissa, two, who had been taken by their father the day before in violation of a court order.

Darnell Oliver opened the door and then slammed it shut. He picked up a fifteen-inch butcher knife and told the police to go away. Adams and Taylor immediately requested the aid of Emergency Services and the Hostage Negotiating Team, and Detective Bill Clark, a negotiator on duty six blocks away at the 67th Precinct stationhouse, was on the scene in minutes and began trying to talk to Oliver through the closed door.

Bolz, who had been at headquarters twenty minutes away (as the squad car flies), arrived a few minutes later and began a backup operation. The Emergency Services team was on the scene by then, in full battle regalia.

At 10:55, twenty minutes after the closed-door negotia-

tions had begun, Oliver asked Clark to get him some methadone. That was a break because it gave police a bargaining
chit.

If Oliver were an addict and had asked for heroin, there
might have been a problem. But as a methadone patient, he
could be granted his request—at the proper time. The counselor at his methadone clinic and members of his family were
summoned and interviewed so that Clark would know as much
about Oliver as he could.

Bolz sent for the police photo unit and, at noon, they set
up on the roof of the house, lowering a TV camera to the top
of a window which delivered pictures of the interior of the
apartment. Among the items the camera revealed was a gas
mask at the base of a chair that Oliver was sitting on.

The mask bothered Bolz, not because the police planned
to smoke the man out but because it seemed to hint that there
might be more to this job than showed on its face. "A dumb
family fight," he told Sergeant Bob Louden, "and it's the kind
that's just liable to explode in our faces." Then he remembered that it was Friday the thirteenth.

Clark continued this conversation with Oliver and, at
1:15, convinced the man to let him and Bolz speak to him
through the kitchen window, which opened onto the rooftop of
a garage next door. At 3:30, Clark sent in one vial of methadone and Oliver downed it. The second one, Clark told him,
would be handed to him in exchange for the little girl. And at
3:45, that bargain was consummated and little Clarissa came
bounding out into her mother's arms.

As 5:00 P.M. approached, Oliver talked of giving up, but
said he had some chores to take care of first. He went into the
bathroom to dress and to use a depilatory cream on his face.
"A skin condition," he explained. "I can't use a razor."

Then he walked to the kitchen and took a slab of bacon
out of the refrigerator. Using the very knife that he was holding
on his son, Oliver sliced the bacon and cooked it. "It'll spoil
while I'm in jail," he said.

The surrender ritual? The James Barker incident was
fresh in Bolz's mind.

At 5:35, Oliver agreed to let Clark enter the apartment,

not through the door but through the kitchen window so he could be assured that it was not the precursor to a police charge. Oliver still had the knife in his hand and the boy at his side, and for ten minutes he and Clark talked, emotionally at times, about the young man's future. Bolz was at the open kitchen window now, both hands resting in plain view on the sill. He had already loosened his revolver so he could match any quick move Oliver might make on Clark.

Finally, Oliver said he was ready to give up. He placed the knife on the table and stepped forward.

Clark reached for his handcuffs. Instinctively, Oliver backed away and reached back down toward the knife.

"Bill," Bolz called from the window, "put the cuffs away. We don't have to worry about the cuffs now."

There was more calming talk and again the issue of surrender came up. Now Bolz was ready. "Darnell," he told the man with the knife, "we won't throw any cuffs on you. Just hold your hands out to Bill and he'll hold his out to you."

From then on, this would be standard procedure—reach out for the perpetrator with open arms, a warm, positive body action exactly the opposite of the cold, negative effect of the handcuffs. Once the perpetrator's hands are in the cop's he is just as immobilized as he would be if he was manacled with the cuffs. A quick toss, or frisking, and the cuffs could go on.

And that is the way it happened. There were smiles all around on Martense Street for another successful negotiating job. But Bolz would always remember the one face without a smile—little Darnell Oliver, Jr., weeping, as his father was led away.

Darnell was old enough to have the experience etched in his mind. Robert Mason, Jr., being seven months old at the time, was spared such memories.

Robert's father, who was twenty-three years old, had fought with his wife about custody of the infant one spring morning and then taken the baby to the roof, eight floors above St. Nicholas Avenue, in Harlem, and threatened to jump. It was 8:30 A.M.

Mason was literally tottering on the ledge of the building

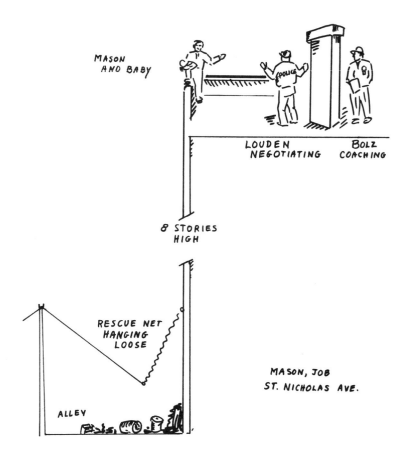

MASON
AND BABY

LOUDEN
NEGOTIATING

BOLZ
COACHING

8 STORIES
HIGH

RESCUE NET
HANGING
LOOSE

MASON, JOB
ST. NICHOLAS AVE.

ALLEY

when the first police arrived. They began setting up a net on the ground, but any such rescue effort, especially in view of the age of the baby, was chancy. The best approach was to talk the man down.

Sergeant Robert Louden was the first negotiator at the scene, and he and Officer John Elter went to the roof, where they were joined a few minutes later by Bolz and a pair of Legal Aid attorneys familiar with Mason's background. The negotiators began establishing a rapport with Mason, but theirs was a terrifying task. This was no gunman who needed to take aim and fire. It was an emotionally overwrought individual inches away from plunging himself—and his young son—to their deaths.

Once, when Louden told Mason, "Don't worry about it, things have a way of jumping up," Bolz almost choked.

"Bob!" he whispered frantically, "don't use words like 'jump.' Please!"

Mason said he had been to Family Court and felt that he had never been given the right to argue for custody of the baby. "That's all I want, man," he told Louden, "a chance to tell my side to the judge."

Louden said he would personally guarantee that Mason could have his day in Family Court, but the man on the ledge shook his head.

"No good, man," he said. "I want it in writing."

So Louden procured some paper and a pen, wrote out the promise that Mason would be granted a chance to seek custody of Robert Jr., signed it, and handed it to the man, who accepted it in one hand even as he held his son at the edge of the roof with the other. He looked at the paper, nodded, and said he would come down off the ledge in a few moments.

But how would he come down? He began to empty his pockets.

"Suicide ritual!" Bolz whispered to Louden. "We can't let him do it. He'll take the kid down with him. Ask him if he thinks it might snow."

"What?" Louden said, thinking that Bolz was every bit as mad as Robert Mason. The sun was high in the sky and so hot that the tar roof was starting to bubble up.

"Thought interruption," Bolz told him. "Get him disoriented. Ask him if he thinks it'll snow."

Louden asked and Mason stopped everything, turned around, and gave the detective a weird look.

"Is it going to *what?*" he said in disbelief, moving away from the ledge. Now he was angry. "Say you meant rain, not snow," Bolz whispered. Louden did and Mason calmed down.

The ploy had worked. Louden changed the subject and kept talking. Mason's sister had been ushered to the roof, and Louden asked him to hand Robert Jr. to her. He nodded and did, then turned back to the ledge and again seemed ready to jump. Bolz had indeed spotted the ritual. Louden and Bolz reacted simultaneously, grabbing Mason and pulling him to safety. He was officially charged with reckless endangerment. To those who had been on the roof for the hour of drama, it sounded like an understatement.

CHAPTER THREE

The Ballad of Cat Olsen

The thirty hours of tension embodied in the Floyd Steele case had placed New York's hostage negotiators on front pages around the country and given the team its first large taste of public acclaim. In the sixteen days that followed, Frank Bolz and his group would relish a different sort of honor as well—evidence that their reputation was spreading on the inside, too. Their special nonviolent form of law enforcement was becoming legendary in the city's jails and prisons.

The call had come in mid-afternoon, Monday, June 17. A man was holding his wife at gunpoint on the lower floor of a row house in the Laurelton section of southeastern Queens.

As in so many hostage cases, intelligence—the rapid gathering of relevant background information—would prove vital in helping Bolz and the team bring the matter to a safe conclusion. And, like so many others, this incident was a sad, almost poignant story. Police discovered that the man inside had just been released from jail. He had gone back into the neighborhood, looking for his wife. She was not around, but the stories were. "Oh, man, while you were away that little mouse sure did play!"

The guy went a little bonkers. He rented a gypsy cab, carted fares around all day, got smashed on Twister wine, and then went to his wife's house. When she refused to admit him, he fired a shot through the door and pushed his way in. Neighbors called police. And now, fresh from jail and cuckolded as well, the poor guy was in the middle of World War III, with Emergency Service trucks, police, sharpshooters, bullhorns, and the works down on 223rd Street. The price of teaching his woman a lesson in faithfulness and loyalty would come high.

It was in this spirit that Bolz approached the apartment after he was briefed on the man's background. The talk was gentle at times, but often argumentative as well. The man had already asked negotiator Kenny Bowen by phone for cigarettes and a bottle of wine, and Bolz sent for them.

After a great deal of discussion about how the wine would be passed inside, the gunman agreed that Bowen should leave the wine on a bedroom windowsill overlooking the garbage-strewn rear yard. Bowen carefully edged along the side of the building, guided in part by Bolz's instructions, relayed to him by radio from an observation team on a rooftop across the courtyard. Bolz did not like the idea of sending another man on such a mission, but as the discussion progressed, it had been Bowen and the gunman who worked out the deal and it was Bowen he was expecting to see. If he had seen anyone else at that window, the gunman might have suspected a trick and fired away.

"Are you ready to come out?" Bolz asked after the wine had been delivered.

Almost, the man said. First, he wanted to take his wife into the bedroom and make love to her. "I'm gonna get laid," he had announced to Bolz earlier; and in the background the police could hear his wife screaming, "He's going to rape me!"

The negotiators were in a dilemma. Members of the press were on the scene and they could hear the screaming. Yet to send the Assault Team in might cost the woman her life. Friends and neighbors told police the couple had cohabited for six years. A rape would certainly be an indignity and an assault, but was it a fate worse than death under those circumstances?

The man took his wife into the bedroom. "I'm going to leave the phone off the hook so you can hear that I'm not hurting her," he said.

"That's all right," Bolz said, "you can leave the phone off in the kitchen." The police did not need a tape recording of what they were about to be forced to allow him to do. After the act was consummated, he calmly handed her his gun and they walked out of the apartment.

It was 8:30 in the morning ten days later that the phone rang in the seventeenth-story Brooklyn apartment of Brenda Scott. Her friend and fellow worker, Paul DeTouche, was calling to make sure she and her three-year-old daughter, Rikisha, were awake. The voice at the other end belonged to Ricardo Washington, Rikisha's father, and he had a disquieting message for DeTouche. "Brenda and the baby ain't going nowhere until we straighten some shit out," Washington said. DeTouche called the police.

The apartment house was part of the Ebbets Field complex where the famed Brooklyn Dodger ball park once stood. When two officers from the 71st Precinct arrived, they encountered DeTouche, who told them that Washington was a guard at a state-run community prison for narcotics addicts. "I know he carries a gun," DeTouche said. "I've seen it."

The officers called for a supervisor, Sergeant John McCarthy. Rather than knock at the door, McCarthy decided to phone the apartment. Washington repeated what he had told DeTouche and then he put Miss Scott on the phone and she screamed for help. It was 9:30 when McCarthy established a temporary field headquarters in a dry cleaning store across the street and called for hostage negotiators.

When he received the radio alarm, Bolz was motoring across the Williamsburg Bridge on the way into headquarters. He flipped on the siren, placed his portable red light on the roof and almost pushed traffic off the bridge. He made a "U" turn at the base of the bridge on Delancey Street and headed back over the bridge toward Brooklyn. Bolz had spent most of his career working in Brooklyn. He made it to the Ebbets Field apartments in six minutes, just ahead of Detective Al Cachie, who had come from the 67th Precinct in Flatbush. Bolz and Cachie went to the seventeenth floor and set up shop in an apartment across the hall from Brenda Scott's.

From DeTouche, neighbors, and brothers of both Washington and Miss Scott, Bolz and Cachie pieced together the situation.

Ricardo (Richie) Washington and Brenda Scott had lived

together for about four years but had split up a year ago. In recent months, Richie had complained bitterly that the woman was keeping his young daughter from him. Only the week before, he had arrived at the apartment, shoved Brenda out of the way and had taken Rikisha, returning her that night. A police complaint Brenda had filed against him was still pending. Richie had arrived Wednesday night, and he and Brenda had been up since then, with him alternately haranguing her and begging her to marry him. He had told her that he would not let her or the little girl leave.

After Al Cachie phoned the apartment, he explained to Washington that he was a hostage negotiator, and the man at the other end of the line started to laugh. "I know you guys," he said. "You're the cops who gave that dude out in Queens some wine and a piece of pussy last week before you busted him."

Cachie smiled. "You'll never believe this," he called out to Bolz, who was standing in the hall, observing the closed door to the apartment. For the next ninety minutes, Cachie and Washington talked. "You love the kid," Cachie told him. "You love her. You don't want to cause her any trouble."

At 11:40, Washington agreed to let Brenda and Rikisha go, but he remained behind. Now it was technically no longer a hostage incident, but what police call a "barricaded" case —an alleged perpetrator, possibly armed, refusing to come out.

Washington was talking about going downstairs the fast way, out the window, but the Emergency Service division had stretched a jump net across the building just below the apartment so that Washington could not be certain of executing a successful suicide. Cachie and Bolz were now telling him that the situation could be resolved. With hostages' lives on the line, Bolz had been loathe to risk allowing civilians to talk directly with Washington. But now he let Willie Lewis, the man's brother, and Keith Scott, Rikisha's fifteen-year-old uncle, talk. Keith was an instant negotiator. "Come on out, man," he demanded. "I've got to get in there and get some stuff!"

Forty minutes after he had let Brenda and Rikisha go,

Washington agreed to surrender. "One thing, though," he told Cachie. "I'd like to go for a ride through Prospect Park before you book me. I want to see the trees before I go to jail."

Cachie agreed. And after Washington came out, he and Cachie took a leisurely ride through the nearby park—a hilly swath of green which was designed in the nineteenth century by Frederick Law Olmstead and is considered by connoisseurs of such things to be prettier than Olmstead's other gift to the city, Manhattan's Central Park. At the end, Cachie reported to Bolz. "Frank," he said, "he never had a weapon. We don't have to charge him, do we?"

Of course, they did. And Cachie seemed overwrought at the idea, demanding to know why Washington could not simply be allowed to walk away. Years later, the hostage negotiators would remember Cachie's reaction as the first dramatic evidence that the police themselves were far from immune to the Stockholm Syndrome, the state of psychological transference, in which a captor's victims slowly begin to identify with his crisis.

But that would be just one of the lessons Frank Bolz would take away from the Ebbets Field job. The other thing he would never forget was the glimmer of recognition in Ricardo Washington's opening line: "You're the cops who gave that dude out in Queens some wine . . ."

When asked why he robbed banks, Willie Sutton uttered six of the more memorable words in the annals of crime analysis. "Because," he said, "that's where the money is."

Sometimes, however, people have other reasons.

In August, 1972, barely two weeks before the Munich Massacre, three men walked into a neighborhood branch of the Chase Manhattan Bank on a quiet street in Brooklyn and announced a stickup. Two of the men, twenty-year-old Robert Westenberg and twenty-one-year-old Donald Matterson (who also used the name Salvatore Naturelle), were homosexuals who had talked of getting enough of a stake to head west and open a beauty shop. The third man, a twenty-seven-year-old employee at another Chase Manhattan branch, had planned the caper. His name was John Stanley Wojtowicz and he also was homosexual. Married and the father of two, Wojtowicz desperately needed cash so that his other "wife," Ernest Aron, could afford to undergo a sex-change operation.

Westenberg panicked during the early stages of the robbery and fled from the bank. Matterson, whose drug habit had earned him a prior jail term, was so fearful of going back behind bars that he decided he would rather die first. And he did —shot down by an FBI sharpshooter at Kennedy Airport fourteen hours after the start of the robbery. Wojtowicz would serve more than six years in prison. Three years into his term, he became famous when he was brilliantly portrayed by Al Pacino in the film *Dog Day Afternoon*.

The movie was playing all over New York City in October, 1975, and one of those who saw it was a twenty-three-year-old Long Islander named Raymond (the Cat) Olsen. The next afternoon, Olsen walked into a small Greenwich Village branch of the Bankers Trust Company at closing time, with a Colt .38, a sawed-off rifle, a bag he said contained "a bomb," and a large portable radio, and announced that he was conducting "a seizure."

And indeed he was. Ultimately, Olsen would be charged with robbery, among other things, on a technicality. But he had gone to great pains to demonstrate as best he could that the last thing he wanted to do was to rob the bank. "I'm completely broke," he told a radio reporter by telephone a while later. "I walked in here with two cents in my pocket. When I get broke, I do crazy things."

Olsen was a high school dropout who dabbled in drugs. Mostly, he hung out. He had been placed on probation at age seventeen after a conviction for burglary in his native Nassau County. There had also been a half dozen drug arrests, a trip to San Francisco's Haight-Ashbury section, and then a return to New York. In the days before he walked into the bank, Olsen had become a regular in Washington Square Park, playing his guitar, smoking pot, and dating a girl who became known, rather logically, as "the Mouse."

When he entered the bank, there were ten others there —five employees and five customers. One of the employees immediately pressed a button setting off a silent alarm in the local precinct. Two detectives attached to the Major Case

Squad—a centrally located unit that handles all bank robberies —were in the neighborhood. Within seconds, the detectives, John Stein and Tom Hallinan, were staring at Olsen and his armament through the bank's storefront window.

The pair moved quickly—but carefully and wisely.

They had to assume that they had come upon the gunman in the midst of a robbery, and any act that might provoke a shootout on busy Sixth Avenue at midday was inherently irresponsible. Consequently, Stein and Hallinan directed all pedestrians out of the line of fire and then hit the ground in the classic prone position, using only the four-inch sidewalk curbing for cover.

Inside, Cat Olsen backed off to an interior position and told his hostages to relax. He was a member of the Symbionese Liberation Army, Olsen said, and he was going to hold them in an effort to gain freedom for Patricia Hearst, William and Emily Harris, and "that Japanese girl," Wendy Yoshimura.

Outside, police, still assuming that they had cornered a bank robber in the act, were rapidly mobilizing. The bank was located on the east side of Sixth Avenue between 12th and 13th Streets. Because Sixth Avenue was one-way uptown, the key points of diversion became 11th Street at Sixth Avenue— for autos heading north on Sixth or heading west on 11th Street and planning to turn right onto Sixth Avenue—and 12th Street at Seventh Avenue for autos attempting to drive eastward on 12th Street toward Sixth Avenue.

Several police officers noticed an Emery Air Freight truck parked at the curb, and when its driver returned, they ordered him to pull it onto the sidewalk just to the side of the bank, affording them good cover. "My boss is not going to believe this," the driver said plaintively. In fact, before long his boss would be watching the truck on television. Another cop, a detective named Tom Sobota from the 6th Precinct, raced into a grocery-delicatessen next door and called the bank.

"My name is Ray," the man at the other end said. "They call me 'The Cat.' This is a seizure, not a robbery. I want ten million dollars in gold and I want Patty Hearst, the Japanese girl, and the Harrises set free."

During the next few minutes, Sobota maintained sporadic

contact with Olsen, trying to calm the young man and to make sure he understood that the police were taking him seriously. And then, less than half an hour after the siege on Sixth Avenue had started, Frank Bolz walked into the grocery store and took command.

When the call came, Bolz and his boss, Inspector Robert Johnston, Jr., were at headquarters, conferring with one police official from Vancouver, British Columbia and another from Pakistan. Bolz rushed from the office, pausing long enough to invite his visitors to come along for an actual look at how the team handled a negotiation.

In fact, Bolz himself was wondering how many more times he would play this scene, scrambling from behind his desk like a fighter pilot, stopping for the ritualistic trip to the men's room, and then racing to the scene, with his trademark —the blue baseball cap—cocked just a bit off to one side of his head.

Bolz was becoming something of a legend in a department that does not like its legends to be lieutenants. And by October, 1975, the pressure was mounting. In order to provide him with enough time for his increasing duties as head of the negotiating team, Bolz had been granted a flexible administrative slot in the Special Investigation Division of the Detective Bureau. But in early summer, 1975, the Chief of Detectives, Louis Cottell, had ordered him transferred to his own command in the Auto Crime Squad.

"I can't do it," Bolz had protested to his boss at SID, Deputy Inspector Dan MacMahon. "There's no way I can run a squad and also have time for all the hostage negotiating work."

"What do you want me to do?" MacMahon retorted. "Tell Louie you can't handle it?"

Privately, Bolz had other reservations about the proposed new assignment as well. In recent months, the Auto Squad had been shaken by scandal over incidents that had actually occurred more than two years earlier. There was every indication that further revelations would follow. When such a situation exists, the spilled blood tends to splatter all those standing nearby. Earlier in the year, he and Harvey Schlossberg had been ordered to begin training eight other detective lieutenants in negotiating techniques, with an eye toward making one of them Bolz's successor.

"What do we do?" he asked Schlossberg. "Do I train the firing squad to shoot me or let them learn on their own?" He and Schlossberg debated the question. They could not let the newcomers go into the field poorly trained, whatever the future. So Bolz and Schlossberg decided to teach the eight lieutenants all they could.

Cottell was a popular old-timer who had been the lone member of the Old Guard retained during a housecleaning of department hierarchy. He associated the idea of negotiating with thugs and psychos with the New Wave cops he despised. At the Floyd Steele job in Hollis, he alone among the brass had failed to personally congratulate Bolz and St. John. Now, in August, 1975, with Bolz's transfer to the Auto Squad already announced, there seemed little recourse.

But happenstance would change that. Several weeks later, Bolz was at the Police Department's upstate recreation center at Tannersville, holding forth at the Steuben Association's hospitality villa at the annual Patrolmen's Benevolent Association convention. That afternoon, a hostage situation had been resolved successfully in nearby Albany. That night, Police Commissioner Michael Codd spotted Bolz and asked if the city cops had played a role in the Albany resolution. "We trained both the Albany police and the FBI people who were in there," Bolz told him.

Codd beamed and told Bolz how proud the department was of his work. "Well," Bolz answered, "if I'm doing such a good job, how come you transferred me to the Auto Squad." Codd seemed concerned and asked Bolz to drop him a note, explaining exactly what the duties of Hostage Negotiating Team chief entailed.

It was too late now to become bashful. Bolz fired off a two-page, single-spaced job outline. Within a week, he was back in the Office of the Chief of Detectives in a corner office as far from Cottell as the Detective Bureau could arrange. And his commander, Johnston, had passed on the word: no more press conferences, no more notoriety. Any requests for information were to be handled by the Detective Bureau training officer. "I'm under house arrest," Bolz confided to a friend. He had won the battle, but the Chief of Detectives was an awful enemy to contemplate in terms of a war.

Bolz had no way of knowing, as he sped down Seventh Avenue and careened past the police barrier at 12th Street, that a disoriented twenty-three-year-old gunman named Cat Olsen was about to provide him with all the opportunity he needed to get out from under the hammer.

Bolz went as far as he could on 12th Street and then pulled the car onto the sidewalk and put on a small, fiberglass bulletproof vest and his blue windbreaker. He could send subordinates back for whatever tactical equipment the situation up ahead might dictate. He glanced up at a vaguely familiar building, the exterior of St. Vincent's Hospital. He had last been on this block one night five months before—the night his father, Frank Sr., had died.

There was little time to contemplate life's ironies now. The scene on Sixth Avenue looked, in fact, all too much like the set of *Dog Day Afternoon*. The delicatessen where police had set up their closest command post was on the same side of the street as the bank, three stores down. Tom Sobota described the conversation he had conducted with Ray Olsen. Leo McGillicuddy, the FBI's chief hostage negotiator (and a Bolz trainee), walked into the store. Since this was a federally insured bank, the FBI also had jurisdiction in the case.

Immediately, Bolz moved to include McGillicuddy in the discussions. Borrowing from his experience as a telephone tapper, Bolz grafted a line from the phone in the delicatessen to a tape recorder that was equipped with a loudspeaker so that any conversations with Olsen could be heard by others as they were being recorded. He looked over his shoulder and surveyed the scene. More and more cops were gathering inside the store. Not sixty feet away, an armed man was holding ten hostages. But in the delicatessen, a counterman was slicing bologna for sandwiches and nonplussed neighborhood residents were casually touring the aisles, doing their Monday

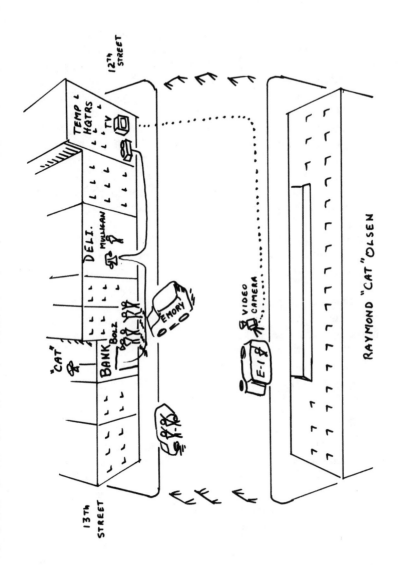

afternoon marketing. Only in New York, Bolz thought with a smile.

There were three lines into the bank and Olsen already had used one of them to call the wire services and radio station WNEW-FM. He asked the station to play music by the group, The Grateful Dead, and added that he wanted to meet his favorite disc jockey, Scott Muni. Bolz could only manage brief conversations with Olsen at first, because now others in the media were catching on and placing calls *into* the bank. As Olsen watched another of the phone lights flash, he would excuse himself and place the police on hold.

"What do I want, man?" he told one of the callers, veteran New York *News* police reporter Edward Kirkman. "I want the Harrises freed. I want Patty out of jail and that Oriental girl too. This is a seizure, man. I'm fed up with this fucking country. I have one other guy in here with me. We have a bomb and enough guns to do whatever we want."

What, Kirkman wondered, could be done to avoid bloodshed.

"Get those fucking cops away from the door!" Olsen answered. "I can see them running around with their rifles and shotguns. They want to blow us away. If they try anything, we will kill all ten hostages. Why not? What have we got to lose? Tell the cops we are wise to their fucking tricks. We won't be fucked like those guys in *Dog Day Afternoon*. We want a limousine. The limousine is to be bulletproof. I'm going to throw a few shots into it just to check." In fact, he had seen *Dog Day Afternoon* for the first time a week before.

At first, Olsen had demanded that an airplane be taxied to a halt on Sixth Avenue right in front of the bank, but Bolz's genuine incredulity had helped convince him that such a demand was unworkable. He also had demanded a conversation with F. Lee Bailey, Patty Hearst's attorney at the time, and the FBI was trying in fact to locate Bailey—if for no other reason than to try to ascertain whether Olsen really might be connected to the SLA. Police, still uncertain of just who was involved in the takeover, had placed a television camera across the street and were examining a frozen frame of Cat Olsen. Within the hour it would help them verify that he was, indeed, the same Raymond Olsen who had a burglary conviction and a string of drug arrests in Nassau County.

The bank was one of those small neighborhood branches designed to reach out for customers in their own locales. The space was more appropriate for a clothing store with narrow frontage on the well-traversed avenue but considerable depth allowing for racks of clothes or shelves of goods. Under the circumstances, Bankers Trust had arranged for a modicum of security. A couple of assistant managers' desks were placed in the front, but the tellers were separated from their customers by counter-to-ceiling bulletproof glass in an area that could be reached only through a locked door. Behind the tellers' area was a rear office. After he announced his "seizure," Olsen had ordered the bank manager to lock the front entrance and he had herded all ten hostages into the back office.

Emergency Service officers were trying to get as close a position as they could. A metal door guarded the sidewalk entrance to the basement—constructed that way so that goods could be unloaded directly from the street into a basement storage area. Danny St. John crawled to the doors, smashed the locks; Police Officer Frank Gallagher and several of his fellow officers slithered down into the basement, following the noise above to position themselves underneath Olsen and his captives. Several others circled to the rear and decided to try the back door. What they apparently did not realize was that Olsen was only a few feet away. He wheeled and fired into the door, sending the cops scrambling for safety.

"Ray, what was the shot all about?" Bolz asked a moment later.

"Get those fucking cops away from the back!" Olsen shouted into the phone.

"Okay, Ray," Bolz said, and, shouting away from the receiver, he called, "Will you pull everyone away from the rear of the building."

The police now knew that their man not only had weapons but was ready and willing to fire them. And that posed new challenges for the men poised to fire back. St. John, of Emergency Services, walked into the delicatessen and pulled Bolz aside. "Frank," he said, "we've got to do something. We've got all those FBI guys out there with rifles and flak vests under the sport coats. And I've got my guys. We can't have two firearms battalions out there. There'll be a disaster. We've got to do a single."

It was a valid point, but the touchy jurisdictional issues involved were such that the question of what to do about it might have provoked trickier negotiations for Bolz than any challenge presented to him by Cat Olsen. He walked over to Leo McGillicuddy, who said he understood the problem. McGillicuddy then walked back to where the agent-in-charge of the FBI's New York office, Wally LaPrade, was standing. A few minutes later, McGillicuddy was back. LaPrade, he said, had agreed to withdraw the FBI sharpshooters. For now, this would be a city police operation with the FBI observing and ready to help.

The FBI agents outside would hear, soon enough, why they had been pulled back. And in the years to come several of them would never miss a chance to needle Bolz when their paths crossed at various jobs and conferences. "The first chance I get for my mom back in Wichita to see me on TV," one liked to say, "and *you* got us put off!"

Inside the bank, the officers in the basement heard a commotion upstairs. One of the five customers, a twenty-four-year-old actor named Peter Holden, had tried to jump Olsen. But the Cat scrambled away and now he held a gun to Holden's head, bracing against a wall so that nobody could come up behind him and screaming profanities at Holden and his girlfriend, a twenty-one-year-old actress named Susan Hammett. Olsen pulled a pair of handcuffs from one of his pockets and ordered Miss Hammett to handcuff Holden.

"Get out of here!" he shouted at the young man after the handcuffs were in place. "I know you'll try something again and I want you out of here!"

But Holden said he would not leave without Miss Hammett, and, after a momentary standoff, they both turned and walked toward a door leading to the basement, betting their lives that the agitated gunman would not shoot them. He did not. Seconds later the couple virtually fell into the arms of the police officers stationed in the darkened cellar downstairs and were escorted to freedom.

By opening the door, Holden and Miss Hammett had also set off a loud burglar alarm located in the very office where Olsen and the eight remaining hostages stood. "Shut that goddamned thing off!" he ordered the assistant manager.

"I have to go outside to do that," the man responded, and Olsen assented. The assistant manager calmly walked forward, through the tellers' area and into the customer section, unlocked the front entrance, and walked out. For a few seconds he appeared uncertain of exactly where to go, walking first in one direction and then the other, and all along remaining in the line of fire. Finally, he was beckoned to safety. Bolz, Johnston, and Cottell—on the scene now—conferred and decided to allow the alarm to continue blaring. It might distract the gunman and could become a point of future negotiation.

Olsen's response was to herd his flock of seven hostages back into the tellers' area where the alarm was less noisy. Downstairs, the police officers were hearing it loudest of all and they plugged their ears with live bullets. The change of position above them had provided a source of information to the cops in the cellar. They could now see much of what was going on up there through cracks in the floor.

With the sound of the alarm muted and the conversations with reporters growing repetitive, Olsen was allowing Bolz longer snatches of his time. Yes, he said, the police could send in sandwiches. "And a six-pack of Budweiser," he added.

"Budweiser?"

"You got Heineken's, I'll take that," Olsen said.

"No," Bolz decided, "I don't think they're going to give up Heineken's. Maybe Budweiser. Maybe even Rheingold. You know, they're losing all their breweries here in New York. We've got to do what we can for New York beer, know what I mean? Heineken's is made in Holland and they do all right by themselves. Maybe Budweiser is okay. How about Rheingold . . ."

Bolz realized in mid-sentence that he had competition. Olsen was listening to a radio account of the siege.

"You're getting to be a real ham, aren't you," Bolz

added, quickly changing pace to try to reattract the young gunman's attention. "But you've made a good point already. Are you already a member of the SLA?"

"I'd like to be," the Cat said. "But, no, I'm not."

"You need a better opportunity than that," Bolz counseled, "because you've got a lot on the ball. What's your father do?"

"He's a schoolteacher. But I'd rather not get him involved."

Bolz took the cue and started talking about the food again —"Salt and pepper on those sandwiches?"—and then the situation and a gentle first approach at assaying the prospects of a surrender.

"Things are moving," he said. "You know your point's been made because you've listened to yourself on the radio. So any time you want to knock this thing off. You can knock it off. You've got this whole damned place up on its ass, you know that? One of the things you've got to remember: if you want to make the Eleven O'Clock News tonight—in time for pictures or anything like that—you've got to come out before seven thirty. Know what I mean . . ."

But Cat was back listening to the radio, this time a disc jockey on the station he had called, and Bolz was back on "hold." Bolz used the time to work out a plan for safely sending food into the bank while, if possible, simultaneously establishing face-to-face negotiations.

"The guy on the radio said I was looking cool," Olsen said, back on the phone. "Some jerk. Nothing's looking cool, man. I'm feeling lousy."

"Why're you feelin' lousy?" Bolz asked. "You're not using anything, are you, Ray? . . . No? . . . Then, why feel lousy? We're doing all right. We haven't had any problems. And we just figured out how we're going to get the food into you. We're going to throw you a rope and then we're going to put a shopping cart on the rope. And you can have somebody pull the rope in through that inside door, you follow me? Or you can pull the rope in yourself because they're inside, the hostages, and they can't get past you."

But the Cat seemed unconvinced.

"When the door opens, how do I know the cops won't rush in here?" he demanded.

"Hey, Ra-a-a-y. Let me tell you. I'll be there. You can trust me. Hey, all you have to do is close the door. You'll see me. You'll see my hands. I will personally push the wagon to that front door and throw the rope in, right to the other door. All right? Then, when the rope is by the door, stay right there. I'll have my pants rolled up and all that silly garbage with no weapons. I'll turn around and give you a look-see. Then I'll stay and make sure nobody rushes at the door. If you like, I'll close the front door, too. Then, after you've got the food inside, I'll open it again."

Olsen was concerned that police sharpshooters could pierce the bulletproof glass with their high-powered rifles.

"If we wanted to do that," Bolz said straightforwardly, "we could've done that a long time ago."

"Except," Olsen noted, "some people were going to go down with me."

"The point is, Ray, if we wanted to blow you away, some guys out there could do that. But that's not our *shtick*. You understand? What would we gain out of that?"

"People could go home," Olsen said.

"Hey," Bolz laughed. "We're all on overtime. What's the difference! The point is, like I said before, you did this for a cause. You believe in something, right? Or else you wouldn't be doing this, right or wrong?"

Olsen asked about the $10 million in gold and Bolz decided to end such talk by making light of his request. It would be impossible to move such a shipment without days of red tape, he declared. At least he could produce roast beef sandwiches and beer, Bolz thought to himself, and until he gained the young man's trust he wanted to deal in matters he could control, like whether the sandwiches should be on rye, rolls, or Italian hero bread (which was his next question).

Finally, Olsen seemed satisfied with Bolz's plan, adding a somber warning: "Don't rush the door, man. It'll be the biggest mistake you ever made."

"Hey, man," Bolz responded. "I'm telling you. Don't fuck with me because *I'm* afraid."

"Well, don't try."

"I won't try."

"Can you promise me? Can you promise me you're not going to try to rush the door? I'll be in the very corner. And all the hostages will be in front of me. They'll be the first to go."

"Hey, listen," Bolz said. "I'm promising you because *I* don't want to go. They tell me it'll be about five minutes. So talk to me in the meantime."

Bolz sighed. It was important to intersperse small talk with all the strategy to take the edge off Olsen, first so he would be less likely to harm his hostages and second so he might eventually let down enough to surrender or be taken.

"Oh boy oh boy oh boy," Bolz said with a long sigh. "I think I'm going to have a sandwich while you have your sandwich."

"Go ahead," Olsen said.

"Yeah," Bolz complained, "but they won't let me have any beer."

"Well," Olsen said, with all the indignance of a taxpayer, "you're on duty."

"Yeah, so I can only drink milk."

Actually, Bolz had downed a quart of milk soon after arriving at the delicatessen. He had learned on previous hostage jobs that it steadied him. They talked about Olsen's last job as a messenger, which ended when he was arrested for possession of marijuana.

"That's a shame," Bolz said. "Once they knock that thing out there'll be a lot of kids who won't get records—hey, I worry about my kid, you know? I've got a young teen-age kid and I'm worried that someday he'll get busted for some silly shit experimenting. And how the hell would that look?"

"It would look pretty bad."

"You know, he'd still be my kid, no matter what," Bolz declared. "So you've got to do the right thing for your kid and try to straighten him out and do the best you can."

"Yeah," the Cat said. "They had my father on the radio. Isn't that *too* much. N-E-W had him on."

"You talked to N-E-W before, didn't you?"

"We talked to them for a little while," Olsen answered,

lapsing into the first-person plural he had used at the outset when he was seriously pretending to have an accomplice. The police were now certain that he did not, but in truth they had given the first two escapees, the actor and actress, a long look, suspecting for just a moment that their escape might have been a bit too pat.

"I don't want to see my father around," Olsen cautioned. "If he comes down, don't send him in."

"Absolutely not," Bolz assured him. "Of course not. No . . . Here's what I wanted to ask you. Like I said before, I want to ask you this quietly. Now if you want to make the Eleven O'Clock News, the move has to be made early. You understand what I mean?"

Yes, Olsen said, and now Bolz was speaking in a stage whisper. "If you want time for a press conference or something like that, that'll be worked out. Either as you're coming out or if you want to sit down later with a press conference. Do you follow me?"

"But how? You guys have marksmen who'll shoot me down. Just recently, somebody on the West Coast, he was going——"

"This is not the SWAT team of Los Angeles," Bolz interrupted. "Remember that. This is the City of New York. And for two years we've been *futzing* around and nobody's ever been hurt. Not a hostage. Not a perpetrator. Not a cop."

"In *Dog Day Afternoon* Sally was shot," Olsen reminded Bolz. "He was shot in the heart underneath the wing of the plane."

"That was at the airport," Bolz said. He was almost beginning to enjoy this line of dialogue, winking back at McGillicuddy. "That was the FBI. You know the FBI. You've got to watch them mothers. There're some bad suckers out there at the airport, I'm telling you."

"Well," Olsen said, "how am I going to get out? The only way is the airport."

"Well," Bolz said, back to his phony whisper, "why don't you come with me? We'll set up this news conference and you can do your thing. You know from the very beginning that you wanted to make your point for Patty Hearst and the

Harrises and them people, right? Let's eat first and then you've got to move if you want to be somebody and we'll work it out."

Bolz introduced Olsen to Joe Mulligan, his backup negotiator. Mulligan took the phone in one hand and he held one of a pair of field phones in the other. Another cop accompanied Bolz out the door with the other field phone, so that Olsen could still communicate with Bolz, through Mulligan, if any problem developed.

None did. Olsen sent a hostage named Anthony John out to fetch the shopping cart and he carefully pulled it back into the tellers' area.

Cottell had accompanied Bolz outside and he said, "Tell him you and I will go in and meet him halfway." But Bolz did not like Olsen's demeanor. "You and *who*, Chief?" he said, adding, "I don't think he's ready yet, Chief." Bolz remained outside for a time and then walked back to the delicatessen.

"Hey, Frank," Olsen called to him good-naturedly after they had restored phone contact, "you're the one in the baseball cap."

"I told you I'd be straight with you," Bolz said.

"At this point," Olsen said a moment later, "I have more confidence in you."

But not enough confidence, it turned out, for Olsen to agree to resume his discussion with Bolz face-to-face. So they continued to talk over the phone. Yes, Olsen said, tell the delicatessen owner that he would pay for the sandwiches and beer.

"Your money or the bank's money," Bolz said.

"My money," Olsen said. "I haven't even touched the bank's money."

"Haven't touched the bank's money?" Bolz said. "Well that's a smart move because that way we have no robbery."

"But you still have an attempted robbery," Olsen insisted.

"We wouldn't," Bolz said.

"I didn't come in here to take the money," Olsen reminded Bolz.

"You did it to make a point," Bolz agreed. "And that's

the idea. You're making your point. Consequently there's no intent for a robbery.''

Olsen offered the horn to one of his hostages, assistant bank manager Larry Haber, who seemed willing enough to stand up for his captor.

''The point he's making is never once did he ask for money. He came in here wanting to make a statement about the radical scene, I guess. And he's never asked for money, never gone for money, and never threatened us. And he's let us go to the bathroom.''

Bolz was very happy to be talking to one of the hostages. It would provide him with more evidence upon which to gauge the mood inside the bank, and it would allow him the chance to communicate with the captives. At its best, such communication could help the cops decide if and when they might move in. Otherwise, it would be a tool of reassurance and a method of impressing the reality of their situation on the hostages. Hostages were most susceptible to the curious Stockholm Syndrome—an extreme condition of psychological transference named for the Swedish bank vault siege in which the captors' victims seemingly became their willing accomplices when they were being held in an informationless vacuum.

''Nobody should do anything stupid,'' Bolz told Haber. ''This guy seems to be a nice enough fella. Don't anybody do anything stupid. Everything will be all right. Understand? And the cops aren't going to do anything stupid either. They're well trained, well disciplined.''

Haber said he understood and then offered the police the names of all the hostages—himself, three female employees (he was so nervous he forgot the name of one of them), and three customers—the hospital worker from St. Vincent's who had met Bolz for the food, a sixteen-year-old neighborhood youth, and a man named Patrick Loughran. It took about three transmissions to get that one right, and Bolz, the German cop in a department traditionally dominated by men of the Auld Sod, laughed and wisecracked, ''Don't worry about it, all those Irish names sound alike to me too.''

Haber said that everyone in the bank was relaxing and listening to WNEW-FM and he asked if the station could broadcast a correction. It was repeating the erroneous information, the manager said, that the siege began when Cat Olsen was trapped during an aborted robbery. Bolz promised to seek the correction. "You *will* face the problem of an unlawful imprisonment," he reminded Olsen a few minutes later, trying to sound benevolent yet honest. "But that type of horseshit is soft."

Olsen was silent for a few seconds and then he said, "I think in about an hour I'm ready to walk out of here."

Bolz tried to pursue the issue without sounding anxious. *He* had to be playing Olsen, not vice versa. "Well, listen, if you can do it between eight and eight thirty, we'll set up the press conference for you," he said. "Then they'll make the Eleven O'Clock News. I'll meet you at the front door myself."

Yes, Olsen agreed, that sounded like "the only way to go." The airport would expose him to FBI sharpshooters. "They'd just as soon blow me away," he said. "Hey, the guys are yelling, 'Let's get some more beer here.' "

Bolz proposed that another six-pack was worth the release of two more hostages. "The people say no," Olsen said, laughing.

Bolz laughed with him. "They want to stay?" he asked incredulously.

"We're all here together," Olsen said. "Besides the beer isn't for me. I'm not much of a beer drinker, actually. It's for them."

Bolz decided to try riding the good mood.

"Listen," he said, "are you ready now? The earlier you do it, the more play you get. Then, you also get Channel Five at ten o'clock. And Channel Two. Chris Borgen is another guy, he's a good guy. He wears some shitty clothes sometimes, but he's not a bad guy, really." Borgen, a former cop, was, typically, the only newsman in the delicatessen.

"This'll get out to Frisco," Bolz said, trying to prolong the mood.

"It's a hell of a way to make it, isn't it?" Olsen said.

"Listen," Bolz said, "everybody's got to do their thing. You're a man. You didn't hurt anybody. That's the main thing."

"Let me finish my sandwich," Olsen said.

The fish was not ready to be pulled onboard just yet.

Bolz tried to prolong the dialogue, dredging up anything to keep the conversation going and always gently reminding Olsen that he was running out of time for optimum media exposure. Olsen, in turn, was reminded for some reason about his experience as a Hare Krishna follower.

"I was an active devotee for a long time," he said. "You see the whole thing is if you're an active devotee you have to keep following the principles. You can never eat meat. No meat-eating and no intoxication whatsoever, no sex life and no gambling."

Bolz knew his basic Henny Youngman.

"If there's no drinking, no gambling and no *futzing* around," he said, "what the hell is left?"

And Olsen, in turn, sounded like he was parodying Terry Southern.

"You see there's a verse in the Bakhvadar," he said earnestly. "It goes, 'One may artificially repress the desire of the senses even though the sense of material enjoyment remains. You see, experiencing such desires enriches you. If you can get a little taste of the Hare Krishna madre, then you can become fixed up in consciousness."

"Yeah," Bolz said, "but the bell business—ding, ding, ding, ding—"

"But those are very old."

"That's the *shtick?*" Bolz said. "I don't knock it."

"Hey, listen," the Cat continued, "you know about anthropologists? They're involved in tracing back history. Well, they can trace back five thousand years and no further. But the Vedic scriptures go back millions and millions of years, from the time the first male was put on the planet. Everything is in the Vedic scriptures according to the Sanskrit."

On the radio, a Grateful Dead album came on, dedicated, as per his request, to the Cat, and then there was Scott Muni, outside the bank now, trying to fulfill the police request that he correct the earlier newscast.

"We really don't have a serious crime at that moment,"

Muni told his audience. "The only crime we have is that some-one has hostages in the bank next door to where I am now. And I realize that he doesn't want to get into any more trouble than there possibly is at the moment. We had told you that he went to hold up the bank and that's not true. What he really went to do was to impress on people that there is a person in need of a friend and help. The message is that if he'll come out and give up the hostages, everything is okay . . ."

Bolz whistled into the phone to Cat. No need to have some bug-eyed disc jockey do any more negotiating than necessary.

"Yeah, I heard him," Olsen said. "I really enjoyed his rap. He said, 'There's a guy in here who really needs a friend.' The point is, that I didn't attempt a holdup."

"Well, the rest of it was his *shtick,* he's talking—"

"He's talking jive. Talking about all those hostages who are trapped. You'd think I was Billy the Kid."

"Nah," Bolz said. "Not Billy the Kid.'"

"What's the matter with Billy the Kid?" Olsen asked. "You hate Billy the Kid?"

"I dig Billy the Kid and John Dillinger and Joey Gallo. And all those other guys who did their thing, man," Olsen said. "You either do it or you don't do it, man. Either your fear overcomes you and you can't do it or——"

"The point is," Bolz interrupted, "it took a lot of heart for you to be in there."

"It took a lot of heart," Olsen agreed.

"You're nobody's fool. And you've got nothing to hang your head about."

"Hey," Olsen said. "They're asking for more beer."

"Before I give you more beer," Bolz said, "I've got to be able to negotiate and say, 'I got something for something.' "

"All right," Olsen said. "If we let one hostage loose, do we get a six-pack?"

Bolz asked Olsen to release all the remaining females. "Listen," the Cat complained, "I know what these guys'll do. They'll say, 'More beer.' And then I'll have to let another girl go. We won't be here more than a couple of hours. Listen, I'm on the spot. I've got the light. And let me have it for a couple more hours. Hey, it's all right. I don't want to make the Ten O'Clock News anyway."

"So you'll make the Eleven O'Clock," Bolz said. "Hold on a minute. Let me come out there with the beer and you let one of the girls bring the wagon out, all right? 'Cause we've got to get the guys ready. We don't want to get anybody shook up out here."

But inside, things were not going precisely according to plan. The young woman who had been advised that she could leave in exchange for the beer became confused and walked through the first door she saw—the wrong way. She wound up in the clutches of the Emergency Service cops in the basement. Olsen ordered a second young woman to walk to the front, fetch the six-pack, and then go back outside to freedom.

As she reached Bolz at the outside door, the woman started to cry. She fell into his arms and hugged him. Instinctively, Bolz's eyes filled with tears as well and he did not mask them as he gently guided the young woman to another cop behind him. Frank Bolz had a daughter. Saving lives could be an emotional experience even for a pro.

It was Olsen who told Joe Mulligan about the first girl's wrong-way exit. "I hope she didn't faint," he said. Mulligan acknowledged that the girl was safe and Olsen didn't seem to mind that she had been liberated from him. "Okay," he shouted to Bolz out front. "I'll be talking to you!"

And a few minutes later, Bolz was back on the phone, slightly out of breath. "Hey, Ray, baby," he said. "That broad made a mistake."

"Yeah, I know," Olsen said. "Everybody makes mistakes. Except me."

With that, Olsen took the phone receiver and placed it next to his radio, treating the city police and the FBI to two more selections from a Grateful Dead album, courtesy of WNEW-FM radio. Well, Bolz thought, maybe it's better than having to hear Scott Muni trying to psych the kid out.

Except that now Cat Olsen himself was imitating a DJ, coming back on the phone as the final chord faded. "How're you doing? You hear it?"

"Yeaahhh," Bolz said, playing the straight man. "Hey, boy, you're doing fine."

"Everybody out there relaxed?"

"Everybody's relaxed," Bolz assured Olsen. "In fact, I

hear when you come out they're going to give you a 'hip-hip-hooray!' Because the people really feel good about the fact that you did the right thing. That's the word from the people out by the barricade.''

"A good response from the crowd?" Olsen asked.

"Good response from the crowd," Bolz assured him. But a few seconds later, the line was dead again and Bolz was cursing into the phone. He decided to take a closer look. He walked outside and around to the door of the bank and was out there when Cat returned to explain to Joe Mulligan that he had taken time to urinate into a money bag. "I had to take a pee!" he shouted out at Bolz.

Bolz returned to the phone. Under most circumstances, Cat Olsen's act of urinating into a money bag would have been considered somewhat bizarre. Yet he certainly could not have turned his back on his hostages and used the men's room. Indeed, he had forewarned his remaining female hostage and she had turned away from him.

"Listen," Bolz said, "she's got class and you've got class. Hey, anybody whose got as much heart as you've got is all right, really. It's moving now to the time. If you're ready, I'll stand by the door, like I said, and let them walk out one at a time."

"I got two weapons," Olsen said. "I got a revolver—a Colt Cobra—and a sawed-off .30.30."

"What you do is, you put them down on the floor."

"I'll throw them out where you can see them," Olsen said.

"We'll look at each other and touch each other's hands," Bolz said. "Nobody's going to shoot me, nobody's going to shoot you. Like I told you, there's no question about that. How many years have we been doing this? Okay, I'm going to come to the door, all right?"

"Wait a minute."

"Take your time," Bolz said. "I'll stand here. You want to hear the Grateful Dead?"

"Hey, listen, they got my old man on the radio."

Bolz liked Doug Edelson, from WINS, who had reached Olsen's father, but he was hating him at precisely that second.

Olsen waited a good couple of minutes before returning to the phone. "I was just listening to the radio and I heard President Ford propose something for twenty-eight *billion* dollars," he said. "He's talking about twenty-eight billion and they won't give me ten million?"

Frank tried to pick up on the surrender plan, but Olsen said there was a problem. The hostages were concerned for his safety, he explained. They didn't want to leave him alone in the bank. He put Larry Haber, the assistant manager, back on, and Haber and Bolz worked out an alternate plan. The five remaining hostages would encircle Olsen and the group would exit as one. "Like a big pinwheel," Bolz said. Was it a case of transference? He believed that accounted for some of the hostages' expressed concern, but he thought that more than likely their real fear was walking out the front door of the bank and getting caught in a cross-fire.

Were things all set now? Not exactly. Haber told Bolz that Olsen had decided, literally, to play with some of the bank's cash. "He's just counting some money for the hell of it," the manager said. "Wrapping it and giving it back to the teller." Haber and Bolz made small talk. "How much is he up to?" Bolz asked finally. "A hundred thou?"

"This little bank doesn't have a hundred thou," Haber replied. "It's mostly tens and twenties."

Olsen was sitting cross-legged on the floor, his guns in his lap, making neat little piles of bills, like a kid preparing to start playing Monopoly. He told Patrick Loughran that he could go to the bathroom. Olsen was still counting money. Ultimately he stopped at $2,500. "That's all?" Bolz said. "All that time and all he's got is twenty-five hundred? Hey, listen, I'm telling you—if you went to rob a bank, it wouldn't even pay. You want to know something? It's not a perfect world."

The money counted and stacked, Olsen put his hat on. "It's a felt hat with a pheasant band," he explained. "It cost me forty bucks. It's from Italy. And the sunglasses cost thirty bucks. I have seventy dollars on my head."

"Let me tell you, you're all right," Bolz said. "Listen. Don't come out like a *schmuck*. Come out standing straight. You've got the people on your side. You watch them cheer when you come out. I'll bet ya. I'll bet you a beer that they cheer when you come out with the hostages.''

"How many years do you think I'm going to get, really?''

"There's no *years* at all in this kind of operation,'' Bolz said. "It's months. It's not a federal crime. It's not a robbery. Nobody was hurt. Understand? So you've got possession of the weapon.''

"Let me tell you the story of how I got the gun,'' Olsen said. If nothing else, at least he was talking in longer sentences now. The trick was to let him talk himself out, without lingering on a subject that would make him jumpy.

Olsen spun a yarn about flying to Richmond, Virginia, and paying a hippie fifty dollars to walk into a gun shop and buy the Colt .38 for him. Pieces of the story did not make sense, but that was not Bolz's problem. If Olsen was trying to con the cops about the gun, perhaps to protect a friend, let him think it had worked.

"Listen,'' Bolz said after the story had run its course, "are you ready? I'm ready. I'm tired. I'm standing all this time, too.'' It was dark now. The city, on police orders, had arranged for the street lights on Sixth Avenue to remain off, so the police could see into the bank but Olsen could not see out. And Bolz warned him that when he was ready to come out, the television lights would be turned on. He again assured the young man that he would not be shot.

"All right,'' Bolz said finally. "I'm going to walk out to the front door.''

"Why?'' Olsen asked.

"To meet you.''

"Oh,'' Olsen said. "I'm not coming this second.''

"Oh,'' Bolz said, "I thought you were ready. Excuse me. I'm sorry.''

"I'm kind of concerned,'' Olsen said. "It's not you, but one of these guys that's on duty.''

"Oh, no,'' Bolz said. "Our guys are pretty well trained, disciplined. They're just as happy not to do anything, because if it all works out then we have no problems.'' He again assured Olsen that nobody would shoot him.

"All right,'' Bolz said, "how about eight thirty? I'll be out by the door, okay?''

Quietly, Olsen said, "Okay."

Bolz reviewed the surrender procedure, and Olsen interjected: "The first thing they'll do is hit me in the kidneys."

"No, they won't!" Bolz said with the air of an impatient coach. "I'll be with you and nobody's going to punch you anywhere. Will you stop that baloney! You see the movies too much. Are you familiar with the Miranda decision? Did you ever hear of the Knapp Commission and all that? There are no fat cops that steal apples no more. What kind of garbage is that?"

"All right," Olsen agreed.

"All right? I heard the line about the fat cops on television one time. Joe's going to talk to you here. I'm going out to the front door. When you're ready to come out, you tell Joe, Joe'll tell the guy on the other phone and he'll tell me, okay? Beautiful. See you at the front door, Ray."

But Bolz was barely out of the delicatessen when Olsen told Mulligan, "Listen, give me another hour."

"Aw, come on!" Mulligan said.

"Give me an hour!" Olsen screamed into the phone. "Gimme an hour, man. I want one hour! . . . I want to meditate for an hour."

Mulligan told him that Bolz was at the front door and the lights were on.

"I don't give a fuck about the lights!" Olsen told him in anger, resorting to profanity for the first time since the volatile opening minutes of the siege. "I want to meditate for an hour, man."

He fell silent. The Grateful Dead were back on WNEW-FM, and the Cat placed the receiver against the speaker and turned the volume up full blast. In the meantime, Olsen told the woman to whom he had handed the money to leave the bank and take the money with her. Olsen's idea, apparently, was to secure every unlocked dollar in the bank so he could never be charged with robbery. Unfortunately, by gathering up the loose cash and sending it out of the building, he had achieved exactly the opposite result—earning himself a robbery indictment.

But that would be for the lawyers to talk about later. "Anthony just used the bathroom," Olsen told Mulligan. "I sent the girl out. We've got no more females. We have four hostages at this point. We've got a sixteen-year-old kid, a thirty-eight-year-old man, a thirty-year-old man, and a black guy in the bathroom.''

Mulligan thanked him for releasing the last woman. "Why do you have the black guy in the bathroom?'' Mulligan asked.

"He's going to the bathroom," Olsen said. But by then Anthony John was doing nothing of the sort. He was down the back stairs, into the basement, and on his way to freedom, leaving only the bank manager, the sixteen-year-old, and Patrick Loughran—a slight man who had consumed four roast beef sandwiches and half the beer, making up for the anxious noneaters in the crowd.

"You're making me nervous," Mulligan told Olsen. "Hey, listen. Why don't you do this? Think about this. You've got a good rap going with Larry, right? You know those other people in there? They gotta be jumpy. Why don't you cut them out. You got Larry.''

Anyone who knew Joe Mulligan and had just heard him talking about "a good rap" had to smile. Mulligan was Marine all the way. He had plenty of neckties, every color you could imagine, and every one of them was emblazoned with an eagle, globe, and anchor, the Marine insignia. He looked and sounded like he could go back to the Parris Island drill field that day. But give Joe credit. He was in there trying, talking to this twenty-three-year-old guitar-picker from Washington Square Park about what a good rap he had going.

Then Olsen demanded that Scott Muni call him. Bolz, standing at the bank door now with Louis Cottell alongside him, was asked what he thought. "No," he said immediately. "Tell him we'll give him the press conference *after* he's out. We can't give that away before. Otherwise we lose our rationale for his walking out of there.''

Inside, Mulligan was stalling, and Olsen was not taking it well. "I have three hostages and I want to talk to Scott," he declared defiantly. "That's my last demand.''

Mulligan was doing a song and a dance. Scott Muni had gone elsewhere. Muni couldn't be located. Muni was trying to set up the press conference. "Can you see Frank from where you are, Ray?" Mulligan asked.

"I'm not *bothering* to see Frank from where I am," he snapped. "Nothing happens until I talk to Scott. I mean I haven't gotten anything I wanted yet. If I don't get this, I'll sit and wait."

"Well," Mulligan reminded him, "you also told Frank that you would talk to him by the front door, so Frank is out there and—"

"Forget that! Forget what I told Frank. Whatever I told Frank don't mean shhitt! I mean that's all just a load of crap."

"He's trying to do his best," Mulligan said.

"Fuck," Olsen snapped. "So am I and I'm in here like a rat."

"No, you ain't like a rat."

"I'm like a rat in a corner, man."

Scott Muni was in the delicatessen, but Bolz sent word that he was to be allowed only a personal phone conversation —nothing on the radio. And, thus, when the conversation did take place it was rather anticlimactic.

Bolz remained at the door to the bank. Occasionally, he could see Olsen peering at him. Reporters from various news agencies were starting to call him again, further reducing meaningful phone contact. In the delicatessen, Cottell reached a decision: cut the phone lines. It ran against everything that Frank Bolz and the hostage team psychiatrist, Harvey Schlossberg, taught. You don't sever any line of communication. But Cottell *was* the boss. An officer with an axe cut the coaxial phone cable leading to the bank. Frank had a tight smile. Lou Cottell had been a fine detective in his day. The bad ones don't make it to Chief. But this just wasn't his way, and that was a sign, to Frank Bolz at least, that it was no longer his day.

Bolz was standing in the doorway. Because of the bullet-proof glass separating him from Olsen, he had to shout to maintain a conversation. It was not the best circumstance in which to attempt to calm someone down. Several times he had to remind Olsen to lower his sawed-off rifle—a weapon that was certainly capable of piercing the glass. And for lengthy periods of time, nothing was said at all.

Bolz found himself thinking, suddenly, about his father, who had died just up the street five months before. He knew that dozens of reporters and camera crews and hundreds of spectators were at the barricades, but for him the darkened street might as well have been completely abandoned. He had to take a leak, but he would rather piss in his pants than give up his position. Cat Olsen had to know that he was there for the duration.

The clock was moving and he had lost sight of Olsen. He could see the three hostages in some state of agitation now, pacing the floor and looking down. He tried to establish hand-signal communication with them and was successful to a point. The manager, Larry, clasped his hands and put his head on them as if to tell Bolz that the captor was asleep.

Actually what he was trying to impart was the information that Olsen was meditating. Why the agitation? Three times in the period between 10:30 and 11:30, police would learn later, as he sat out of sight of the outside world behind the tellers' counter, Olsen placed the .38 to his head and pulled the hammer back—a split second short of blowing himself away.

At 11:15, the Cat suddenly pulled the gun away from his head, looked up, and said, "You guys want to go now?"

Olsen handed his two weapons to Larry Haber. The cops in the basement, who had been peering up through the cracks in the floor for all those hours, could not quite make out what was happening, but they saw the hostage with both the .38 and the rifle and assumed he had disarmed Olsen. They rushed up the stairs and grabbed him.

After eight and a half hours, it was over.

Bolz never did meet Cat Olsen. He walked back to the delicatessen, went to the bathroom, called his wife, Ruthie, and then sat down for the first time in eight hours and popped open a beer. He would have to bring the car around to Sixth Avenue and pack up all his gear, but he wanted to wait until the press had dispersed.

Frank McLaughlin, a former newspaper reporter who

was Deputy Commissioner for Public Information, sent word for him to come out and talk to the reporters, but Bolz sent word back that he had been barred from holding any news conferences. A few seconds later, McLaughlin walked back. "I just talked to the Chief, Frank," he said. "It's all right. Come on out."

The press coverage was worldwide in scope. "Special Breed of Cop for Very Touchy Case," the *Daily News* headlined. "Police Hostage Group Employs a Heavy Weapon: Psychology," was *The New York Times* headline. "The Hostage Saviors," shouted a headline in the Australian *Sunday Telegraph*. "Special Force Saves Lives By Talk."

Raymond (the Cat) Olsen would eventually plead guilty and receive a four-to-twelve-year sentence, but in Frank Bolz's eyes he would be remembered most as the man who had saved the Hostage Negotiating Team.

There was another news conference at headquarters and then a trip to the Claddagh Pub down the block for the debriefing, the effort at group therapy designed to bring the negotiators down slowly. It had come by accident after the Floyd Steele job, but now, like so many other devices picked up by the team along the way, it was a formal part of the program.

Pat Loughran, the hostage who had enjoyed the best-catered siege in memory, was there, too, downing still a few more beers. And so was the cop from British Columbia who had begun his day listening to Bolz and Johnston discuss how the team operates.

"Where," Bolz wanted to know, "is the other guy, the Pakistani?"

"Oh," someone said, "he took off at seven o'clock. He was really disgusted with us. He said, 'You can see him, why you no shoot him.' "

Ah, well, there was no pleasing everybody.

CHAPTER FOUR

"I'll Blow Up
the Building"

For all of four decades, the Empire State Building was the tallest structure in New York, rising 102 stories above 34th Street. Then the Port Authority of New York and New Jersey constructed the World Trade Center, two solid rectangles rising higher than the Empire State Building and all others.

Perhaps it was because of such symbolic singularity that the Trade Center would be a magnet for disturbed or perturbed men. Or, it is perhaps because one of the Center's sky-high towers is almost entirely occupied by offices of the State of New York—the ultimate bastion of unassailable bureaucracy —that a man would resort to violence in the face of frustration.

It happened for the first time at 10:30 A.M. on March 16, 1976, when a man who said his name was Gosundi Wusiya walked into the seventy-third-floor office of Norman Silverberg, a special aide to the State Commissioner of Industrial Relations. Wusiya had been at Silverberg's office the day before, complaining about his inability to collect unemployment insurance in New York. He had last worked for about a year in Albuquerque, New Mexico, he told Silverberg, but had been paid "off the books" and had resigned as a result of a dispute with his bosses. Silverberg had suggested that his visitor file an appeal, but Wusiya had seemed unimpressed. He said he would return the following day "to talk to the Commissioner," Louis Levine.

Now, he shoved a desk against the lone door to the office and blocked Silverberg's path as the twenty-seven-year-old employee sought to leave. "Sit down," Wusiya ordered, "and you won't get hurt. Don't move. Don't try to leave. I'm with an organization called Vanguard and we've done this before, in New Mexico. I want the Governor here. I have something to talk over with him."

Silverberg asked for permission to call his superior, Harold Stern, in the next office. Stern sprinted to the door—and found it locked. Then he called the police.

Actually, Gosundi Wusiya's private war against his perception of governmental indifference had begun two years before. Up to that point he had been something of a successful young bureaucrat himself, an executive with the quasi-governmental New York City Off-Track Betting Corporation under the name of James Andrew Johnson. He had earned $22,000 as director of organizational development, spending long hours paying special attention to the needs of minority employees hired to staff the city's betting parlors.

James Johnson had been an activist, but a considered, subdued activist. He had been elected president of the tenants' association in his apartment house on Manhattan's West Side and had impressed his neighbors by directing a sophisticated battle that succeeded in reversing a rent increase. At OTB, too, his superiors knew Johnson as a man who fought quietly to gain as much meaningful employment for minorities as he could.

But in August, 1974, Johnson had tendered his resignation and announced that he was going west, to Albuquerque, New Mexico. His associates at the Off-Track Betting Corporation began to wonder about Johnson when they received a newsletter from him announcing that he had adopted the African name of Gosundi Wusiya, had become a vegetarian, and was dedicating himself to pacifism. None of those actions were particularly objectionable, but they didn't sound like things the James Johnson they knew would undertake.

In the autumn of 1975, a small news story on the wire from Albuquerque confirmed to those who connected Johnson with his new name that he had indeed changed. Gosundi Wusiya and a second man had invaded the New Mexico State Employment Security Commission, declared they were "desperate for work," and barricaded themselves in an office, demanding jobs and a conversation with Governor Jerry Apodaca.

Apodaca did, in fact, talk with the two men, who said they represented a minority-oriented self-help group called Vanguard. They subsequently surrendered and were arrested. But there had been some public sympathy with the cause; and, with the acknowledgment that no weapons had been used in the takeover, charges against Wusiya and the other man were dropped. He soon returned to New York and began working with Ebony Associates, an organization that was attempting to organize the minority employees of the Off-Track Betting Corporation.

Almost immediately after taking control of Silverberg's office, Wusiya availed himself of the telephone, first calling a local television news program personality and then the New York City office of the FBI, demanding a jobs program and a conference with Governor Hugh Carey. Numerous reporters and television camera crews tried to reach the seventy-third floor, but the Police Department's press relations unit held them on the forty-fourth—a "sky lobby" elevator transfer floor. Soon after that, however, some reporters figured out that they could phone the man in room 7303 as easily as the police could—and, as usual, their calls would hinder police efforts to communicate with Wusiya.

Lieutenant Frank Bolz and five members of his Hostage Negotiating Team rushed across town to the World Trade Center and rode to the seventy-third floor. They arrived at 10:59 and, from an office adjoining Norman Silverberg's, Sergeant Dan Linehan called Wusiya and began negotiating. There had been no mention of a gun or any other weapon—and the police certainly were not going to raise the issue—but Bolz and Linehan had to assume that Wusiya had one. All other employees were evacuated from the seventy-third floor.

Wusiya did not rant. He spoke to Linehan in measured, almost robotlike sentences. "We are . . . demanding . . . a . . . meeting . . . with . . . Governor . . . Hugh . . . Carey . . . We . . . are . . . demanding . . . one hundred thousand . . . jobs . . . for . . . young . . . black . . . and oppressed people . . . in the city . . . We are demanding . . . amnesty

. . . for our . . . actions . . . We are demanding . . . the presence . . . of Melba . . . Tolliver'' [the TV newswoman he had called initially].

Linehan brought the state labor commissioner to the phone, but that only seemed to annoy Wusiya. "Don't call me again!" he counseled. "The . . . only . . . person . . . I want . . . to speak to . . . is . . . the Governor . . . Don't go bothering me again!"

The Police Photo Unit had supplied a TV camera to the negotiators, who were anxious to gauge Wusiya's setup inside Silverberg's office. But how would they get the camera inside? For a time, they considered trying to drill a small hole through the wall. Then somebody remembered that the entire building had dropped ceilings. So as Wusiya paced the floor, talked to Silverberg, and answered an increasing number of calls from radio news reporters anxious for a few seconds of his voice on tape, a police officer poked through the ceiling outside the office, reached over, and gingerly removed a single ceiling tile.

When the camera was in place, it became apparent that Johnson was not armed. Outside the door, Emergency Service officers waited. Inside, Silverberg was beginning to establish his own dialogue with Wusiya, suggesting that the man take him along to talk to state officials. The New Mexico incident undoubtedly had left Wusiya with a sense of immunity from punishment for what he considered an act on behalf of righteousness.

"I'll tell you what we're going to do," Silverberg heard his captor say finally. "We're going to talk to *him*." When the officers outside heard Wusiya pushing the desk aside, they were poised for action. When he opened the door a bit, they sprang from the hall and grabbed him.

It was just a few minutes past noon. James Andrew Johnson was charged with unlawful imprisonment, harassment, and obstructing governmental administration. In New Mexico, he and an accomplice, Carroll Woodward, had faced as much as fifty years in prison. "When we went into that office," Johnson had explained to an Albuquerque reporter after his conversation with the Governor, "the only thing on our minds was to demand a job. The abduction was not planned. But sometimes you have got to be ready to prepare strategy and to do that which is best for that particular time.''

This time, he would not escape without paying a price—in prison.

The next time their assignment took Bolz and his team back to the World Trade Center, the issue would be far more personal and the stakes a lot higher.

It was Monday, July 10, 1978, and coincidentally, Frank Bolz had spent much of the morning in Tower Two of the World Trade Center, testifying at a license revocation proceeding.

One evening some months earlier, Bolz had spotted a motorist driving erratically on the Long Island Expressway. He began tailing the man and called the Highway Unit for help, but the unit's dispatcher reported that each of two cars in the vicinity was otherwise involved and it might be a few minutes. Eventually, negotiator John Byron, driving to a meeting, picked up the transmissions on his radio, pulled onto the highway, and cut the driver off, forcing him to a halt on the shoulder.

At that point, one of the Highway Unit cars pulled up. But the highway cops had never seen the man driving. No, Byron said, he couldn't make the arrest. He was late for his meeting. Bolz had not arrested anybody in years. (It is the policy of the negotiators never to make an arrest on the job because publicized court appearances stemming from negotiations might cause a loss of future credibility.) But Bolz, accompanied by the highway cops, escorted the driver to the Forest Hills precinct stationhouse, watched as the intoxication test was administered (it was positive), and then completed the paperwork.

Eventually, the driver pleaded guilty to a reduced charge. But the State Department of Motor Vehicles summoned Bolz to a July 10th hearing into whether the driver's license should be suspended. When Bolz arrived at the sixty-fourth-floor offices of the department, the driver had not arrived, but the administrative judge who was presiding agreed to take his deposition. And, shortly after 10:00 A.M., Bolz left for One Police Plaza several blocks away.

As Bolz completed his testimony, another administrative judge, named Louis Jerome, was calling a different hearing to order in the offices of the State Workmen's Compensation Board twenty-eight floors below.

In addition to the judge, those in the small hearing room were Adeline Walker, the court clerk; Clarence Douglass, the court stenographer; Sidney Duzant, a representative of the state insurance fund; Wladyslaw Fraczek, the appellant whose case was to be heard, and Anton Gasperik, Fraczek's attorney.

It was a rather involved case.

Fraczek, a former Polish soccer player, had defected to West Germany while on a playing tour in 1974 and had come to the United States the next year. He went to work at a machine shop in Brooklyn, but soon after that he accidentally cut two fingers with a power saw and fell from a ladder, injuring his head.

Fraczek had received medical benefits plus a Workmen's Compensation award of $6,500, based on the decision that he had suffered a 40 percent loss of his middle finger and the complete loss of the use of his index finger. The last weekly installment had been paid in November, 1977, and the following month Fraczek asked that his case be reopened, on the premise that he had never been compensated for his head injury, which he contended had led to dizziness, headaches, and a loss of memory that were preventing him from seeking further employment. The matter was rendered more complex because the employer claimed that Fraczek had failed to wear safety equipment that could have prevented the accident. And it was complicated still further by the fact that Fraczek spoke little English and that his attorney, Gasperik, ostensibly translating for him, possessed merely a rudimentary knowledge of Polish.

Shortly after 10:00 A.M. that Monday, Jerome examined the file, noted that necessary new physical examinations of Fraczek had never been conducted, and postponed the case for three months, pending their completion. Gasperik had informed Fraczek a few minutes before that a delay was very possible. Now he began trying to convey the essence of the action to his client.

Suddenly, Fraczek stood up and started shouting, in Polish, "I've been coming here for three years! I want this settled now!"

He ran from behind his place at the applicant's bench to the door, just beyond the judge's bench, and slammed it shut and announced in Polish, "Everyone will stay!"

As Gasperik translated, another state insurance employee, Charlie Cates, looked through the window in the door but walked away when he spotted Duzant frantically signaling him to stay out. When a department attorney, Sal Ciaccio, approached a moment later, the judge tried to shoo him away, but Ciaccio misunderstood and entered the room. Miss Walker, the clerk, was closest to the door, and she ran out as he came in. A moment later, a security guard peeked in, heard Fraczek shout at him in Polish, and left for help, and Ciaccio fled with him.

Fraczek returned to the bench and pulled a peculiar-looking olive-colored device from a plastic bag he had carried into the hearing room. "This is a bomb," Fraczek said in Polish. He wheeled over a blue suitcase from where he had parked it in a corner of the room. "In that case," he said, "there is eighty pounds of dynamite. If the bomb explodes, the building will explode and everyone will die."

"What does he want?" the judge asked Gasperik after hearing the numbing translation.

"He wants to be healthy like he was before," the lawyer said after conferring with Fraczek.

"Tell him I'll give him a pension for life," Jerome ad-libbed, but it was too late for such a promise.

"I only want my health back," Fraczek stated with obvious emotion.

And by the time Captain John Collins of the Port Authority police arrived a few moments later, an impasse had been reached—Fraczek with his green device and his suitcase, standing near the door; Jerome still at his bench; Gasperik, the attorney; Duzant, the state insurance official, and Douglass, the stenographer, elsewhere in the room. Collins ordered the floor evacuated and the city police notified.

It was 11:00 A.M. At police headquarters, Bolz had just

walked into his office when the call came. "Police Officer Zontini, Operations Unit, reports a suspicious device at Number Two World Trade Center, thirty-sixth floor, and a possible hostage situation. Circumstances unknown at this time."

Back on the thirty-sixth floor of the World Trade Center, Bolz immediately sent for Detective Myron Kopchynski, a Ukrainian-born member of the negotiating team with a working knowledge of several dialects of Russian as well as Polish. Then he tried to organize things on the floor, where a variety of police and state officials were buzzing around like hornets outside a disturbed nest.

The state had an information desk just opposite the elevator bank and that seemed to be the right place for a temporary headquarters. A thirty-five-foot corridor separated the desk from the entrance to a common vestibule for six hearing rooms, three on each side. Fraczek was holding forth in the middle hearing room on the right. Miss Walker and Ciaccio were able to outline the situation in the room and to describe the purported explosive device. They said it was metallic and was shaped like a bulb at the bottom with a cylinder protruding from it that served as Fraczek's handle.

By then, the negotiating team's television camera had been brought up by the Police Photo Unit. It was about the size of a cigar box, and Bolz placed it against his side, under his arm, ran the wire down his pants leg, and practiced surreptitiously panning from side to side as he watched the monitor to determine what angle he would need to get a shot inside the door of the hearing room so that a frame of the device Fraczek claimed was a bomb could be frozen and shown to members of the Police Bomb Squad for analysis.

When Kopchynski arrived in about twenty-five minutes and began trying to make contact, Bolz followed him down the hall, but neither Fraczek nor his bomb could be seen from that angle. After a few moments, the lawyer opened the door and conversed with Kopchynski. Bolz, backing him up, slowly panned the camera from side to side, then up and down. The camera was actually on its side at the time, so the men at the monitor had to tilt it on *its* side to retain a proper perspective.

What they saw caused them grave concern. Unlike military bombs or weapons, homemade explosive devices are almost impossible to analyze externally. They would not be able to predict the manner of detonation or the type of explosive.

Fraczek ordered the door closed after a few seconds. Kopchynski was peering into the room through an eighteen-inch square window in the door. Fraczek, speaking in Polish, asked Kopchynski for two things—a typewriter and the opportunity to speak with Bolslaw Wierzbianski, editor of the *Polish Daily News*.

It was 11:50, and Fraczek said he would say no more until his requests were fulfilled. At noon, the police sent water into the room. At 12:15, when a state official broadcast a message over the public address system authorizing all employees to evacuate, Fraczek grew angry, but he made no move.

Shortly before 1:00 P.M., Fraczek acknowledged that Kopchynski was Ukrainian and said that, although he hated Russians, he liked Ukrainians. Both Poland and the Ukraine, Fraczek noted, had after all been captured and enslaved by the Soviets. But when Kopchynski tried to expand the dialogue into a more personal discussion of Fraczek's case, the Polish man said no, he did not want to discuss the matter with anyone but the Polish newspaper editor. When Kopchynski pressed the point, the door was literally slammed in his face.

With pictures of the device not definitive enough to identify it, Bolz decided to utilize the camera in another fashion. He carefully placed it against a wall opposite the door to the hearing room, camouflaging it with some papers. Then he returned to the temporary headquarters for a microphone and, carefully crawling back down the corridor now, placed it against the door to the hearing room, so that police would be able to see the door and hear what was going on near it throughout the siege.

In the meantime, other members of the negotiating team were compiling a dossier on Fraczek, and it had already produced one piece of unwelcome news: he appeared to have enough background in chemistry and electronics to be capable of constructing an explosive device and, in fact, had discussed with acquaintances some of his exploits as an underground antigovernment saboteur before his defection from Poland. Yes, they said, he had talked of blowing things up.

Wierzbianski, the editor, was on the way. Fraczek had no known relatives in the United States, but many in Brooklyn's tightly knit Polish-American community knew him and they were beginning to offer assistance. Among them was a neighborhood priest, Father Longrin Tolczek, and a Polish-American physician, Dr. Nadrowsky, who had treated him for his work injury and had referred him for psychiatric counseling.

A picture was emerging of this former soccer star who claimed to have a bomb. He was as fanatic in his loyalty to the American dream and to the cause of Polish independence as he was bitter toward the Soviet Union and communism. And in recent months, he had become preoccupied with the frustrations of his unemployment and his inability to communicate, blaming both on the effects of his accident. Fraczek had been ill-tempered and easily provoked since his accident and had grown more and more committed to religion as an answer to his problems. When someone asked him how he was keeping busy, he would say that battling doctors, lawyers, and the state had become a full-time occupation. Just a week before, he had brought some literature handed to him by a member of the Reverend Sun Myung Moon's Unification Church to his parish priest. The priest expressed doubt. "If everyone lived like that," Fraczek had replied, "it would be a better world."

His accident had indeed caused him some neurological problems, according to a physician who had examined Fraczek, and he was taking medication to ease his psychological problems. That information would have been useful in the hearing room at 10 o'clock. Now, at 1:30, all it did was tell the police that the man they were confronting inside the hearing room might be psychotic.

Shortly before 2:00 P.M., Wierzbianski arrived, somewhat startled, and said that frankly he could not remember ever having met somebody named Wladyslaw Fraczek. "But I do go to a great many functions in connection with my work at the paper," he said. "Perhaps we have met and I don't remember."

Bolz was always reluctant to allow an outsider to speak directly with someone in Fraczek's position. And the editor's disclaimer further heightened his concern. Earlier, Kopchynski had tossed a field phone through the door, and Fraczek had ignored it. Now Kopchynski told Fraczek that a message could be sent to the editor via police on the field phone, but that he could not be reached directly from inside the hearing room. The disgruntled Pole said nothing.

If Fraczek was play-acting, he was doing it well. His hand never moved from the handle coming out of the base of his contraption. And, once, when he shifted position and moved the blue plaid case he said contained the dynamite, it had not moved without some pull. *Something* was in that bag.

One interpretation of Fraczek's threat had provided police with the information that there were eighty *sticks* in the suitcase. That would be about forty pounds. But another person recalled hearing eighty *pounds* mentioned. Bolz asked to speak with a munitions expert. He had counted about seventy-five people on the floor—negotiators, Emergency Service police, local Manhattan police, Port Authority police, men from the Bomb Squad, a variety of detectives, state employees —and he was beginning to consider the number of lives that might be on the line if whatever Fraczek had in there were to go off.

"If he has eighty sticks of dynamite," a Bomb Squad expert told Bolz, "what would happen is that all the glass would blow out first. Then it would go up through the hanging ceiling and across and the pressure would probably bring down the ceiling. That would be the initial explosion. Then the implosion would come. You see the explosion would create a vacuum and whatever didn't go flying out would be drawn back in. Anyone standing in line with a window would probably be cut to shreds. That's eighty sticks."

Bolz looked around. Two of the building's outer walls were all glass. The floor would have to be cleared of all but essential personnel, and those who remained would have to be positioned so that they could see nothing but solid walls wherever they looked.

"All right," Bolz asked the munitions expert. "What if he's got eighty *pounds?*"

"Now," the man from the Bomb Squad said, "you're talking about an explosion."

Bolz conferred with Chief Dan Courtney, head of Manhattan South and the commander at the scene. They decided then to move the temporary headquarters on the thirty-sixth floor as far from the hearing room as possible and to clear almost everyone off the floor. A new command post was established on the forty-fourth-floor sky lobby. Extra cables were attached to the television camera, the listening device, and the field phone, and they were run up a staircase to the forty-fourth floor. When it was over, Bolz listed all those who remained on thirty-six and counted them up. Another bad omen? It was thirteen. "Maybe we should send somebody else up there," he said, "or maybe bring somebody back down."

A state engineer was on the floor now with the blueprint. Each of the Trade Center's giant towers had been built with four cores, he explained. "If we lose one of the cores," he said, "the building will sustain itself. But if we lose one and part of another, the Observation Tower could wind up in Jersey City."

Kopchynski was periodically trying to make contact with Fraczek without success and, from the forty-fourth floor word was passed down that the editor and the neighborhood priest had derided his efforts. Kopychynski, they said, was speaking in a Ukrainian dialect and such was Fraczek's hatred of anything Russian that it was most likely exacerbating the situation. Sure, Bolz thought, they want to come in and talk. Everybody always thinks they could end it in a second. Kopchynski reminded Fraczek that the police had sent in a typewriter and suggested he write a letter to be published in the paper.

At 3:10, Fraczek asked to speak to a Polish-speaking physician who had been treating him and who was also running for local political office in Brooklyn. "If he doesn't come in one hour," Fraczek said, "then you won't see me or any of these people ever again."

He also asked to see a priest—not Father Tolczek, but a second man, a Polish-speaking priest. He needed the priest "to hear confession and grant absolution," Kopchynski reported. It was the most direct threat he had issued, and when

Gasperik translated the pronouncement for the other hostages, the police could hear yelling in the room.

Bolz decided to allow Wierzbianski, the editor, to speak directly with Fraczek, after instructing him to avoid revealing to Fraczek the he was actually in the building. They had a brief conversation in Polish.

Fraczek said he had met the editor on a subway once, and he begged for the man's help. "How can I help you?" Wierzbianski asked finally, and there was no definitive response.

Gasperik was stationed at the door now, and relaying messages. Fraczek told him to ask the police to send in "a urinal." Kopchynski handed Gasperik a wastebasket. "Close the door," he shouted at Gasperik after that.

Courtney came back down to check with Bolz, and the two walked down the hall together. "You know," Bolz said to him, "this guy may have nothing. If it turns out he's got nothing, you could be the laughing-stock of the department tomorrow. We could go in. It's your decision."

"Hey," Courtney said, "I can take the heat. I can take it if somebody laughs. I can't take it if somebody's hurt."

Bolz thanked him. He was the expert on these occasions but never the decision-maker. It was left for the brass to consider his opinion and make the decisions. And Courtney was one of those commanders who truly believed in the concept of negotiation.

The problem this time was that Fraczek had proven to be a stubborn subject. No rapport had been established with him, and the only real conversation came in short, grudging questions, demands, and replies. He had clearly developed a contempt for Myron Kopchynski, whether it was because Kopchynski's Polish insulted him, or more, as Bolz suspected, because the detective represented an authority that Fraczek detested. He turned down an offer of food, and, at 4:10, he again threatened to blow up the building if his physician was not brought to him. As if to punctuate his declaration, Fraczek picked up a field phone and threw it at the negotiator—an act that could be interpreted easily in English, Polish, Russian, or any other language.

This further limited communication. Minutes were turning into hours. An army of press personnel was kept in a herd on the ground floor this time (with the forty-fourth-floor sky lobby that had been used as a media area in the Gosundi job now the police command post). Nadrowsky arrived, as did a second doctor and Fraczek's roommate, and each was ushered up to the forty-fourth floor, but he was not given direct access to them.

Sergeant Dan Linehan sent word to Bolz: the neighborhood priest, Father Tolczek, might be a productive force, but the roommate was emotionally upset and ought not be allowed near Fraczek. But Bolz had decided that the priest, any priest, was the last person he wanted in the room. "Not if he's asking for absolution," he told Courtney. "No way."

At 5:40, Fraczek again demanded a priest. He wanted absolution, he said again, "and then everything will be over." And, lest that phrase should be misunderstood, he added, "Everything will be dust."

Shortly after that, Fraczek was shouting. He had heard a noise from overhead. A member of the negotiating team, Jimmy Cowan, had recalled the effective use of overhead observation in the Gosundi Wusiya job and had begun, on his own, to try it on Fraczek. But the noise had alerted him.

It would be left for Cowan to explain, some hours after that, why he would move into such a sensitive area without checking first—an act symptomatic of the psychological need of even a disciplined cop to "do something" in the face of frustration. What Bolz urges such unoccupied negotiators to do is to supply more and more background on the perpetrator by talking with friends and relatives and making inquiries of agencies and corporations. But those chores tend to seem mundane to them, with such drama unfolding a few feet away.

A few minutes after the ceiling fiasco, Bolz could hear Fraczek shouting again. The "urinal" was leaking. It was quickly removed and replaced. But Bolz was not concerned about leaky urinals by then. He was worried about the possible ignition of eighty sticks, or maybe eighty pounds, of dynamite. Through it all, Fraczek was still carefully holding the handle of his curious device.

Two Bomb Squad cops were on the floor in full regalia, wearing large balloonlike suits with hoods that made them resemble a cross between beekeepers and space cadets. The suits had been purchased from an English firm. They were constructed of twenty-five layers of Kevlar®, a bullet-resistant fabric.

With negotiations at an impasse and nobody being brought to him, Bolz began worrying about the possibility of a Phase Two—Fraczek's deciding he would move. In such an event, Bolz and Courtney decided, Fraczek would have to be forced out away from the core of the building and its elevator banks, to reduce the risk of an explosion leading to structural damage.

"We cannot permit him to move," the chief said simply. "If he starts to move, we are simply going to have to take him and if it goes off, it goes off."

"All right," Bolz said. "Let's take one of the Emergency Service containment men, give him a shotgun, and put him in a bomb suit. Then if he has to take him out, at least he's got half a chance if it explodes."

Courtney agreed, and the man was chosen, outfitted, and given his instructions. "If he comes out and tries to head in toward the building, warn him and then, if necessary, take him out."

To the police commanders, the idea of the tower toppling over must have seemed remote. Even after hearing the expert analysis of what eighty pounds of dynamite could do, they had evacuated only the twenty-fifth through the forty-third floors. But as Bolz contemplated an armed confrontation with Fraczek, his mind wandered for just a moment. Had he kissed Ruthie good-bye in the morning?

If you're dealing one-on-one with a guy with a gun, at least you have a chance, he thought. You can make your own cover and avoid exposing yourself. But here, I have no options. If this thing goes down wrong, if this guy decides to commit suicide with eighty sticks of dynamite, it doesn't make a difference what *I* do, I couldn't do a thing to save my life. And neither can anybody else up here.

Bolz had never contemplated operating from the forty-fourth floor himself—a move that might have been defensible in terms of strategy. He knew that if he put somebody else in his place to back up Kopchynski and that man later was blown to pieces, he would have trouble living with himself evermore. Certainly, the guilt would render him useless as a cop. Had he kissed Ruthie good-bye before leaving East Meadow in the morning? Bolz couldn't remember. Maybe he ought to give her a call—just say hello and that everything was fine. No, he decided. In more than five years, he had never called before a job was complete. She was a smart woman. Even an innocuous call would probably scare her half to death.

Chief Dick Nicastro, the top aide to Chief of Detectives James Sullivan arrived at 7 P.M. and was briefed.

"So what are we going to do?" he asked Bolz.

"Nothing," Bolz said. "We're going to sit and be patient. At this point that's all we can do. Look, if he was going to kill anyone in there, he would have done it already. If he's suicidal, he'll wait for the right time. Now he's indicated he wants a priest for absolution. So he's not going to do it until the priest gets here. He's going to wait. So let's wait."

Inside the hearing room, the four hostages were beginning to grow concerned about the standoff, and police could hear occasional discussions, some of them loud. With the door closed and communication virtually cut off, police would not be sure exactly what was happening. Now operating *with* authorization, Emergency Service police were painstakingly slicing the wallboard and spooning pieces of the cinderblock wall out of the rear of the hearing room, like jailbirds trying to tunnel silently from their cells.

At 7:15, the doctor left, and at 7:35 so did the editor. The police had candidly informed them that under the circumstances they would not be utilized for further discussion with Fraczek. Then, at 7:36, there was sudden movement.

Actually, it was the fruition of nine hours of planning. Clarence Douglass, the court stenographer, had watched Fraczek carefully and decided (1) the man was probably bluffing, and (2) in any event, if Douglass summoned the courage to make a break for freedom, he could beat Fraczek to the door.

Periodically, Fraczek would order Gasperik to open the

door, and he would demand to know where the priest was; Kopchynski had told him, "We're trying, my friend, be patient." Now as Gasperik opened the door and Kopchynski and Bolz moved into position, they saw Douglass bolting from the room, carrying his stenography machine case under his arm like a football.

For the first time in hours, Bolz smiled. Such are the ways in which people are patterned. Clarence Douglass was running for his life—but he would never think of leaving the bulky machine behind. He had been trained to carry it with him.

Bolz watched for a reaction from inside, and in a few minutes it was forthcoming. Upset by Douglass's escape, Fraczek ordered Gasperik to tape newspaper over the window in the door, and the lawyer began to comply. But suddenly, spurred by Douglass's move, Jerome and Duzant were on their feet, screaming at their captor.

"I'm not going to stay here any more!" Duzant shouted at him. "I'm leaving right now."

As he said that, Jerome, the administrative judge, picked up a New York State flag that adorned the room and charged at Fraczek, like a picador moving toward the bull. Jerome was outweighed by perhaps sixty pounds, and once Fraczek evaded his ersatz spear, he began pummeling the judge with a vengeance. Duzant and Gasperik would tell interviewers later that they leaped to Jerome's assistance. In fact, they stood frozen in their tracks.

Sergeant Swanson of Emergency Services and two of his men had been crouched in their containment position across the vestibule from the hearing room for almost nine hours. "Let's go in," he told them. One cop grabbed the green grenadelike device from Fraczek and tossed it into one of the far rooms. Two others tackled the man and pinned him to the floor.

It was over—almost. Fraczek was led to a room down the hall, handcuffed and searched. Kopchynski was trying to recite his Miranda decision rights to him in Polish. The thirty-sixth floor was starting to fill up with bosses, Port Authority police, backup negotiators—all those who had been cleared off the floor and others who had arrived in the interim.

A few minutes later, Brandy, the Bomb Squad's trained bombsniffing German shepherd, was led into the room and suddenly sat bolt upright. That was the signal for explosives.

"The dog sat down!" one of the cops shouted. Up on the forty-fourth floor, the smiles of success were supplanted by new looks of consternation. Downstairs, the thirty-sixth floor could have been the soundstage for a Mack Sennett comedy, with everyone near the newly liberated hearing room charging toward the other side of the building.

In fact, Brandy had sat down because, after all the hours of waiting, she simply was tired. Bomb Squad personnel—who had shed their protective bomb suits by then and were down to tee-shirts—opened the suitcase and found not eighty sticks or eighty pounds of dynamite, but four loaves of black bread, a Polish Bible, and some other Polish books.

In a nearby room, Fraczek said he would explain how to disarm the explosive grenadelike device, provided the police brought him his cross and Bible. Walter Donach, a Polish-speaking police officer from Brooklyn, who had been preparing to spell Kopchynski at the door, was brought in to help translate. But in any language, it sounded like double-talk.

The Bomb Squad decided to transport the second device via armored truck to its detonation range at Rodman's Neck in the far reaches of the Bronx before trying to dismantle it. What they discovered inside the "grenade" was a flattened Coca-Cola can. The words "God Bless America" had been inscribed on one side of it, along with the opening stanza of Emma Lazarus's poem that is at the base of the Statue of Liberty: "Give me your tired, your poor, your huddled masses yearning to be free."

The police viewed the contraption as a carefully constructed dummy grenade and saw in it proof of premeditation. But Fraczek was already taking a different stance, and constructing his defense in the process. The device was a "figurka," he said, a religious symbol. He had talked of blowing up the building in a moment of frustration and, later, had made threats when he realized how much attention he was getting.

But Fraczek swore that he had planned no such thing and that much of the siege, like much of his underlying problem with the State Workmen's Compensation Board, had been the product of mistranslation.

Fraczek was booked on kidnapping and other charges, but the Polish-American community hired a prominent attorney for him and he was released on bail to await further legal action. Later he went back into court to apply for permission to leave the country—so he could travel to Rome to attend the coronation of John Paul II, the first Polish pope. He went and returned.

In fairness, there never had been a weapon and there seemed little likelihood of Fraczek repeating the incident. But Frank Bolz knows how scared *he* was. He can still hear the munitions expert talking about explosions and implosions and then telling him, ". . . the Observation Tower could wind up in Jersey City."

CHAPTER FIVE

Rules
of the Game

As the years passed and the cases multiplied, there were many with common denominators. The Hostage Negotiating Team learned to spot various patterns. Some of them were repeated often enough to be labeled rituals—elaborate patterns of behavior that differed little from one case to the next. But the most obvious rule of all was that no two cases were ever exactly alike and that each had something to tell Bolz and the team to help them in future situations.

They even tried to prepare themselves for the case they hoped would never come, the one in which their best efforts would not succeed in saving a hostage's life. "The guilt associated with that death will be overwhelming," Schlossberg told them. "You have to be prepared for it, to understand that if and when it happens, it will not be your fault; that it will have come despite you, not because of you."

But as one case followed another to safe, successful completion, more than a hundred had gone by without the death of a single hostage after negotiations had commenced. It was a record that gained recognition throughout the world and brought Bolz invitations to lecture everywhere. His advice was easy to compose. All he had to do was simply recount the facts of job after job, explaining that the idea of talking first and shooting later (if at all) did more than spare hostages and perpetrators. It saved the lives of cops as well.

When John Ferrero walked into the pizza parlor around the corner from his apartment in the Bensonhurst section of

Brooklyn, he was a twenty-three-year-old time bomb, a mixture of alcohol, methadone, and munitions.

Ferrero was a drug addict. When he was seventeen, he had been arrested twice for auto theft and once for robbery. At nineteen, he was locked up for possession of heroin, and at twenty he was back in jail, again charged with robbery. In need of hundreds of dollars a week to feed his habit, Ferrero probably had committed more crimes than he could remember before entering the methadone maintenance program.

Such a program replaces heroin with methadone, a substance that is nonaddictive and can be administered orally. It is designed to satisfy an addict's hunger for heroin without providing the subsequent "high" that heroin would. Combined with proper counseling, it can stabilize an addict, allowing him to lead a reasonably normal life, dependent upon his daily dose of methadone much the way a diabetic is dependent upon insulin.

The hope is that, eventually, the addict will be physically and psychologically strong enough to reduce and discontinue his dependence, but in fact that was just a secondary goal in New York and other major cities when they started financing methadone clinics in the 1960s. The cities were more concerned with getting drug-hungry addicts away from street crime—so concerned that there even had been serious talk of a heroin maintenance program, a plan inaugurated in England on the theory that it would be safer and cheaper for taxpayers to give the stuff to addicts for nothing than provide it through robberies and burglaries.

For a time, Ferrero seemed to be adjusting well to the methadone program. He had landed the first steady job of his life, running the duplicating machine in a Wall Street brokerage, and had become involved romantically. But after a year, the brokerage laid him off and, with his background, another job was impossible to find. He collected unemployment insurance and paid more and more attention to an old hobby—guns. He papered his apartment with large display posters of guns. And he started drinking—despite warnings from his brother Charley and their father that booze and methadone could kill him. And, on February 25, 1975, Ferrero had broken up with his girlfriend.

He was obviously drunk when he walked into the store-front pizza parlor shortly before 9:00 P.M. and ordered a forty-cent slice of pizza and a Coke. There was one other thing about him that caught the attention of the owner of the parlor, Tony Barretta. As Ferrero ate the slice of pizza and sipped the Coke with his right hand, he cradled a sawed-off .22-caliber rifle in his left. Barretta never complained when Ferrero didn't cover the seventy-six-cent tab and then reached over the counter and picked up a square cardboard pizza box, into which he placed the rifle. Barretta took a deep breath when the customer half-staggered out the door, and then called police.

"Intoxicated man in front of pizza parlor with a machine gun at 24th Avenue and 63rd Street," was the radio call to officers Peter DeMattei and William Nappa, who were patrolling Sector B in the eastern portion of the 62nd Precinct.

It was a fairly quiet precinct, in large measure because its eastern portion, at the shores of Lower New York Bay, contained a number of comfortable homes owned by some of the most lethal mobsters in the country, men whose very presence seemed to discourage street crime and who did away with each other in a manner that rarely if ever involved other civilians or the police. Thus, the report of a man with a machine gun was enough to attract a crowd of cops. Officers John Diana, Tom Rausch, Anthony Vitale, and George Carruthers rushed to the scene when they heard the call.

Witnesses told the police that Ferrero had gone into an apartment house on 23rd Avenue and had fired several shots into a rear courtyard. They went to the house, knocked on the first-floor apartment door that bore his name, but elicited no response. A minute or two later, after they had fanned out to search the neighborhood, the officers heard three more shots. A neighbor pointed to the door of Ferrero's apartment and the first two cops in the hallway, Diana and DeMattei, noticed that there was a key in the door lock.

When there was no response to a knock, they opened the door and walked into the apartment. "Police officers! Anyone back there!" Diana called out. From a darkened room in the rear, a shotgun blast roared past them, and Ferrero emerged. The two cops tried to pry a Rossi .12-gauge shotgun from him and it broke in two. But as they grappled, Ferrero had come close enough to the apartment door to slam it shut, with DeMattei and the other cops out in the hall—and Diana one-on-one with Ferrero inside in the kitchen.

DeMattei didn't use the key this time. He kicked the door down. By then, Ferrero had retreated to the rear and re-emerged with his semi-automatic sawed-off rifle. He fired three shots toward DeMattei at about the time Diana was firing three shots at him with a Smith & Wesson service revolver. None of the shots hit.

After the volleys of gunfire, Ferrero had reappeared with a hand grenade. "I'll kill you cops!" he shouted. "I'll blow you up!"

He pulled the pin and tossed the grenade onto the floor. Diana warned the others to take cover and fired three more shots in Ferrero's direction. From the doorway, Carruthers fired three times as well and Vitale fired once. None of the shots hit—but the grenade continued to roll out of the apartment door and into the vestibule. Everyone in the large room raced for the outside door, but their escape was not necessary. The grenade did not explode.

Ferrero remained in the interior of the apartment and Diana stayed one room away. Nappa and DiMattei circled behind the apartment, into the late-night February chill of the courtyard, cutting off the possibility of a rear escape. By then, members of the Police Emergency Service Squad and Hostage Negotiating Team had been alerted and were speeding to the scene. Four trained negotiators—Al Cachie, Dick Auletta, Bob Marshall, and John Rainey—arrived within minutes and they were joined by Lieutenant Frank Bolz and Assistant Chief Jules Sachson, highest ranking officer in the Brooklyn South command on duty at the time.

Bolz had been at a Long Island movie theater on a sort of busman's holiday when the call came. He had been watching *The Taking of the Pelham 1-2-3*, the movie about the hijacking of a New York City subway train. He was impressed in two ways when he entered the vestibule of the apartment house. First, there were the Art Deco surroundings, almost ghostlike now with all the furnishings gone and some of the wall paint chipping. A lone pedestal table was the only stick of furniture in what had once obviously been a rather fancy apartment house. Not that there wasn't a lot of brass in the vestiblue—all of it festooned to the shoulders of a variety of high-ranking officers who had responded to the call.

Rainey, a Brooklyn homicide detective, stood at the apartment entrance and started talking to Ferrero. The conversation was disjointed and, from Rainey's standpoint, shed no light on what had made the young man erupt. But while they talked, Bolz was outside assembling information. A priest, who as chaplain at Rikers Island prison had known Ferrero, was escorted to the scene; he entered the apartment and spoke with the armed man. Charles Ferrero, Sr. and Jr., John's father and brother, arrived, but Bolz decided against allowing them inside. Each was distraught, and Bolz decided the appearance of either might trigger a negative reaction.

Often, when rational contact cannot be established with someone in John Ferrero's position, it is a small, seemingly inconsequential act that puts the first crack in the stalemate. In this case, it was a cigarette that Rainey offered him. He tossed it about twenty feet into the darkness and in a moment he could see the flicker of a match. Ferrero smoked the cigarette in silence, and after it was finished he apparently decided it was not much of a peace offering. With only a scream to warn Rainey of what was coming, he fired a rifle shot into the wall just beyond the detective.

Rainey retreated into the hallway, but after a moment he tried to pick up the conversation. "How about a cup of coffee, John?" he asked.

"Okay," came the reply. "You can bring it here, but take off your gun first." Rainey complied, in part. He pushed the container across the floor toward Ferraro with a broomstick.

"This is as far as I go," Rainey told him. "I'm not armed. Come take the coffee, John."

What Ferrero could not know was that the coffee container had been carefully—and tightly—sealed with a plastic lid by Bolz, so it would be difficult to open.

Ferrero walked forward. He had placed the rifle down and now carried a handgun. He pointed the gun at Rainey with his right hand and knelt to pick up the container with his left. The detective stood his ground, making no move. Slowly, Ferrero walked back, stopping about twenty-five feet away in a rear hallway. But he could not pry the lid off with one hand, and so he placed the gun in his waistband.

As Ferrero worked the cup lid off, the gun was slipping, ever so slowly, down below his belt. When Rainey could no longer see any portion of it above Ferrero's waistband, he sprang. It was over in no more than five seconds, Rainey sitting on top of Ferrero and Cachie, Marshall, and Auletta standing alongside.

It was 11:03, exactly 124 minutes after the first radio call, when John Diana announced to Ferrero that he was under arrest. A total of eleven shots had been fired—seven by the police—and all had missed. The "grenade" proved to be a dummy. But police found 135 live .22-caliber bullets in the apartment, meaning that Ferrero could have fired for half the night. Not one exchange between Rainey and Ferrero could have been categorized as rational discourse. Yet, except for the one shot following his cigarette, the talk had replaced gunfire and led directly to the capture.

In his recommendation for Rainey's citation, Bolz said that in entering the apartment initially and again after he had been fired upon, the detective had perpetrated "an act of gallantry and valor at imminent personal hazard to life with knowledge of risk above and beyond the call of duty." But even beyond his pride in Rainey's bravery, Bolz felt the effort reflected workmanlike precision on the part of his crew of negotiators, a sense of when to wait and when to move in a manner that guaranteed optimum preservation of all human life involved. "They exhibited all the attributes of complete professional law enforcement officers," he wrote. More and more, as case after case was brought to conclusion without injury, that second adjective—"professional"—was being applied to Lieutenant Bolz and his team.

If there is a pattern to it, nobody has yet decoded one. For Frank Bolz and his team of hostage negotiators, the timing of the cases has been about as erratic as the behavior of their subjects. During the first fifteen weeks of 1975, only the young man who walked out of the corner pizza parlor with his sawed-off rifle in a pizza carton had provided the team with a serious challenge.

One day in late March, for a time, Bolz visualized his own little Munich after a band of thirteen youthful radicals invaded the South Vietnamese Embassy in Manhattan, trapping a young Vietnamese woman. But the scene outside the building on First Avenue and 48th Street was actually about as tense as a carnival, with twenty-five placard-waving, chanting members of the Revolutionary Student Brigade predicting (correctly, it would turn out) the imminent fall of Saigon.

As soon as those demonstrators inside discovered that the release of the young woman was foremost in the minds of police, they sent her out, almost apologetically. They hadn't meant to seize any hostages, a leader of the group said. The woman (in the embassy to arrange a crafts exhibit) was just there. And within minutes of her release, Emergency Service Division officers battered down the door and arrested everyone inside for criminal mischief.

And that had been the extent of the hostage negotiators' major work for four months, until the week of April 14. Then, within thirty-nine hours, the team confronted two situations that would test it on several levels and underscore some important lessons for its growing handbook on the do's and don'ts of its dramatic trade.

The trouble began on a Monday evening in a fifth-floor apartment in the Bronx.

The apartment belonged to James and Shirley Faison and their five children. Three of the Faison children were out with friends, but the eleven-year-old twins, Linda and Leon, were in the apartment, playing with a neighbor's eleven-year-old daughter, Loriann Goode. Otelia Faison, a twenty-nine-year-old cousin of James Faison's, was also visiting, waiting for a boyfriend from New Jersey, Terry Hammonds.

Hammonds arrived at 7:30, and in a few minutes he and Otelia were arguing. When Hammonds shouted that he had a gun that could settle everything, Shirley Faison had the presence of mind to sneak out of the apartment and call police.

Officers Dan Coviello and James Herzog answered the call and knocked at Apartment 5A. Suddenly, the door swung open and a woman—Otelia Faison—sprinted out. And, just as suddenly, three shots were fired from the other side of a long, dark corridor leading to the interior of the apartment. The officers fired three times themselves and then all was quiet again.

None of the shots hit anyone. As the two cops put out a radio call for help, Terry Hammonds grabbed the neighbor's girl, Loriann, and put his gun to her head. Police riflemen, equipped with bulletproof vests, were dispatched to the roofs of adjoining buildings where they could gain a sight line to Apartment 5A. The call went out to the two Bronx negotiators on duty, Detectives Jimmy Graham and Fred McGarry, and, high atop police headquarters at the other end of Manhattan, someone pushed a button, sounding the ever-present beeper on Frank Bolz's belt.

Bolz had been nearby, attending a meeting of the Steuben Association. By the time he reached 1647 Washington Avenue, McGarry and Graham had already started to talk to Terry Hammonds through the half-open door to Apartment 5A.

The building was a classic New York City tenement with four apartments on each stairwell landing. Graham and McGarry positioned themselves on the stairway leading to the roof and Bolz stood behind them, alongside, as backup negotiator. At the other side of the landing, two members of the Emergency Service assault team, Kevin Barry and Charles Craig, were in position, lying face down on the cold marble steps, waiting to fire their Ithaca deerslayer shotguns or to storm the apartment on command if that became necessary.

It became clear, almost immediately, to Graham that Hammonds was incapable of discussing whatever problems he had with any sense of rationality. "I'm here to help you, not to hurt you," the detective told him. "Just stay calm and you won't be hurt."

Downstairs, other members of Bolz's team were talking to the two women who had escaped, trying to gather as much information as they could about the situation inside, as well as the background of the gunman, radioing the bits and pieces

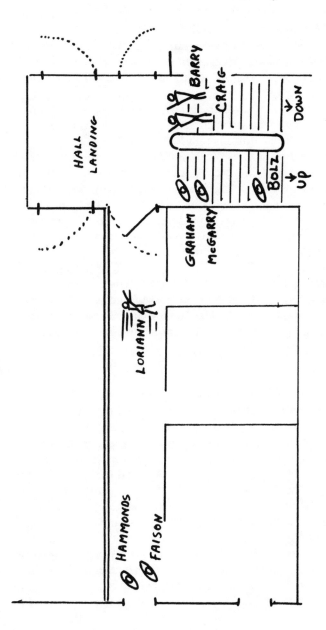

HALL LANDING

BARRY

CRAIG

DOWN

BOLZ

UP

GRAHAM

McGARRY

LORIANN

HAMMONDS

FAISON

1647 WASHINGTON AVE

they could glean to Sergeant Ken Bowens on the roof. William Terence Hammonds, they were told, was separated from his wife and had had a stormy relationship with Miss Faison. Three months earlier, after a similar blowup, Hammonds had wounded himself, possibly with the same gun, in the same fifth-floor hallway.

A check with New Jersey police produced the information that he had been arrested fifteen times. "I've got his yellow sheet, Frank," Bowens told Bolz over the radio.

"A minute, Kenny," Bolz said. "Let me write this down. Okay, shoot . . . No! Hold it! Hold that! . . . Just read me the sheet, Kenny." There were stifled smiles on the landing. "Shoot" can mean only one thing on the Emergency Service Division radio frequency. Bolz rolled his eyes, grateful that none of the police sharpshooters had mistaken his innocent request to Bowen for a command.

After Bolz learned the identities of the four hostages held by Hammonds, he had asked Graham to try to gain the release of the children. And, after police tossed him a pack of cigarettes as a show of faith, Hammonds did release the twins, sending Linda out first and then, an hour later, allowing her brother to walk out the door.

It was almost midnight, four hours after the siege had begun, and now just two hostages, James Faison and Loriann Goode, remained inside the apartment with Hammonds. Down on the ground floor, twenty-eight-year-old Emma Goode was pacing, repeating, "My baby . . . ooh, my baby . . ."

On the fifth floor, Graham and his backup, McGarry, were reduced to making small talk with the gunman, when they spoke at all. The hallway was dank and dark, illuminated by a single, naked sixty-watt bulb on the twelve-foot ceiling. And the ancient marble stairwells were cold. Shortly after one, Bolz walked back up to the roof, more to break the tension than for anything else.

From the rooftop, the police could see a panorama of New York's skyline, with the outline of the George Washington Bridge in the distance, and every minute or two they could hear another plane descending onto the runways at LaGuardia Airport just across the East River. But, closer to them, were the realities of the Bronx. They kept reminding each other not to attempt to take any positions on the next roof because it wasn't there. The building next door had burned, and little more than four walls remained.

On a rooftop across the street, an Emergency Service team was gazing into the apartment with a special night-vision device that amplifies light, so that a lit cigarette provided them with a view of an entire room. The problem was that the device itself emitted an eerie green light that silhouetted the cops' faces for Hammond, who shouted, "Get those motherfuckers off that roof or I'll blow them off."

"Hey," Bolz radioed, "get your coats over your heads." They put the coats over the device and then their heads, like old-time still photographers, and continued to observe the apartment without further detection. Bowen told Bolz that a stepbrother of Hammonds, an Army recruiting noncom named Lorenzo Wrenfro, had been located in Connecticut, and, at the suggestion of Bronx Field Area Commander Anthony Bouza, state police there had agreed to drive him to the Bronx.

Bolz nodded and went back downstairs. Now that we've got him nice and calm, he thought, all we need is some family member to start him up again.

In the hallway, all had been quiet for some minutes. Then, the police heard something. Steps. It was steps. Someone was running down the corridor. "What is it?" Bolz barked and, when the footsteps continued, he shouted, "Halt!"

But the steps grew louder and Bolz yelled, "Stand aside!" to Graham and McGarry and added, "He may be charging us!" On the opposite side of the landing, Kevin Barry and Charles Craig prepared to fire. Then a figure bolted forward through the open door and Bolz screamed, "Hold your fire!"

The little girl, Loriann, had rushed into the arms of the detectives. "Why didn't you say it was you?" Bolz asked, and she looked up at him and shook her head. With all the interviewing of James Faison's wife, her two children, and Loriann Goode's mother, no one had thought it important to tell the police that Loriann was a deaf mute.

When she raced through Bolz's command to stop, she

could easily have been mistaken for Terry Hammonds, gun in hand, and killed by either Barry or Craig. It had been a moment of cool courage for the two shotgun-wielding officers on the marble staircase and neither they nor the four detectives who looked on will ever forget it.

Downstairs, as little Loriann explained, in sign language, how she had feigned sleep to get Hammonds's guard down before making her run, a Connecticut state police car pulled up with Sergeant Lorenzo Wrenfro.

Bouza, who earned a reputation as a scholarly, somewhat rebellious police commander before his retirement, chatted with the man and told Bolz that he believed the Army sergeant should be given a chance to talk his stepbrother from the apartment, where now just a single hostage remained.

"We bring these people here for intelligence, not to use as intermediaries," Bolz told Bouza. "It's stable in there. We wouldn't want to do anything to rile him up."

But Bouza was insistent, suggesting that both Wrenfro and Otelia Faison, the girlfriend, be brought to the apartment door to talk with Terry Hammonds. When Bolz tried, gently, to dissuade him from the move, the suggestion became an order. Bouza was the highest-ranking officer at the scene and he was in command. Standing nearby, another high-ranking officer had listened to the exchange. He pulled Bolz aside.

"Frank," he said, "I'll lean on him if you want."

From the outset, the relationship between Bolz, a detective lieutenant, and the assortment of high-ranking commanders likely to surface at the scene of a negotiation had been somewhat unclear. On the one hand, he was in charge of the negotiating team. On the other, he was subject to the chain of command. And, from personal experience, Bolz was painfully aware someone bucking the authority of superiors in the NYPD might win the battle but was almost certain to precipitate a no-win war. He agreed to escort the brother and girlfriend to the fifth-floor landing.

"We want to be able to pull them out at the first sign of trouble," Bolz told Graham and McGarry. Bouza said he agreed. And after a few moments of recognition, then small talk, Bolz heard his worst anticipations confirmed.

"Come on," Wrenfro told Hammonds, "lay that gun down and walk on out of there. You're embarrassing me, you're embarrassing the whole family. You know what Mom and Dad are going to say when they hear 'bout this?"

For the first time in hours, the voice at the other end of the corridor grew emotional. "They're going to kill me," Hammonds told his stepbrother. "As soon as I set foot out there, they're going to gun me down. I just want one thing. I just want one thing. I want you to send my body down South. I don't want to be buried up here near these white motherfucking cops."

"Hey, man, there's a brother, right up here," Wrenfro said, trying vainly to calm Hammonds. He glanced back at Craig, still poised alongside on the marble staircase. There was the flash of a match inside and the smell of smoke. Hammonds had started a small fire in a trash basket.

"Terry, that's not going to accomplish anything," Graham said. Hammonds screamed some epithets in return and said he was going to kill Faison and then himself. But a few moments later, after further reassurances from Graham, he doused the flames.

It had been eight hours now, but until Wrenfro had raised the subject, there had been no racial references in the exchanges with Hammonds. Now, however, the gunman seemed preoccupied with the issue, and Bolz told Graham to ask Hammonds if he might not like to talk to Craig. A few minutes later, Craig, already wearing a bulletproof vest, handed his shotgun to another officer and went to the door.

"Hey, brother," he said, "I just want to talk to you. I'll put my gun down." And he made a big show of removing his sidearm and holster and dropping them to the floor in the apartment corridor near the entrance. For the next fifteen minutes, Craig made small talk, assuring Hammonds that he would not be hurt, occasionally asking if he could come farther inside.

Finally, Hammonds agreed to give up. Craig, with Graham and McGarry alongside, slowly started to walk the remaining twenty feet toward the other end of the corridor, where Hammonds held his gun to Faison's head. He was to hand over the gun when they reached him. For Craig and the others it was the longest walk, made step by step while continuing to assure the gunman that he would not be harmed. Then as they moved almost to him, Hammonds suddenly pulled the gun from his hostage's head and pointed it at the three cops. They lunged at him, simultaneously pinning him to the floor, wresting the gun away and freeing Faison.

"I would've come out a long time ago," Hammonds told police as he traveled in handcuffs to the 48th Precinct stationhouse, "but I was scared one of you guys was gonna blow me away."

It was mid-morning the following day, when two New York City Transit Authority police officers first spotted Gilbert Caban on an IRT subway train.

Officers Raymond Conley and Joseph Mailberger were on anticrime patrol, dressed as unkempt hippies. They were looking for a teen-aged Hispanic mugger whose specialty was pulling a knife on elderly women as they rode in near-deserted subway cars. It fit the pattern of a previous crime in which Conley had arrested Caban, a seventeen-year-old from Brooklyn. When Conley saw Caban, on the 14th Street station of the IRT Seventh Avenue line, he nodded to Mailberger and the two began trailing Caban.

Whether Caban was their man or not, Conley and Mailberger decided within minutes that he was up to something. He had moved on and off a variety of trains, obviously not intent on reaching any particular destination.

At the Franklin Street station, two women, Theresa Gernan of North Bergen, New Jersey, and Ann Carney of the Bronx, each fifty-eight and both waitresses, waited for the local train that would transport them to their place of work at a posh brokers' luncheon club on the thirtieth floor of a skyscraper overlooking the Battery at the very southern tip of Manhattan.

When they boarded the train, Caban followed them into the first car, and Conley and Mailberger got on the second car. The two women found seats at the front of the car, a position that Transit Police themselves recommend for safety because of its proximity to the motorman's cab. But only seconds had passed before Caban approached them, pulled a knife, and demanded their money. Mrs. Carney screamed and fled, apparently surprising the assailant. She banged at the motorman's door and then rushed away toward the rear of the car.

Conley had positioned himself at the front door of the second car. When he perceived the situation, he slid open that door and the door into the lead car, pulled his revolver, and ordered Caban to drop the knife. But Caban sat down next to Mrs. Gernan and put his knife to her throat. "One step closer and I'll kill her!" he warned Conley. The train was easing into the busy Chambers Street station, a block from New York City Hall, and the motorman was peering from his cab. Conley, who had already broadcast an alarm on his own walkie-talkie, yelled for the motorman to toot his horn as a signal to Transit Police at the station.

When the train pulled to a stop at the station, a conductor opened the doors and all the other passengers raced off. They rushed to find the dispatcher at the end of the platform; after conferring with police, he signaled the train's crew not to start it up again. On the first car, cops were multiplying, and Caban, literally cornered, seemed to be getting more agitated by the minute.

Normally, Frank Bolz is at One Police Plaza, just three blocks east of the station, and would have arrived a few minutes after the call for negotiators went out. But this day, Bolz was in the far reaches of Brooklyn, training negotiators at Floyd Bennett Field. He made the twenty-five-mile trip in twenty-two minutes.

The first thing he saw after he entered the car worried Bolz considerably. Conley, trying to talk Caban into releasing Mrs. Gernan, had dropped to his hands and knees; "I'm begging you, man," he said. "Let the lady go."

What Caban needed to see in the police who confronted him at that moment was cool, subdued authority. As well intentioned as the young transit cop begging for Mrs. Gernan's release might have been, he was heightening tension by displaying just the opposite—a lack of control and an abandonment of authority. You urge, cajole, reason, even order on occasion. When you employ emotion it is under a controlled situation, designed to elicit a specific reaction. You never beg.

Because it was a knife that Caban was wielding and not

a firearm, the police "observers" did not fear for their own safety, and they started to pile up like kids in the grandstand. Bolz had the uniformed city police commander order the car and the platform cleared. That also brought Conley back to his feet. By then, police had checked Caban's record and produced a Manhattan Legal Aid attorney named Carol Halprin who had represented him on other charges.

Throughout the ordeal, Caban's victim seemed to be the calmest person in the car. When he told police he was thirsty, it was she who produced a stick of chewing gum. Once, when he responded to a suggestion that he give up with a menacing wave of the knife, she protested, "Look out, you're mussing my hair!" She told him at another point, as everyone awaited Miss Halprin's arrival, that he was making her late for work and her boss would be angry.

After the Legal Aid attorney arrived and was ushered into the car, it was over in a matter of minutes. "I'll do what I can for you, Gilberto," she told him. He thought for a second, nodded, and held the knife out to a transit patrolman. It had been an hour and forty minutes since Officers Conley and Mailberger first spotted Caban, and fifty-five minutes since he had pulled the knife.

As the cops whisked Caban off, Teresa Gernan collapsed. She was taken to a nearby hospital in a wheelchair, treated for shock, and released. Her co-worker, Mrs. Carney, had accompanied her to the hospital, and the two waitresses went to the club, newspaper reporters at their heels. The manager gave them the day off with pay, and the Transit Authority provided some very special service—a ride home in a chauffeured limousine.

Terry Hammonds, who held a gun to the deaf mute girl's head in the Bronx, was not the only initiator of a siege who became too scared to surrender. Fear is a denominator common to many such individuals. Often it is an element that drives them to act in the first place. Once surrounded, their fear is translated into an expression of concern that they will be shot down if they give up.

Billy O'Malley, serving a term at Sing-Sing prison for

robbery, had been granted a one-week furlough in March, 1976, to make arrangements for possible employment following his release. The State Department of Correctional Services allows such furloughs on the premise that they help ease the pressures of a convict's ultimate return to society. But there is one pressure point built into such releases themselves—the clock. Inmates know they had better be back at or before the appointed time. Men have spent days in solitary confinement for a few minutes' lateness coming off furlough.

Billy O'Malley had been due back at Sing-Sing March 18. He didn't make it and had not shown a day or even a week later. A prison officer called police on Staten Island on the morning of March 30 and said he believed Billy O'Malley was staying in his sister's apartment on Park Hill Avenue.

Officers from the 120th Precinct went there and found no one, but a neighbor thought that maybe they had been looking for Billy's other sister, just across the way. The door was locked. Billy was inside, but he refused to come out. Inside with him were his sister and two friends. In a matter of minutes, a quiet street in the city's least populous borough began to resemble a war zone, complete with a police blockade, Emergency Service trucks, and sharpshooters in bulletproof vests. There was still no firm indication that the man inside was armed or, for that matter, was holding any of the others against their will.

By the time Lieutenant Frank Bolz and the hostage negotiators arrived, Billy had phoned the New York *Daily News* and requested that a reporter be dispatched to the house "to insure that I'm not hurt." Bolz started talking to him by phone, assuring Billy that he would not be harmed. At thirty-seven, he was no kid. But he seemed obsessed, if not petrified, with the notion that unless reporters were there to see his surrender, the police might rough him up. As he had been on many jobs, Lieutenant Stanley Carris of the Emergency Service Division was with Bolz.

Bolz sent word to a pair of reporters from a local paper, the *Staten Island Advance,* and one of them volunteered his New York City police press card. It was slipped under the door. But Billy still resisted.

Then Bolz asked O'Malley, ''Billy, have you ever heard of the Hostage Negotiating Team from anyone else in the joint?''

Yes, O'Malley said, he had and that the team had a reputation for ''never blowing anyone away.'' Bolz played upon that theme for a time, and finally, at 9:30, O'Malley opened the door and walked out. Inside, the three ''hostages'' said they couldn't understand the fuss. Billy, they said, was just scared and, for that matter, so were they. Warily, they accompanied police to the 120th Precinct stationhouse—concerned mostly about Billy's safety. No weapon was found in the apartment. By midday, Billy O'Malley was on his way back to prison. And in the following morning's editions of the *Daily News,* Billy O'Malley's story had been reduced to a single paragraph.

In May, 1976, the City of New York announced that it would be forced to lay off 3,200 municipal hospital workers as a result of a budget deficit. The hospital employees union decided to protest by calling a strike. And as a result, all hospital supervisors were ordered to release in-patients deemed to be in less than dire need of hospitalization.

On the alcohol detoxification ward at Van Etten Hospital in the Bronx, it was easy for those in charge to select Jack Salazar and John Thomas for release. Just that day, the pair had been spotted drinking in the hospital. They had lowered a rope of knotted bedsheets from a second-floor window to a compatriot on the street, who then tied a bottle to the bottom sheet. At 4:30 that afternoon, Salazar and Thomas were sent away.

They celebrated their release by hoisting a few that evening. And the evils of booze seemed to become more apparent to the pair of detoxification dropouts with each succeeding drink. By midnight, they concluded that their eviction from the hospital had been as prime an example of urban injustice as they could possibly imagine. What they had to do, Thomas told Salazar, was get some guns, go back to Van Etten and take over.

They returned at 1:20 A.M., slipped past a guard in the lobby, and walked up to the detoxification ward on the fourth floor. A registered nurse, Susan Augustus, and a licensed practical nurse, Lillian Tinner, were on duty, watching over the ten remaining patients. "You don't belong here," Mrs. Augustus told the two intruders as they appeared at her office door. "You've been discharged. And I want you to leave right this minute."

"We're not going to leave," Salazar announced. "We are going to take over this place. We want to be rehabilitated."

When Mrs. Augustus walked toward her desk to call for help, he pulled a gun and put it against her head. "Lie down on the floor," Salazar ordered. Then he turned toward the other nurse and added, "You, too."

By then, there had been enough of a commotion for the patients to awaken. Several walked into the office, and one of them demanded that the nurses be allowed to stand up. "All right," Salazar said, motioning for the two women to rise. "But I've got a bomb in this bag, and if any of you move on us, I'm going to blow this whole damn hospital up."

It was Salazar who went to the phone. He called his attorney and urged him to come to the hospital. "And you'd better hurry," he said, "because I've got a bomb here and it's set to explode in twenty-six minutes." Calls to a television station and a newspaper followed. In each, Salazar pleaded for the continuation of the detoxification program.

Two local police officers were in another part of the large hospital complex, where they had gone with a patient. They were alerted to the situation on the fourth floor and rushed to the scene. But the doors to the ward had been locked from the inside.

The Emergency Services Division was alerted and rushed a crew to the scene, ready as always to move in with flak-vested assault teams. Detective Louis Hernandez, a Bronx-based negotiator, was Bolz's first man in the building. He arrived at 2:30. By then, Bolz himself had been contacted in his Long Island home and was on the way, monitoring the Emergency Service radio frequency for late developments and doing a cool seventy-five miles per hour through the virtually empty parkways leading to the Throgs Neck Bridge that connects eastern Queens County to the Bronx.

Hernandez could see the two men through a pair of foot-square panes on the locked doors. When he leaned against the doors to call through the crack between them, both Salazar and Thomas pointed their pistols directly at him. "We want treatment," Salazar called to him. "We want to be rehabilitated. We are going to hold this center until we are guaranteed that it will not close."

But inside the ward, a schism between the two gunmen was clearly developing. Thomas had ordered Mrs. Augustus to open a medicine cabinet in her office and hand him some drugs. He wolfed down twenty-four Librium pills, washing them down with a paper cup of milk. He was primarily a spectator as Salazar pleaded, eloquently at times, for better hospital treatment. But whenever Salazar talked about terms upon which he would surrender, Thomas became agitated. Several times, he trained his gun at the head of his accomplice and told Salazar, "We're not giving up. I'll kill you first."

Steve Hyman, Salazar's attorney, arrived in the hall outside the ward entrance—relieved to discover that although twenty-six minutes had passed, there had been no explosion (and in fact, police would discover eventually, there was no bomb). He told Hernandez that Salazar was the father of a seven-month-old infant and had always appeared to be sincere. At 3:30, Patricia Rainford, the hospital's associate administrator, arrived. She delivered much the same message. She had called the ward and had spoken to Salazar, Mrs. Rainford told Hernandez, and he had indicated both a willingness to surrender and an overriding fear that he would be killed, by police if not by his accomplice.

Now, she, too, tried to negotiate with the men through the crack in the door. "We know you are in need of help," she told them. "We want to help you."

"Who are you kidding," Salazar shouted back. "All you are going to do is lock us up, if you don't kill us first."

But both Mrs. Rainford and Detective Hernandez persisted, and the course of nature was on their side. Thomas, the far more unbalanced of the two gunmen, was obviously feeling the effects of the Librium on top of the alcohol he had consumed earlier. Bolz was on the scene now, pleased that Hernandez seemed to have the situation under control.

At 3:50, wobbly now and close to losing consciousness, Thomas approached the locked doors. He was waving his gun wildly now, and Hernandez grew concerned that, in his semi-stupor, the man might fire without warning. It was obviously a concern of Salazar's as well. He motioned for Thomas to exit first after unlocking the door.

Thomas stumbled from the ward, holding the gun by its barrel now, and handed it to Mrs. Rainford, who gingerly handed it to Hernandez. But Salazar was still inside. "I want my lawyer here, right here by the door," he said. He was deathly afraid that the police would shoot him as he emerged. Hernandez motioned Hyman to approach the door and Salazar walked through, into the arms of police, who found no weapon. He had wrapped it in a towel and placed it on a table inside the ward, where the practical nurse, Lillian Tinner, was holding it.

Both men were arrested, but Thomas did not go directly to jail. He was rushed first to the hospital's emergency room to have the Librium pumped from his stomach. And the root of the problem, at least as Salazar had perceived it, remained. By August, 18,000 municipal hospital workers—including the two nurses in the detoxification ward on the fourth floor at Van Etten Hospital—walked off their jobs for four days to protest cutbacks and layoffs. They, too, were breaking the law, violating a court injunction against the strike. But at least they carried picket signs and not guns.

Sea Gate is an island within an island. At the tip of Coney Island at the southwestern edge of Brooklyn, it is an enclave of private homes and small apartment houses separated from the rest of the borough quite literally by a security gate. In the past few decades, Coney Island has become less of an amusement park than a welfare ghetto of high-rise housing projects and decrepit bungalows, making Sea Gate seem even more isolated than its founders had intended—separated from the city's other middle-class bastions by miles of crime-ridden streets and surrounded on three sides at the mouth of New York Harbor by some of the most polluted salt water on earth.

It was 9:30 on a November night when the call came from Sea Gate. "A man with a gun" was in an apartment on Lime

Avenue. The two patrol officers who pulled up heard him screaming from the third floor. In a moment they saw a nineteen-year-old girl—only she was screaming at them, pleading with them to leave. No, she shouted down, she was not being held against her will. Her common-law husband (a polite term for lover in New York State, where there is no such thing as common-law marriage) was very drunk and he had a butcher knife, the girl said. "I'm afraid he's going to hurt himself or anybody else who comes up here. Please! He'll be all right! Just go away!"

The two cops did not know what to make of the scene. They alerted their superiors to a possible hostage situation. All that did was to bring roughly half the Brooklyn South police command, including hostage negotiator Joe Strano, to Sea Gate.

Strano walked up to the third floor and knocked at the door. The girl came to the door and again begged him to go away "before something terrible happens." Strano stood his ground. Nobody wanted to hurt her boyfriend, he told the girl. But she wasn't helping matters by staying inside with him. The young man, who was twenty-one years old, approached the door. "Donald," Strano said, "Ellen loves you very much. She's worried about you. We're worried about you. We don't want you to do anything foolish."

Donald told Strano that he was very upset and that he didn't care who was worried about him. As the detective spoke, members of the Emergency Service Division readied themselves for a possible assault on the apartment. Ellen was very upset, but she did not seem to be inebriated. Strano told her that if she left the apartment voluntarily, the police would take every step to safeguard her boyfriend. "You're concerned about him," he said, "but we're concerned about you." At 10:25, she agreed to leave. Her boyfriend made no move to stop her, but he also did not follow her out. It took another ninety minutes of talking to convince him to leave. He was immediately straitjacketed and driven to Coney Island Hospital.

At the hospital, a physician told the police what they already knew—that Donald was very drunk. There was no reason to admit him or to believe that his underlying mental state posed any immediate danger to himself or others. He would be released. That was the medical diagnosis. But what about the legal diagnosis? Had the man committed a crime?

No, his girlfriend insisted, that had been no threat to her safety. And she had never been held against her will. The State of New York has two volumes full of criminal laws, and, after a great deal of discussion, the police decided that Donald had broken none of them. Two hours of tension and a full-scale mobilization had led, in the end, to nothing more than an "aided" case.

On a June morning on Staten Island, another anonymous call was to lead Officers Robert Richardson and Brendan Gavigan to the home of a forty-seven-year-old civil servant named Sal. An armed man, the caller had said, was holed up in the house.

When Richardson and Gavigan went to the front door, Sal opened a window about six inches from the bottom.

"What's the problem," one of them asked.

"They're after me," Sal told them. "They're following me."

Sal refused to allow the police to enter and also refused to come out. He said that his wife and teen-aged daughters were in the house with him. Within minutes, the house was ringed with cops. Five relatives of the man were found and interviewed. They told police that in recent weeks Sal had been increasingly depressed and had expressed the certainty that people were after him. They also said that he had a long-barreled revolver, a shotgun, and a bolt-action rifle somewhere in the house. The Emergency Service Division and the hostage negotiators were summoned.

When Assistant Chief Jimmy Meehan, a Staten Island commander, began talking to Sal, he learned no more than the cops knew already. Yes, Sal said, he had a rifle in the house —for his own protection. He certainly would not hurt members of his family, he said, but he would not leave, and he would not let them leave either. "You have to understand," Sal said. "I'm a hunted man. They're after me."

Bob Louden arrived and began coordinating efforts, but throughout the day virtually nothing changed. Nobody went into the house or came out, and police were continually reassured that nobody was in danger.

Finally, at 6:30 that evening, Meehan had a novel idea. He gathered the supervisory personnel and told them, "I really don't think we have a true hostage situation here. What if we walk away and call it a draw?"

There were further conferences and finally a decision. The negotiators and emergency cops would be withdrawn and a token crew would keep the house under surveillance, ready to respond and call in reinforcements at any sign of trouble. The following morning, the two girls walked out of the house and went off to school, as if nothing unusual had occurred—and the last of the police departed.

Some branches of the department are geared to making arrests. For them, such escapades would be considered frustrating washouts. But for Joe Strano, Jimmy Meehan, and the hostage negotiators, they were something quite the opposite—the ultimate success story. Potentially lethal standoffs had been brought to conclusions with no shots, no arrests, and no tragedies.

Sometimes Bolz winds up at a hostage job dressed, you should pardon the expression, to kill. He was at the posh Plaza Hotel, attending a retirement party for Al Whitaker, the head of the New York office of the U.S. Secret Service, the night the William Holt case broke in the 77th Precinct in Brooklyn.

Holt lived with his wife, Margaret, and their two-year-old twins, Marlin and Marlynda. He and Margaret had quarreled, and Holt stabbed her twice. She ran into the hallway and shouted for a neighbor to call the police. When officers Richard Parker and John Sugden arrived, they found Mrs. Holt bleeding in the hall. She pointed to the apartment door, which Holt had locked. Mrs. Holt, who had suffered only superficial wounds, was taken to a local hospital.

The officers broke into the apartment and came face to face with William Holt, who was completely nude. Holt grabbed the two children and ran to a bathroom about fifteen feet down the corridor. The officers stood their ground and called for help. Detective Joe Strano arrived to help negotiate, followed minutes later by Bolz, who had replaced his dinner jacket with a windbreaker, but was still wearing dress slacks.

Parker was handling the situation like a pro, and Bolz motioned to Strano to allow him to continue negotiating. Parker commiserated with Holt and slowly gained his confidence. At about 11:30, two hours after Parker and Sugden had arrived, Holt said he would come out, but he asked for a few moments to get dressed. Bolz nodded to Parker, who said that was fine. At 11:45, Holt walked out with his kids. He had had no weapon. The knife he used to stab his wife still lay on the kitchen table.

"Great work," Bolz told Parker. "It's your collar."

"Do we have to lock him up?" the cop asked. "He really hasn't done anything. His wife's not hurt bad, just a family dispute, really."

Like Al Cachie that day in Prospect Park during the Ebbets Field apartments job, Richard Parker was undergoing a form of the Stockholm Syndrome, the psychological transference that puts the negotiator so close to the perpetrator of a siege that he cannot easily separate himself and step back into his peace officer's role when the siege ends.

A reporter can be a negotiator's ally or, inadvertently at times, his enemy.

When Bolz can use the presence of the media to assure a worried gunman that he will be arrested without being attacked by police, he is thankful for the press. If the police ascertain that someone conducting a siege is listening to the radio, they can even use the press to help advance negotiations. They did it to let Cat Olsen know that they understood he had not been trapped in the bank during a routine holdup. And they did it again, in 1977, to tell a band of Croatian nationals who had invaded the Yugoslav Embassy that United Nations Secretary General Kurt Waldheim had received a copy of their demands.

But when newsmen phone their questions directly to a perpetrator—or, worse, begin to play amateur psychologists —while the police are forced to sit by helplessly, they are no longer journalists but participants, and quite likely unqualified for that role. Once, on St. Patrick's Day in 1977, a reporter literally walked into a hostage situation—allowed in by the police, in fact—and he is not likely to forget it.

John Johnson is a tall, handsome, articulate black television newscaster at Channel 7, the ABC television station in New York. Johnson has built up a following in the city, and it was not unusual that someone in trouble would call him for help.

The call that would eventually put Johnson on the wrong side of a .45-caliber automatic pistol came from Father James Lodwick, an Episcopal priest at St. Edward the Martyr church on East 109th Street in East Harlem. Father Lodwick said that he had been asked to place the call by a parishioner named Charles Butts, who was holding both Father Lodwick and the fifteen-year-old son of the church superintendent, who was also Butts's nephew, as hostages.

Johnson called the police and then raced uptown to the scene. Several officers from the 23rd Precinct had arrived before him and were setting up operations outside the church. Concerned that the police would charge the church, Butts ordered the priest to leave and to inform the police that he meant no harm and had merely done this to dramatize his desperate desire for help. He had been released from jail earlier in the week, awaiting a trial for armed robbery, only to discover that his wife had left him and his five-year son had been taken away by the Bureau of Child Welfare. Butts had spent the preceding days trying, unsuccessfully, to get somebody in authority to listen to his plea for the return of his son, and he had gone to Father Lodwick for help. After the priest told him he could offer little more than sympathy, Butts had pulled the gun.

When Johnson arrived, he went to a corner pay telephone and called into the church, speaking directly with Butts, who asked that he come inside. Johnson said he would try, confident in his own mind from previous experience that the police would not let him enter, but hopeful that they might allow him to participate in some form of electronic communication.

But Johnson had outguessed himself. What he did not

know was that the officers who responded to the call had received the somewhat erroneous information that Johnson had called police from inside the church. When he showed up at the door, the officers assumed that he had been allowed out by the gunman to make the call and, as a matter of good faith, was expected back inside. To the newsman's surprise (if not abject horror) he was allowed to return. Too embarrassed to suddenly back off, Johnson entered the church. Now, Butts had two hostages again, one of them handed to him by police.

Bolz had been about to start eating lunch at the Claddagh Pub down the block from headquarters when the call came. By the time he and Emergency Services Captain Danny St. John arrived at the church, Johnson was already inside. Bolz took up a position at one of the front windows, where he could see the situation clearly.

For the next two hours, Butts spilled out his troubles to Johnson as well as to Bolz on the telephone. St. John was at the door. Slowly, as the dialogue proceeded, he seemed more relaxed, thankful that, at least, somebody was listening to him. At times he placed the gun down on the priest's desk. At 2:15, when the gun had been there for some minutes, Bolz nodded to St. John, who rose from his crouch, sprinted into the church, burst through a pair of Dutch doors, and pinned Butts to the chair.

Johnson grabbed the gun and brought it out to the police. That night, he would tell viewers the inside story of how he had talked Charles Butts into submission, but for the moment he was very shaken. "Don't ever let me do that again," he told Bolz. "Never."

A week after John Johnson's nightmare, a hapless forty-one-year-old ex-convict in the Bronx discovered that one plus two equaled five, not three, and it all added up to another successful operation for the Hostage Negotiating Team.

It started at 1:00 P.M. at the Fordham Hill housing complex, when a plumber noticed someone loitering on the seventeenth floor. He called the building manager, Roger Lorigan, who dispatched a security guard to investigate. The guard encountered the man, Jack India, and asked him to come down to the ground floor, where Lorigan was waiting. Lorigan, who had already called police, began to question India.

A young housepainter named Edward Blanchard walked into the lobby just as two 46th Precinct patrolmen pulled up to the building entrance. Seeing the cops, India grabbed Blanchard, pulled out a gun, and backed into the elevator. The cops, Joseph Harney and William Kivlehan, raced down a staircase to the basement, beating the elevator car there.

India saw them and quickly pressed the "close" button, but not before Harney could wedge his nightstick into the door's path. India—face to face with the two cops now—grabbed Blanchard's throat with his left hand and put the gun to his head. "Get your stick out!" he told Harney, "or I'm going to kill the kid."

He complied and India pushed the "up" button. The elevator rose to the eighth floor and returned, empty. They went back up to the ground floor, where a backup team had arrived, and a few moments later heard a noise from the stairway. India, Blanchard in tow, had descended to the second floor, hoping to make his escape. But the police sealed him off and he retreated back up the stairs. A variety of support personnel, including hostage negotiators, were on the way, and those police on the scene decided to stand their ground and wait. They were sure of this much: the gunman and his captive were somewhere up there on the seventeen floors of apartments.

Frank Bolz arrived at 2:00 P.M. and immediately requested a floor plan of the entire building, which he posted along with a description of India in the temporary field headquarters in the lobby. The police decided to start on the seventeenth floor, going from apartment to apartment, working their way down. As each apartment was searched, word was relayed to the ground floor, where Bolz scratched it off his master list.

The search continued. By 3:00 P.M., the building custodian had provided a list of six vacant apartments, and twenty minutes after that, police received word that a telephone in Apartment 17F was off the hook, a suspicious fact. They raced back to the apartment for a second look, but there was no problem, just a phone off the hook. And the search continued, until 4:50, when word came that something was amiss in Apartment 3B. Bolz rushed to the entrance.

India, in fact, had entered the apartment and taken its occupants, an elderly couple, as additional hostages. He knew he was on floor number three—the number of the apartment told him that much, and he prepared for a possible escape, knotting bedsheets together. He stopped when he believed he had enough length to clear three floors.

But India's addition failed to account for two elements. One, floor number three was actually on the *fourth* story, because the ground floor was just that—on the street level—and the number system started with the second story. Two, the apartment India chose to enter was at the rear and it faced out onto a recessed courtyard fully one floor below the ground. He would have needed five floor-lengths to climb down. When the police entered, he surrendered. They found his gun in a bedroom closet.

Less than twenty-two hours after Jack India's surrender, a man named Luqman Abdush-Shahid walked into the office of the New York City Housing and Development Administration in Lower Manhattan for a meeting that had been scheduled to pave the way for a $300,000 federal loan for the rehabilitation of two buildings in Harlem. Abdush-Shahid was a member of the Sunni Muslims, an orthodox Moslem sect, and also the secretary of the St. Nicholas Housing Development Fund Corporation, created by the Sunni Muslims to sponsor rehabilitation of the building.

Waiting to meet with Abdush-Shahid were Lawrence McGaughey, a lawyer hired by the corporation, three officials of the city agency, Jacob Gelfand, Robert Robbin, and Charles Lavan, and a bank lawyer, John Pearson. What no one in the room knew as Abdush-Shahid entered at 2:30 was that six hours earlier he, his wife, and their four children had been evicted from their apartment in the Bronx, their furniture tossed onto the street by city marshals.

Through the meeting, Abdush-Shahid was exactly as the municipal bureaucrats and his own lawyer had always known him—calm, soft-spoken, constructive. Then, shortly before 5:00 P.M., with the meeting about to break up, he suddenly pulled out a gun.

McGaughey laughed, assuming it was a gag, but he was not laughing for very long.

"I'm serious," Abdush-Shahid warned him and the others. "This is a game, but it is a serious game." He pulled out a copy of his eviction notice and a list of demands and told McGaughey to call WINS, one of the city's two all-news radio stations. An employee of the radio station called police, who rushed to the HDA offices at 100 Gold Street. At 5:20, he released McGaughey with his letter of demands.

"The following demands," his two-page, single-spaced letter began, "represent the Sunni Muslims of America, who are Kushites (Americans of African descent) in particular."

Under that preamble were eight numbered demands. Abdush-Shahid said he wanted "freedom of religion"; a suspension of municipal parking restrictions for two Muslim holy days (just as they are suspended on Christian and Jewish holy days); "equal employment for Sunni Muslims"; allowance for the ritual dress of Sunni Muslims; an easing of legal hurdles toward Muslims abandoning "our former slave master names" and adopting ancestral names; more rights for imprisoned Muslims; visitation rights in prisons, hospitals, and other institutions for Muslim clergymen; and immediate "final closing" of the loan application.

Bolz arrived at 6:00 P.M. It was the first day on the job for a new chief of detectives, John Keenan, and he responded personally soon after that. Police were all over, particularly concerned because just weeks before, another Muslim sect, the Hanafis, had seized three buildings in Washington, D.C., killing a hostage.

The HDA officers were on the ninth floor of the building, which was the national headquarters of the Bache, Halsey stock brokerage firm. Bolz and John Byron went to the floor, where eight Emergency Service assault cops were ready to enter, if necessary. Abdush-Shahid had barricaded the two doors with desks, never realizing that one of the office entrances opened out—and the cops could have pulled the door open at any time. But they chose to wait.

Inside, Abdush-Shahid was treating his captives well, even reassuring them that no harm would befall them. But Bolz was concerned about his contact with a growing number of radio newsmen, and he arranged with New York Telephone to have the three lines in the HDA offices disconnected. They were knocked out at 7:10 and it didn't take long for Abdush-Shahid to figure out what had happened.

"Hey!" he called out to Byron and Bolz, "give me back these phones!"

Twenty minutes later, he had another demand—that his list of demands be sent to the Egyptian news service. That led police to suspect that Abdush-Shahid might follow up with a request that he be transported to Kennedy Airport and given transport to an Arab country, and Bolz sent for a car, just in case. But Abdush-Shahid's next demand, at 8:30, was for a prominent radical lawyer and, after police reported they had been unable to locate him, another attorney.

At 8:05, police had slipped a sensitive microphone under the edge of a rear door to the office, and at 9:20 the first snatch of optimistic conversation between Abdush-Shahid and his captives was transmitted back to them. He had indicated that he might let them go soon.

Gelfand, a heavyset, sixty-six-year-old assistant counsel at the development agency, was heavily into conversation with Abdush-Shahid, whom he had known in an entirely professional relationship up until five hours earlier. Now things had changed.

"I understand what you are talking about," Gelfand said. "I am a Jew and, believe me, I have been discriminated against all my life. I know what can happen in this country, what is happening to you and your people. But this will not solve anything."

Outside in the hall, Bolz was trying to maintain a dialogue through the closed door, but it became clear to him that the hostages themselves were upstaging him. After he offered to trade a radio for a hostage at 9:55, the police monitoring their amplifier could hear Gelfand telling Abdush-Shahid that the hostages would not leave one at a time; that they wanted to go out together or not at all.

When Abdush-Shahid again asked for a radio, Bolz decided to place one near the door without extracting anything in return, hoping that when he heard a broadcast of his activities and demands he would feel free to surrender. But there are always dangers associated with employing variables over which the police do not have complete control. The news broadcast reported that two Muslim leaders had been brought to the building (actually, it was an Arab consular official and an attorney) and Abdush-Shahid then wanted to know just which officials had been produced.

Bolz sent someone to get the two names, hoping that neither represented an enemy sect (and recalling that the Washington takeover had its roots in an internecine struggle between Muslim factions). "Hey," he called to the gunman, "do you still have to go to the bathroom!"

"Yes," Abdush-Shahid answered. "We all do. That's the first demand on the new list."

Bolz picked up on the almost Kafkaesque dialogue. "Listen," he said, "I'll clear all but two of these cops out of here and you can come out and go to the bathroom, all right? You can come out with the hostages in front of you."

"Will the police be armed?" the gunman asked.

"Yes," Bolz said, "they have to be, to protect themselves—unless you send the gun out first."

"Are you going to put handcuffs on me?" he asked.

The surrender seemed so close. It was no time to harp on a phony line.

"I have to," Bolz said. "That's part of it."

"Okay," Abdush-Shahid said simply. He turned to the four hostages and said, "Let us pray," and chanted in Arabic for several minutes. Then he took the shells from the gun and handed it to one of the hostages. At 10:30, it was over.

From a political perspective, the case could not have come at a better time for Bolz and the team. They were under the command of the Chief of Detectives and the new chief, John Keenan, was positively beaming.

The hostages, too, were impressed.

"After my ordeal with Luqman Abdush-Shahid at 100 Gold Street, Manhattan, on Friday March 25th, I learned that you have never lost a hostage," wrote Jacob Gelfand, the man who had commiserated so eloquently with his captor. "I am sure glad I did not spoil your record. Please know that my family and I are tremendously grateful for the magnificent job you and your people did in effecting the release of my associates and myself.''

From the Chemical Bank, whose attorney, John Pearson, had been a hostage, Vice-President Charles Lehind wrote: ''The people of New York City are very fortunate to have Frank Bolz guiding the unit which performs one of the most difficult jobs in this city of ours.''

The message was getting through to average citizens and businessmen as well as cops and crooks. The NYPD had found a better way to fight terrorism. And the judges, too, seemed to be learning that, for their part, they were expected to discourage such acts from the bench.

No one who dealt with Luqman Abdush-Shahid failed to feel sorry for him and his plight. He had simply snapped. But to condone his response would be to encourage others, when they had to be dissuaded instead. After he pleaded guilty to kidnapping, Shahid was sentenced to a term of up to ten years in state prison.

Police Commissioner Michael Codd was one of the department's own, a tall man with a ramrod-straight stride who had risen through the ranks. He had known Bolz for years through the Steuben Association, but more and more Codd was getting to know Bolz the way many other New Yorkers were—as the man in the blue windbreaker and the baseball cap who could talk gunmen into submission. That was gratifying, but it had some potential weaknesses in that it tended to multiply the Hostage Negotiating Team's work, bringing them to false alarms turned in by well-meaning local commanders.

Practically from the outset, Bolz and Schlossberg had felt that the team should not respond to ''barricade'' jobs—cases in which someone who held no hostages was refusing to submit to arrest. But when the Police Commissioner asks for you, you go willingly, and that brought Bolz to the Kew Gardens section of Queens one spring night in 1977, to talk a seventeen-year-old former mental patient named Kevin Maysmith into laying down his gun and walking out.

Codd and his boss, Mayor Abraham Beame, had been

taking a great deal of heat in Queens because in nearby Forest Hills, not more than a mile from Kevin Maysmith's apartment on Metropolitan Avenue in Kew Gardens, a ".44-caliber killer" had struck twice in five weeks, each time killing young women. The city was in a virtual state of panic, and a special task force of detectives had been assembled to track down the man (who would kill twice more a week later in the Bronx, leaving a taunting note that would earn his code name—"Son of Sam"—a place in the annals of American crime). Codd wanted no more shootings in Queens, and he wanted Frank Bolz there to bring Kevin Maysmith out unarmed and alive.

The incident had begun earlier in the evening, after Maysmith and several co-workers went to one local discotheque, then another, and back in the car somebody noticed that Kevin was packing a Magnum. One of those with Maysmith, Michael Rhodes, wrestled the gun away from him, and Maysmith became so upset he stalked off and went home. "Aw," said another of those in the car, Lonnie Mitchell, "it probably isn't even loaded." Mitchell reached out of the window, pointed the gun skyward, and fired. A bullet exploded from the Magnum's chamber. "Hey," he said, "we better get this thing back to Kevin."

They drove to the young man's house and Rhodes walked in and handed the gun to Maysmith's sister. Maysmith appeared, suddenly, pulled it away from her, and raced into his room on the second floor of the house. Rhodes heard some commotion and raced around to the rear of the house to try to see what had happened, but Maysmith spotted him and fired, putting a slug into Rhodes's shoulder.

The young man's mother ran out of the front of the house and called the police. It was 7:45. Shortly after 8 o'clock, a second call came into the department "911" emergency switchboard. "My name is Kevin Maysmith," the caller said. "If the cops come here, I'm going to shoot them."

The Emergency Service Division responded, closing off the busy thoroughfare and establishing positions all around the house. At 8:28, Maysmith called the police again, this time demanding to talk by phone to a friend of his who was in the Queens House of Detention. If he didn't hear from the friend,

Maysmith said, he would kill both his mother and Mike Rhodes.

The police knew that neither Mrs. Maysmith nor Rhodes was inside, but they also knew that Kevin had a history of mental illness. They decided to play along, contacted jail officials, and set up a three-way conversation, which they would carefully monitor.

When Bolz arrived, the conversation was about to start. It's not something I would do, he thought to himself, but first of all, this is not my ball game and, secondly, no lives are on the line at this point except that poor kid's in there.

The friend proved to be a positive influence and, after the conversation ended, Bolz came on the line and tried to talk Maysmith out.

"Look," he said at one point, "you've got no cards, no hostages to play. You'd better just come on out." And at 11:00 P.M., the young man did just that. There was a flurry of activity when police discovered that among the guns young Kevin Maysmith had stowed away in his room was a .44-caliber Magnum, but it was not the gun that had killed the two women. There was more than one psycho walking the streets of New York.

PART TWO

July 4, 1977

CHAPTER SIX

A Man
with an Axe

Independence Day, 1977, broke about as nicely as a summer day can in New York, warm but clear and dry. Frank Bolz was up and out ahead of the sun. His daughter Susan had spent Saturday and Sunday with her parents and younger brother in their East Meadow, Long Island, home and now she had to return to Beth Israel Hospital in Manhattan for the day shift this Monday morning when most of New York and the country would be sleeping late, enjoying the final twenty-four hours of the three-day holiday weekend.

Bolz, who was nine days short of his forty-seventh birthday this Fourth of July, had scheduled himself into a six-to-two tour of duty to adjust to his daughter's schedule.

Family holidays like Independence Day, he knew from experience, often breed the sort of frustration that drive men of sadly ordinary desperation to extraordinary action. All over the city this Monday morning, men and women, in poor sections and rich ones alike, would be at each other or at themselves, coping with any number of personal nightmares on the dark side of the American dream.

Just about all of them would make it through the long weekend. Somewhere, one or more might crack. They would most likely attempt suicide. But, in an era when even a suicide attempt can be shrugged away, one of them just might reach for a knife, grab the nearest unsuspecting human being, and begin negotiating for that most elusive of bargaining goals—peace of mind. Or, on this the 201st anniversary of America's birth, a self-styled radical might decide to publicize his or her

149

cause at gunpoint. If such a situation arises within the five boroughs of the city of New York, it is Frank Bolz's job to be society's bargaining agent.

Father and daughter drove off in Bolz's car, unmarked but labeled nonetheless by its four huge radio antennas, a couple too many for even citizens' band enthusiasts to carry. But at 5:30 on a holiday morning, there was hardly anyone to notice. The parkways to Manhattan, which would normally be building toward their rush-hour overloads on any other Monday, were virtually empty.

Bolz dropped his daughter off at Stuyvesant Town, a housing development on the East River where she and another nurse share an apartment in a section of the development that is so filled with hospital personnel that it is called "Bedpan Alley." Then he stopped at a phone booth and called the man on the midnight-to-eight shift in his office at headquarters. "I'm on the beeper and I'm going up to the Bronx to start checking cars," Bolz announced. Such notification might gain his wife Ruthie some additional sleep by assuring that no one would try to phone him in East Meadow.

Up the East River Drive, past the United Nations complex, Bolz headed north, exercising a cop's on-duty prerogative to set his own speed limit. At the ramp to the Triborough Bridge he passed a patrol car and, with a beep and a thumbs-up sign, established that he was no ordinary speeder. He drove east on the Bruckner Expressway, then onto the Bronx River Parkway, and a few seconds later cruised to a halt at the department's Highway Unit No. 1. It is there that the Hostage Negotiating Team stores one of its cars, which are scattered strategically throughout the city to assure the fastest response time.

It was 6:25 A.M. and the station was loaded with motorcycle cops assigned to parade duty. Bolz alighted from the car, and a few seconds later still another cycle man followed Bolz in. "I thought I had myself one more traffic summons before heading in," he shouted to another cop, pointing at Bolz, and the three of them laughed.

In the garage, Bolz encountered his first piece of bad news this day: the team car was dead, so dead that it would not start even with a jump. That was not an unusual situation.

CARL T. GOSSETT

EYEWITNESS NEWS—LITERALLY

*John Johnson, a reporter for Channel 7's "Eyewitness News"
in New York, got a little too close to the news for his own
comfort the day police mistakenly allowed him into a church on
107th Street in Manhattan. There, Reggie Butts, a distraught
father, was holding a 15-year-old boy hostage. Bolz talks to
Butts* (top), *trying to convince him to give up. Minutes later,
police catch Butts off guard and grab him. He is escorted out*
(bottom), *with a somewhat shaken Johnson trailing behind.*

UNITED PRESS INTERNATIONAL

PROPOSAL GONE AWRY

Five hours after a Sunni Muslim named Luquam Abdush-Shahid turned a meeting about the proposed conversion of a Harlem office building into a hostage situation, he surrenders to police.

NEGOTIATING IN COMFORT

Bolz found a rocking chair on Staten Island (left) *to help arrange for the surrender of a young man who had barricaded himself in an apartment. That's John Byron* (right) *escorting the man out, finally, with Edward Zigo, who engaged in face-to-face negotiations, alongside* (in baseball cap).

ASSOCIATED PRESS

DRAMA ON THE 36TH FLOOR

While a Polish immigrant threatens to blow up the World Trade Center (top), crowds gather below. Eventually (bottom), the man gives up (he had no dynamite), and his elated Workman's Compensation lawyer, Anton Gasperik, recounts his own experiences for the press.

PHOTO BY NEWSDAY

BUS ON THE RUNWAY

Police post an armored truck opposite the green bus (top left) *and use it to create a "cone of security" for their negotiations, after passenger Jimmy Lo* (bottom left) *is shot by Robinson and thrown from the vehicle. After dark, the bus the experts swore could not be moved suddenly lurches down the runway, with police cars and a motley assortment of other vehicles in pursuit* (top right). *The bus* (bottom right) *starts from runway 13L (1), is escorted to satellite area (2), leads police on a frantic chase to the ends of the airport's extensive runways and taxiways (3) and back again and is finally cornered and disabled (4) just a few yards from city streets.*

ASSOCIATED PRESS

PORT AUTHORITY OF NEW YORK AND NEW JERSEY

DRAMA ON A HARLEM ROOFTOP

Robert Mason, distraught after quarreling with his estranged wife, threatens (opposite, top left) *to jump from the roof with his son, Robert, in his arms. Hostage Negotiator Bob Louden asks Mason, among other things, whether he thinks "it will snow." Eventually, the child is handed over to his aunt* (opposite, top right), *and Bolz and Louden restrain Mason* (opposite, bottom), *and join other police in escorting the young man from the roof* (above).

FROM RIDGEWOOD TO UNIFORM

There weren't many places to play where Bolz grew up, amidst the rowhouses of Madison Street in Ridgewood (top left). *Frank got the local precinct to establish a Police Athletic League Center above a pool hall on Myrtle Avenue. It may have been that early contact with the police that convinced Bolz, at 24, to join up* (top right). *In any event, it beat standing above manholes as a telephone splicer's helper. And it led, eventually, to the proud day, which he shared with his bride, Ruth, of Bolz's elevation to captain* (bottom).

Laden with weapons, protective gear, and communication devices, cars like the one at Highway Unit No. 1 are often idle for days at a time and their vital organs often atrophy. Bolz left a request for mechanics on the day shift to force life back into the engine and drove off, heading south now, back over the Triborough Bridge to Astoria and the 114th Precinct, where another of the team's cars is stored.

By 7:10, he was back on the road. He headed out on the Van Wyck Expressway toward John F. Kennedy International Airport and then headed west to Brooklyn along the city's oceanfront on the Belt Parkway. His destination was Floyd Bennett Field in Brooklyn, once a major naval air base and now one of the homes of the hostage negotiators who store equipment and hold training sessions in an old airplane hangar there.

The hangar was locked, so Bolz had to walk across the way to the police aviation hangar, where a duty sergeant was passing the quiet holiday morning with only a police dog for company. The trio, Bolz, the sergeant, and the dog, walked back to the other hanger, where the sergeant went to open the door, then Bolz went to start the two cars parked inside, and the dog just went, on the floor in the center of the building.

His two human companions looked at each other with uncertainty. Finally, the lieutenant said to the sergeant, "Well, they'll know we've been here," and both laughed. The droppings would be left for others to clean, a small if unpleasant reminder of the prerogatives of rank.

Both of these cars were in working order. Bolz called the office, then drove back to One Police Plaza, the modern headquarters building astride the Manhattan approach to the Brooklyn Bridge. It was not to be a lengthy visit. He parked his car in the basement garage, rode the thirteen floors to his office, poured a cup of Sanka—and heard the radio call transmitted over the Special Operations Division frequency: "Sergeant at the 75th Precinct requests Emergency Service Division and Hostage Negotiating Team. Confirmed hostage situation. Man armed with axe holding two-year-old child. Address is 823 Hendrix Street near Linden Boulevard."

Bolz glanced for a second at the sheaf of papers on his desk, a quarterly report on automobiles available to the Resource Allocation Unit of the Tactical Support Section of the Detective Division, his normal duty assignment. This morning the quarterly reports would have to wait. "Let's go," Bolz told John Byron, a sergeant who is a negotiator and also works under him in the Detective Division. Then the phone rang. Detective Bill Herrmann of the Major Case Bureau had heard the radio transmission at his office elsewhere in the headquarters building. "Meet us in the garage," Bolz told him.

Bolz and Byron stopped in the men's room, painful experience with day-long sieges having taught the team to make such a pause unfailingly at the start of every mission. The elevator must have stopped thirteen times, with police officers walking on and off at floor after floor, unaware that the two men in the corner were en route to a desperate man holding an axe on his two-year-old son.

In his mind, Bolz had already mapped the route. The Hendrix Street address was in the heart of the East New York section of Brooklyn, a drug-infested, rat-infested, fire-gutted sprawl of urban dilapidation that was beginning to rival the infamous South Bronx as a candidate for the worst slum in America. He would drive over the Williamsburg Bridge to Bushwick Avenue to Pennsylvania Avenue to Hendrix.

On the way, Bolz, Byron, and Herrmann picked up a second radio transmission of some interest: Chief of Special Operations Joseph Hoffman had landed in a helicopter at the Canarsie Pier and was asking for transportation to the hostage site. Bolz, already moving at a good clip, light flashing and siren wailing, hit the accelerator a bit harder. "Let's beat him there," he said, and the other two nodded.

A block from the scene, the commotion was obvious—police vehicles and pedestrians so cluttered the street that Bolz hopped the curb, barely avoiding a fire hydrant on one side and a utility pole on the other, and cruised to a halt on the sidewalk. Methodically, almost automatically, the trio alighted and moved into action, Bolz pausing just long enough to note with satisfaction that they had indeed beaten the chief to the scene. The time was 9:17. It had taken twenty-two minutes from the call for help to their arrival.

Herrmann pulled a large artist's sketching pad from the trunk of the Satelite and started asking questions of the 75th

Precinct officers, writing their answers on the oversized pages. Who was in the apartment? What did they know about the man with the axe? What about the layout of the apartment? The building? Had any relatives or friends of those inside been located? And so on.

The answers, taped to the side of the car, would provide Bolz and the others with an instant tableau of what confronted them in words and diagrams, which ultimately would provide perhaps the most important information, detailing positions of the apartment's inhabitants as well as its entrances, obstacles, and possible weapons. Peaceful negotiations and a violent charge were not the only options. If the man inside could not be talked into giving up without a struggle, he might be outsmarted without one.

Bolz walked up the front steps and through the outer door into a dark, dingy alcove. The man with the axe was on the other side of a door halfway down the alcove to the right in a first-floor apartment. The door was ajar, held in place by three chain locks, and a police officer from the 75th Precinct, Joe Bisiani, was talking through the crack in the doorway. Behind Bisiani stood Al Cachie, a Brooklyn-based member of the Hostage Negotiating Team who had been at the scene for several minutes.

"He's doing okay," Cachie told Bolz. "He's been talking to him."

Cachie's opinion was well taken. Once, as the principal negotiator in a hostage case on Bedford Avenue not far away, Cachie had established such a strong rapport with his subject that when the man surrendered, Cachie sought and received permission to accompany the perpetrator through his booking and arraignment. Police psychologist Harvey Schlossberg describes this strong sense of identification as the phenomenon of "transference," and Bolz's negotiators are trained not to resist it. Put yourself in the perpetrator's shoes. Convince him the world, as embodied by one cop doing the talking, can understand his problems and help him cope. On Bedford Avenue that day, Al Cachie had attained a remarkable level of spiritual unity with someone who would normally be perceived as his total enemy—an angry man with a gun.

Now on Hendrix Street, the cop doing the talking was a

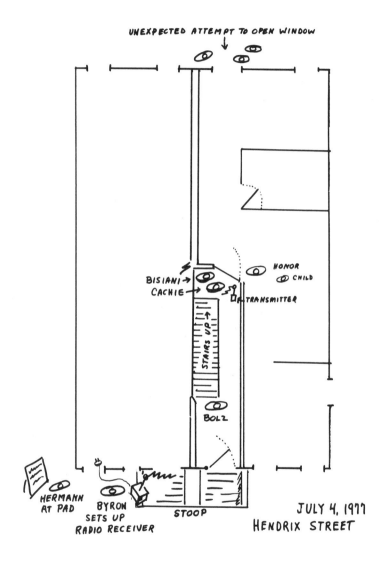

UNEXPECTED ATTEMPT TO OPEN WINDOW

BISIANI →
CACHIE →

HONOR
CHILD

TRANSMITTER

STAIRS UP →

BOLZ

HERMANN
AT PAD

BYRON
SETS UP
RADIO RECEIVER

STOOP

JULY 4, 1977
HENDRIX STREET

novice at this sort of thing. Yet any cop who walks the streets of the 75th Precinct must necessarily know much about its residents and their predicaments. Indeed, the three chain locks on the apartment door spoke volumes about life on Hendrix Street. And, as Bolz assayed the situation, other practical elements favored the retention of Joe Bisiani as the primary negotiator. He had already made contact, and any replacement would put the team back to square one or, worse, arouse the suspicions of the man with the axe.

As Bolz conferred in whispers with Cachie and Bisiani, Byron was setting up a radio relay system so that the conversation at the door could be monitored some distance away. He ran cable from a receiver into the apartment next door to be plugged in. Bisiani was handed a wireless transmitter. From then on, every word exchanged between negotiator and hostage was audible to police standing outside.

By then the name "Kenny Honor" had been penciled next to the word "Perp" on Bill Herrmann's pad. Honor was holding his two-year-old son. His wife and aunt were in the street and hysterical, a natural enough reaction, but one that rendered them useless as potential conduits to the man inside. They *had* produced keys to the door as well as to two of the three security chain locks tethering it almost closed. If Kenny Honor and his axe could be diverted for long enough, someone might be able to cut the last chain and move in through the front door.

Because of the position of the door, perpendicular to the alcove's entrance halfway back, Honor could stand at the door and speak while alternately guarding the infant in a rear room to his right and surveying the action on the street through the front windows to his left.

At one point, Honor complained that a neighbor had burglarized his stereo system. "He's standing right out there in the street," he told Bisiani and Cachie. "He's a burglar. You go arrest him and get my stereo back."

There are times when the temptation is strong to dismiss such statements as paranoic delusions. But on Hendrix Street the police knew better. They approached the accused onlooker, and he volunteered to drive off with them in a squad car apparently under arrest. (Police, in fact, were to learn later that Honor had already confronted his neighbor and retrieved all the components of the stereo system that had not been fenced.)

When the "arrest" did not produce an immediate surrender, Bolz began to worry. He had stationed himself midway between the front door and the entrance to the apartment, occasionally edging closer to the apartment to confer with his negotiators. They were deploying him as the heavy in a good cop, bad cop, Mutt-and-Jeff ruse. If the axe-wielder wanted some minor concession that was easy to grant, Bisiani and Cachie would concede. If he asked for something that clearly could not be granted to him, Bolz would be called over to reject the demand. Again, the rapport: "We're on your side, Kenny. We're doing what we can for you."

Now there was another man in the alcove, a sergeant from Emergency Service who had painstakingly opened two of the three chain locks during moments when Honor's attention was diverted. The sergeant retreated, waited for the chance, and then moved up to the apartment door, bolt cutters in hand. But the chain, manufactured to resist just such an onslaught, was too strong. The noise of steel on steel alerted Honor, and he angrily slammed the door shut, momentarily ending all communication with the outside world.

Now it was up to Bisiani and Cachie to reestablish contact. At such seemingly hopeless moments, the tide can turn back in the negotiator's favor with surprising speed. A man with a hostage *wants* to communicate. And as bizarre as his means for showing it is, police can seize on an equally irrational excuse to reopen the channels. In this case, they turned the trick with help from an innocent bit of law enforcement bureaucracy known as Form UF61, a citizen's complaint sheet.

"Kenny, you have to sign this for us to hold the guy," Bisiani counseled through the closed door, slipping a UF61 under it. Honor said he was thinking about it. In the rear of the apartment, out of his sight line, officers from the Emergency Service Division were poised below a window. They could see the little boy just a few feet away. It would take only a matter of seconds: open the window, grab the child, and end the siege.

Finally, a lieutenant in command of the detachment nodded to his men. But at first the window would not budge, and when it did, the screech it made would have wakened the dead. Honor wheeled and ran for the back, screaming. He returned a minute later, yelling through the door about a double cross.

For once, the negotiators could assure him forlornly that it was not their doing. Bolz and his crew out front had no advance notice of the attempted intrusion at the rear. It was a mistake: a dumb, unwarranted risk. But there would be time to discuss that in the critiques. The two-year-old boy still inside was the only important consideration now.

Bolz made a show of ordering all police away from the back of the building. Again, slowly, negotiation resumed. If Honor was serious about pressing charges against his neighbor, Bisiani told him, then he would have to accompany police to the 75th Precinct stationhouse soon or they would have to let the man go. That made some sense, the man with the axe agreed. The tide was turning. "I'll go with you," Honor said finally. "But first, you have to let us get dressed."

Thus began the last, most excruciating minutes of tension for the team: "the ritual."

It can take several forms. The man inside might ask for a few moments, as Kenny Honor had, to dress. He may want the time to straighten up the place or assemble some personal papers. Negotiators had learned the hard way that these lingering efforts at delay could be something else altogether.

Bolz was watching for any signs as Honor prepared to surrender. The alcove was cleared of all personnel but Bisiani and Cachie. A sergeant stood on the steps outside, shotgun at the ready, on the off chance that this was not a surrender at all but an attack.

Honor opened the door, leaving the boy and the axe behind him. The drama was over.

"Toss him," Bolz barked from the outside and, sure enough, Cachie frisked Honor and pulled a large knife from the man's inside pocket. He had probably forgotten it was there. Outside, the crowd cheered as the little boy emerged and ran into his mother's waiting arms. Earlier, a couple of free-lance photographers had been at the scene, fellows who monitor police radio frequencies and rush to crime sites in the hope of snapping a photo that can then be sold to newspapers. But it was July 4th and even they had departed before the siege's conclusion.

Bolz shook his head. There had been eighty hostage jobs in thirty months. Some were considered big news in the media and others never attracted a line, sometimes for odd reasons. This day, the police reporters were all watching the Parade of the Tall Ships in New York Harbor.

In custody, Kenny Honor regained a bit of his obstreperousness. He wanted his son, the little boy he had just held with an axe for three hours, to accompany him to the police station. Bolz shrugged, then nodded, and father and son climbed into the back seat of a squad car with Bisiani. Byron, Herrmann, Cachie, and Bolz loaded the equipment back into their car and followed, leaving others to complete the gathering of evidence at 823 Hendrix Street. Their job was done.

After a brief stop at the 75th Precinct in Brooklyn, the hostage negotiators went their separate ways, Bolz, Herrmann, and Byron returning to One Police Plaza, where they lugged the radios and other equipment employed on Hendrix Street up to the thirteenth floor for refurbishing. It was a quarter past noon. Herrmann returned to duty with the Major Case Squad, and Bolz and Byron started working on the paperwork they had been about to tackle when the call from Brooklyn intervened. Their day was almost over—or so they thought. Actually it had barely begun.

CHAPTER SEVEN

"Take Us
to Kennedy"

Outside the Port Authority Bus Terminal on Eighth Avenue, all was quiet.

To the north, the sun was glistening off the black-glass storefronts on the Minnesota Strip, a half-mile of the avenue named unofficially for the young prostitutes who are imported from the Midwest to solicit there. The girls are usually at work day and night, but even they were in short supply at noontime, July 4, 1977, in keeping with reduced demand. Most of their usual customers were home in the suburbs or at the beach, celebrating Independence Day with their wives and children.

To the south, on the western edge of the city's garment center, on almost any other Monday in the year men would be careening racks of dresses and sportswear through the streets, vying for space with tractor trailers up from the southern mills with yard goods. But there, too, the streets were virtually empty.

With such an eerie quiet on both its flanks, the bus terminal itself was just beginning to stir. Like the city's docks and airports, the terminal is under control of the Port Authority of New York and New Jersey, a heavily bonded bi-state agency whose indebtedness will be amortized by generations of yet unborn New Yorkers, ensuring among other things that the descendants of the present bond holders will be so well off that they'll never have to set foot inside the bus terminal. Less affluent New Yorkers and their visitors, not so well versed in higher economics, sometimes have trouble with the name of the building, which they often call "the Port of Authority Terminal.'' Presumably, they are happy that something in the beleaguered City of New York still has authority.

By late afternoon thousands of riders would be streaming through the cavernous ground-floor arcade to catch the bus home at the end of their holiday weekend in the Big Apple, many of them trying to usher small children through the terminal quickly enough to blur its surroundings.

In most cities, the long-distance bus terminal is in one of the sleazier sections of town. New York's terminal, being one of the world's largest, also leads the world in sleaze, although from a distance it does cut an impressive figure, a mammoth square-block structure with ramps extending in various directions like arteries from a heart. Its underside first strikes a visitor's sense of smell. Even after its thorough daily disinfecting, a vague odor of urine emanates from the arcade's far corners. On closer inspection, the shops and booths are dingy, and, subtlest but most important of all, the travelers themselves reflect their own sense of disrepair. Out at the airports, the crowds often seem to be a cut above the norm. At the terminal, the clientele is shabbier.

At 1:00 P.M., as Luis Robinson made his way through the arcade, his steps echoed. A derelict was polishing off his first bottle of wine, leaning against the steel gate of a closed hotdog stand, and two zombie-eyed sons of the street were standing across the way. But Robinson barely noticed them. His eyes were on a well-dressed middle-aged man who seemed to be following him through the arcade. He was not the sort of fellow one normally saw at the bus terminal and that concerned the twenty-five-year-old sailor.

I'll bet he's a Fed, Robinson thought. He was returning to Bath, Maine, where his ship, the U.S.S. *Detroit,* was docked. But he was having second thoughts about going back there at all. Earlier, before his leave, he had been arrested, charged with trying to cash a stolen money order for a fellow sailor. They think I'm going to take off and they're watching me, Robinson thought. He ducked into the men's lavatory and walked to the far urinal. A moment later, the man he had been watching walked in after him.

Robinson left the lavatory quickly and started hurrying

toward the loading area for the 1:30 bus to White River Junction, Vermont, where he was to catch another bus to Bath. He had his sailor's white duffel bag slung over his right shoulder. In it was a 765 mm. automatic pistol. He would eventually tell the police he had bought the gun in the spring as protection against some of the white sailors, who had been picking on him. He hadn't told the SPs aboard the *Detroit* about the gun, of course, but he had told them that he thought some of the whites were plotting against him. At times, he even sounded incoherent to himself and that bothered Robinson. He was certain they would refer him for psychiatric tests. But to them, he was just another sailor accused of trying to cash a stolen check. And that, too, bothered him.

Downstairs, where the big green Vermont Transit Company bus sat, engine idling, at its appointed dock, Robinson did not see the man he had left in the lavatory, and for a moment he calmed down. It was 1:31 when driver Norman Bozick rolled the bus up a ramp, slowly negotiated the perennial West Side street construction, and turned uptown onto 10th Avenue for the ride that was to end after dark in Vermont. Most of his twenty-two passengers would depart before then, at waystations in Hartford, Connecticut, and Springfield, Massachusetts.

The passengers were typical of the sort that still ride intercity buses these days—some of them poor, some elderly, some foreign-born, and some who just don't like to drive.

Leon and Anna Nesbitt, an elderly black couple, were heading home to New Britain, Connecticut, and David and Nettie Blassberg, an elderly white couple, to Greenfield, Massachusetts, where Mr. Blassberg, legally blind, worked in the county courthouse as a newsdealer. Israel Maldonado and Carmen Santiago, teen-aged sweethearts from Hartford, were returning with Israel's mother and brother after a weekend visit with another brother in the Army. Maria Reyes and her two children were going home to Springfield after a stay with relatives in the Bronx. Marie Poteau was returning to Hartford with her four children.

Jacqueline Rostom, a Queens woman, was on the way to Vermont where she and her sister had rented a vacation cottage. Rosalie Seabrook and Norma Rochester were going home to Hartford after a weekend together in the Big Apple, as was Priscilla Taylor, who had spent a summer weekend with a girlfriend in the Bronx. Jimmy Lo, a Hong Kong national, was heading for a business meeting in Hartford. Bruce DeBoar, a twenty-year-old East Hartford man, had been in town to visit his girlfriend. Robert Vinas, a twenty-six-year-old Venezuelan, was returning to the International School at Brattleboro, Vermont. Susan Bruso, on leave from the WACs, was on the last leg of a trip home to Florence, Massachusetts.

John McGavern, a fifty-year-old librarian, was going back to Yale University in New Haven. Luis Robinson was already in his seat when McGavern entered the bus and walked past him toward the rear. Robinson's panic returned immediately. Of course, he thought. They switched agents on me. McGavern, like the man in the terminal, was much too well dressed to be riding on this bus.

The big green bus trundled up the West Side, into the Bronx and onto the Major Deegan Expressway, making excellent time in the traffic-free streets. But Luis Robinson hardly noticed the surroundings. He was constantly glancing back at John McGavern. He felt himself losing control, the way he almost had several times aboard the *Detroit*, when he thought the white sailors were planning to kill him. All along, through the weekend at home with his family in New Jersey, he had put off the decision about going AWOL or returning to face the charges and, worse, life in the Navy. He still had time to make that decision—or did he? Who was the man in the suit sitting in back of the bus? I've got to compose myself, he thought. In the tiny bus lavatory, Robinson vainly tried to calm down. But it was no use.

At about the time he emerged from the lavatory, the bus had crossed the Harlem River into the Bronx and was just passing Yankee Stadium. When Norman Bozick, the driver, heard a commotion behind him, he glanced up at the rear-view mirror and saw a young, dark-skinned man dressed in black running through the aisle from the rear, shouting something.

Bozick could not stop on the elevated highway, but he slowed somewhat. The man in the aisle had wheeled now and was heading back to the rear. The driver could not quite make out what many of his passengers had already seen all too clearly. From a small white canvas bag he had brought aboard, Luis Robinson had pulled a gun and a knife, and he was wielding both of them now. He returned to his seat momentarily, then stood up and shouted, "Don't move!"

McGavern, the librarian, was seated nearby, and the gunman approached him, pointed at his face, and fired. McGavern seemed more stunned than wounded at first. "Did someone shoot me?" he asked incredulously. His assailant lifted the fifty-year-old librarian to his feet and herded him to the front of the bus.

"Do you know the way to Kennedy Airport?" he asked Bozick.

"Change the sign, get off the highway, and turn this thing around. I want you to take us to Kennedy Airport." Having no "Airport" sign on his spool, Bozick turned to a blank space. Robinson dumped the wounded man into a front-row seat and turned to the other passengers. They would not be hurt if they followed instructions, he announced. Bozick drove his bus off the highway and turned around. The gunman was gesturing with the knife in his left hand. Those who spoke no English were hurriedly advised of his wishes by bilingual passengers. It became apparent to all that they had been hijacked, and not merely robbed. All passengers were ordered to clasp their hands at the back of their necks.

There was an immediate air of tension aboard the bus as well as a good deal of confusion, owing to the number of non-English-speaking passengers as well as children aboard. But there was no panic and little surprise. Hijackings had been reported too often on television and in the newspapers. Banks and airplanes had been taken over regularly. A bus? Why not? The cooler heads immediately settled on two missions: (1) Keep the children quiet and safe; (2) Think about getting out.

As he moved up and down the aisle, directing the seating arrangements, Robinson began to talk. "No one will get hurt if you cooperate," he shouted. "But before this is over, I may have to kill a few of you. I'm in the Navy and I'm being fucked around and I'm tired of this country and the way it treats my people." As if to emphasize his seriousness, he would punctuate his trips to the front by returning the nose of the gun to Bozick's neck. "If I have to kill you," he announced at one point as the bus rolled through Queens, "I'll shoot the whites first, then the blacks."

He turned to Jackie Rostom. They had exchanged words briefly when the bus was still parked at the terminal, when he had helped her squeeze her luggage under her seat. "Do you think I'm crazy?" he asked. As he spoke, a few live rounds dropped from the white canvas bag he was carrying on his shoulder. "Would you please pick them up for me?" he asked politely. He turned in the other direction and espied Maria Reyes. "Don't look at me like that," he snapped at her in Spanish, "or I will kill you." She turned away.

Robinson noticed Israel Maldonado's duffel bag, not unlike his own, and the comparison brought a jarring thought to his head. "Are you in the Army?" he asked, also in Spanish. "Do you have a gun?" Maldonado shook his head, and the gunman opened the bag and turned it upside down. There was no weapon, but when an Army uniform tumbled out, he kicked at it and spat. He began to offer the passengers a series of dissertations about the unfair treatment of blacks and poor in the United States, now offering his own translations in Spanish. As Norman Bozick drove, John McGavern lay slumped in the front seat, and the twenty-one remaining passengers sat petrified, moving only to shush those children too young to perceive the danger at hand.

As the bus approached the airport, Robinson returned to the front. The gun was in his right hand. With his left, he placed the knife against Bozick's throat and began to act as a navigator, ordering the bus off the Van Wyck Expressway onto a service road and then onto a turnoff.

The turnoff led to a service road adjacent to Building 269, the Port Authority's headquarters at Kennedy. A PA police officer, routinely situated at a gate leading to a runway at the end of the road, smiled when he saw the large green bus roll toward him. Out-of-town driver, he thought. He walked into the road and prepared to give the man directions for whatever terminal he wanted to find in the complex, multistructured airport.

"Bust through the gate!" Robinson ordered. The bus was about ten yards away from the cop when he fired. A bullet shot past the cop's head. He ran for cover behind a car parked alongside the road and looked up in time to see the green bus crash through a steel mesh gate and roll onto the runway.

"Out there," Robinson ordered Bozick, "on the runway." The bus veered to the right and onto the 14,500-foot ribbon of concrete. The gunman ordered the driver to stop and open the front doors. He lifted the semiconscious figure of John McGavern and plunked it down on the pavement. "Now," he said, pointing toward the two blue-and-yellow Port Authority police cars that were in cautious pursuit, *"they'll* understand I'm serious, too."

Robinson took a piece of paper from Jackie Rostom, scrawled a note on it, and beckoned two young black boys, Joseph Plummer and Raymond Poteau. He asked for $6 million and an airplane by three o'clock. He turned to seventy-one-year-old Leon Nesbitt and said, "Take them off and make sure the police get this."

There were bright blue-and-yellow Port Authority police cars shooting onto the runway from all directions now, and Robinson was screaming that the cops still did not understand how serious he was. "Let's get out of here!" he ordered Bozick after a few minutes, and the bus rolled on, making a large circle with the police cars in pursuit.

He ordered all the whites to the front of the bus now, literally surrounding himself with them. "They're not going to keep shooting at me if they think they'll hit one of you by mistake," he said.

Susan Bruso, the WAC, was sitting in the first seat on the aisle. In basic training, she had disarmed bigger men than this one. Perhaps it was learned instinct more than reasoning that governed her. She waited for Robinson to glance the other way and then leaped at him.

He caught sight of her and slammed the gun against her face, sending the young woman sprawling. "You think I'm kidding!" he screamed at her. "What do I have to do to convince you I'm serious! What?"

Susan was hysterical, half-crying, half-shouting, "I'm sorry. I'm so sorry. I won't do it again. I'm sorry."

That seemed to disorient Robinson. He yelled for Bozick to stop the bus and open the door, and he shoved Susan Bruso out. Then he turned to the other aisle seat and ordered Nettie Blassberg to stand up. She clutched at her husband for a moment and then rose.

Robinson placed her in the door well and said, "I'm really sorry I have to do this. But you're an old woman. Your own people made me do this."

Then he raised the gun to her head and fired.

Mrs. Blassberg stumbled to the floor of the well, and Robinson moved to push her out the door. From behind him, Norman Bozick saw his chance. Feet first, swinging out from behind the driver's seat, he tried to kick Robinson out of the door. But, he too, had been spotted. Robinson wheeled and fired. Bozick slumped to the floor, fatally wounded.

If he was a failure at life, Robinson had, in a tragic moment of truth, proven to be an adept gunman. He dumped the bodies of his two newest victims onto the runway. The bus was halted now, it had no driver, and still the brightly colored police cars were advancing on it.

"Drive the bus!" the gunman shouted at David Blassberg.

"I can't," he replied. "I'm blind."

Robinson moved toward the rear in search of a substitute driver, giving some of those behind him at the front a chance to move. Israel Maldonado, Robert Fernandez, and old Mr. Blassberg escaped, clambering out the front doors and running to one of the patrol cars.

Outside, two Port Authority police officers, Robert Arnold and Drew Johnson, risked their own lives to drag Bozick and Mrs. Blassberg from the line of fire. But it would be no use for them. While McGavern, the librarian, had somehow survived, Mrs. Blassberg was already dead, and Bozick would die before he ever reached the hospital operating table.

Another Port Authority officer, Al Itkin, was driving the PA's semi-armored escort truck onto the runway. It is ever at the ready as an anti-terrorist device and is regularly used to escort the crews of El Al Airlines to and from their planes to protect them against possible attacks by Palestinians.

All across the sprawling John Fitzgerald Kennedy International Airport, police and civilian personnel were mobilizing. Word of the crisis on Runway 13 had not yet reached everyone, but not a single employee or traveler in any of the terminals was unaware that something was very wrong. In the sky from Florida to Illinois to the Azores, passengers were informed by plane captains that traffic conditions at Kennedy had necessitated a change in landing site. Confronted with a hijacked bus on a runway, three wounded, and they knew not what else, officials had ordered the entire airport closed to all takeoffs and landings.

CHAPTER EIGHT

A Day
to Remember

At 1:30 on July 4th, Frank Bolz and one of his officers, Dennis Butler, had gone to lunch at the Claddaugh Pub. The place, long a hangout for cops assigned to headquarters, is named for an area of Ireland that reflects its owner's ancestry. Beyond the name it is pure New York—featuring food prepared by an Italian chef and served by a Jewish and a Polish-Irish waitress to background music from a jukebox equipped to offer a variety of ethnic nonsequiturs.

By 2:00 P.M., Byron arrived, and the three men ate and reviewed the morning's job with no small sense of satisfaction. In the end it had been routine and that was something of an accolade in itself. The Hostage Negotiating Team had learned how in eighty incidents in thirty months to convert potential tragedies into minor, unreported incidents, small, repaired rips in the complex urban fabric of New York.

Bolz glanced down at his watch. It was 2:40. "Do you realize," he told his companions with mock anguish, "that I've been eating lunch on my own time for more than half an hour now?" They laughed and Bolz ordered a round of drinks in observance of the morning's successful performance. He would be on the way home by 3:00 P.M., with time to spare before the Fourth of July traffic clogged the roads. Ruthie and Frank Jr. had been promised his presence at a quiet barbecue.

The drinks had just been poured when Bolz's beeper sounded. Before he could flip it off and head for the phone at the end of the bar, it was ringing. "Uh-oh," he said.

"Lieutenant Morris wants you to call him, Frank," De-

168

tective George Mehrmann was saying from the thirteenth floor at One Police Plaza. "It looks like we have a confirmed job out at JFK."

Bolz walked back to his seat at the bar, pushed the drink away, and ordered a glass of milk. Then he went to the men's room. He sent Butler back to the office to stand by and decided that he and Byron would ride to the airport in separate cars, so he could continue on to East Meadow if the job fizzled or ended quickly.

The two cars raced in tandem across the Williamsburg Bridge and onto the Brooklyn–Queens Expressway, the Long Island Expressway, the Grand Central Parkway, and the Van Wyck Expressway. Confusing as it may sound, that is the shortest route from Lower Manhattan to John F. Kennedy International Airport.

Bolz drove straight to Building No. 269, the Port Authority police station at Kennedy Airport. He knew the terrain well enough, having spent many hours working with Port Authority Police on hostage training.

The City of New York does not have one police force. It has at least a half-dozen. Underground, there are Transit Police. In city-run projects, there are Housing Authority Police. There are also Corrections Department guards, court officers, even a contingent of Sanitation Police. Some of these enforcement agencies enjoy rather limited jurisdiction and power. But at Kennedy and LaGuardia Airports (as well as Newark Airport in New Jersey) and along the piers of New York Harbor, the Port Authority of New York administers a police agency that is as large and well equipped as the police departments of many cities in this nation.

At times, relations between the NYPD and the city's smaller forces can be strained by the human emotions of pride and jealousy. But with the potential for danger so great at the sprawling New York airports, the two police agencies have learned to accept one another's roles, leaning over backward on occasion to emphasize mutual respect and courtesy. Bolz knew that one of the men he had worked with closely in training, Lieutenant Orlando Gonzalez, had since retired, and he learned that another, Captain Ralph Cambariotti, was away on vacation. But he was relieved to spot another friend, Lieutenant Jack Stone, who had been appointed to succeed Gonzalez.

"At first when they crashed the fence we thought it was just some nut," Stone explained. "But he wants six million dollars and a plane. When we heard that, we called you guys and the FBI." Stone arranged to have Bolz and Byron escorted through a gate and onto an airport runway where, a half-mile away, just across from Hangar 12, a large Trans World Airlines cargo building, their chore awaited them.

At first glance, the scene resembled a riot action more than a hostage job. Three armored vehicles, an assortment of marked and unmarked patrol cars, and dozens of police riflemen were deployed on various parts of the runway, their attention riveted to a green cruiser bus. Its rear window faced Frank Bolz as he halted his own car near the armored truck closest to the bus, fifty feet away, and prepared to take command. At the moment, he knew virtually nothing of what had happened to set the scene that confronted him, but he *had* been apprised of one thing that would fill the coming hours with tension: two people who had once been on that green bus were dead.

Some things were automatic, no matter how big the job was. Out came the oversized sheets of drawing paper, taped to a car; the field phone; the periscope; a bullhorn; the bulletproof vests. Detective Julio Vasquez had been one of the first members of the Hostage Negotiating Team at the scene; and Bolz was thankful when he heard the earliest briefing, an account from McGavern before he was transported to the hospital to have the bullet removed from his neck. The librarian had told Port Authority Police that the man with the gun inside the bus spoke Spanish.

"If we make contact," Bolz told Vasquez, "you man the phones."

Over a bullhorn, Bolz shouted at the bus: "We're going to send over a hand line. We want to talk to you! We're going to throw a line over! Send somebody out to pick up the line and we'll run the telephone to you!"

One of the large picture windows on the right side of the bus moved out. Byron weighted one end of the spool of tele-

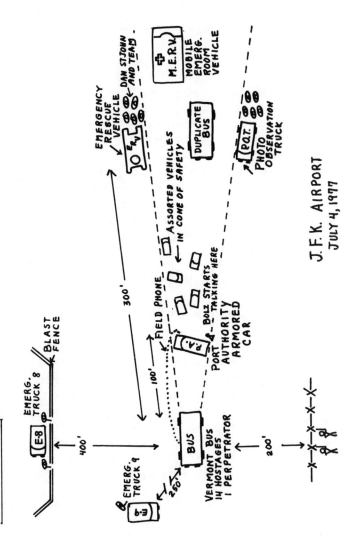

J.F.K. AIRPORT
JULY 4, 1977

phone line and prepared to toss it toward the bus. "Oh, my God," he said suddenly. "It's not long enough."

Frank stifled a laugh. It had been a makeshift existence, nurturing and maintaining a new police unit at the height of the city's austerity program. What was on the spool, like a lot else in the trunk of his car, had been carefully preserved and patched from previous jobs. The "periscope" he was now peering through, for instance, was a kid's toy. And he simply had not broken out a new reel of phone line without using what he had. Nobody could have anticipated a job of this size.

But it would not take long to find some phone cable in the bottom of the trunk. And if eighty previous efforts at hostage negotiation had convinced Frank Bolz of a single thing it was that, deadlines notwithstanding, time was his friend. In a few minutes, Byron tossed his line, and a woman walked from the bus, picked it up, and returned. A field phone was attached from behind the police encampment fifty feet away, and, slowly, it was pushed toward the vehicle, clothesline style.

On the bus, the gunman motioned for Bruce DeBoar to pick up the microphone and make contact. "Tell them they've got fifteen minutes left," he said, consulting a watch he had removed from the wrist of one of his captives on the way to the airport.

"Hello, hello," Julio Vasquez stammered.

"You have fifteen minutes left," Bruce DeBoar said calmly. Vasquez knew immediately that the youthful voice at the other end was not *the* voice, but merely an intermediary. He tried to choose these first words carefully. "Tell him to . . . let him . . . put him on the phone. I can't hurt him in any way."

"He doesn't want to talk to you," Bruce said.

"Plead with him," Vasquez suggested. "This is no good."

There was a pause and then the intermediary was back on the line. "Don't worry about why he doesn't want to talk to you," Bruce said, pleading with Vasquez rather than his captor. "Just do what he says."

Bolz was surveying the scene and he was not happy with what he saw. There was just too much open space on the other three sides of the bus—no way to divert the gunman's attention and sneak up on him. And if the gunman refused to speak directly to Vasquez, he was all the more alert, all the harder to reason with. "Keep trying to get him on the line," Bolz whispered. "Tell him that's the only way we can find out what he really wants."

"We want to do everything he says," Vasquez told Bruce, trying to ease the tone of desperation at the other end. "And we're doing everything possible for him. Tell him to understand that."

"Well," Bruce replied, "he doesn't want to talk to you, so we'll have to settle for this arrangement."

"Is anyone hurt on the bus now?" Vasquez asked suddenly. A jump shift.

"No," Bruce said, "no one's hurt."

"We're trying to get everything that's available for you. Do you understand? Tell him that we're doing everything. We cannot even negotiate within the next five minutes because we haven't gotten the word yet. We're trying to do everything possible, and if we were able to talk to him—if I was able to talk to him . . . does he speak Spanish at all? Maybe I could communicate better with him in Spanish."

"What?" Bruce asked incredulously.

"Does the man speak Spanish?"

"No, not really well. He doesn't want to talk to you, though, so it doesn't really matter."

Now it was the cop's turn to sound impatient. It was not unusual at all for a hostage to slowly become an advocate for his captor. The psychological phenomenon of transference worked in that direction, too. In Europe, a woman once fell in love with her captor in a bank vault. Whole nations of moviegoers rooted for Al Pacino to make it out of the bank in *Dog Day Afternoon*.

But in the hands of a hostage instead of a cop, transference was not a police tool. It was an impediment. As frightened as hostages may be, they are likely to be rational individuals who are not undergoing the kind of confused mental stress that has moved their captors to act. Thus, as police seek to outfox a gunman if they cannot win him over with their sincerity, hostages often become their own worst enemies by lending rationality to a man desperately trying to keep his mental equilibrium.

"Well, it *does* really matter," Vasquez lectured Bruce, "because if I could speak to him in Spanish I could communicate much better with him than in English."

"Well, he speaks English and Spanish," Bruce replied impatiently, "but he doesn't want to talk to you."

By now, the police brass had started to assemble. The chiefs of detectives, field services, and patrol, the three highest-ranking officers of the department, were among the first to arrive; and the Federal Bureau of Investigation was beginning to mobilize its sharpshooters—but it seemed Bolz remained in command. "You can hear it better over there, Chief," he said gently, pointing to an auxiliary speaker Byron had installed a few yards away from the spot where he and Vasquez stood. And the chief meekly obeyed, a general bowing to the expertise of one of his junior officers.

A quarter-mile away, on the other side of the corrugated retaining walls at the side of the runway, television cameramen had mounted the roofs of automobiles, planted their tripods, and aimed at the no-man's-land between the cops and the bus, ready to videotape whatever might happen, even though they could hear none of the exchanges between Vasquez and Bruce and could only guess at what might be happening out there on the runway.

Byron looked across the runway at the cameras and back to where three of the four highest-ranking police officers in the City of New York, the third most powerful man in the Federal Bureau of Investigation, and the chief of security for this mammoth airport were standing, watching Bolz and Vasquez operate, and waiting like everyone else. And what dawned on him was that after all the months of training, all the publicized jobs and the unpublicized ones, at this moment the hostage negotiators were coming of age. "Hey," he told Bolz, "you know you're in charge here. This is your show."

For a second, Bolz did not understand what Byron meant. Then he knew. But he also realized there was another side to all the attention. A failure here, after all the successes, would be devastating to him, the team, and the department.

"Tell him we're getting him a plane," Bolz whispered to Vasquez, "and that we're trying to get the money. Tell him the banks are closed and we need more time."

Aboard the bus, the man who was the object of all their attention was still weighing the renewed police invitation that he assume a more direct hand in negotiations. Vasquez raised the volume, straining to catch the byplay, but he could hear no more than muffled background voices and, finally, Bruce again announced: "No, he doesn't want to."

"Okay," Vasquez said, starting off anew. "His demands are just the plane, right? And money—so far."

"Yes."

"Well, you know, he picked a very bad day," Vasquez said. "We're doing everything possible. It's a holiday. Half the offices in this airport are closed today. The banks are closed. Everything is making it very difficult for us. Why is he giving us such a short time? He has to realize that we have to get all these things from so many different places—"

"Can you get the plane?"

"That is what we are arranging for, sir," Vasquez said. "And that's what I'd like to make clear to him. But he's very stubborn when we're trying to help him in every way possible. We ran a phone out to you. We're trying to get everything for your benefit, for his benefit, and we're trying to do everything possible. And he doesn't want to cooperate in the least. I understand your position. I'm not blaming you in any regard. You're doing great under the circumstances and the stress that you're in. I understand your situation. You can only be an intermediary."

"Yes, I know," Bruce said, sighing audibly. "But he doesn't want to do it that way. It's the only choice we've got." There was a pause. Vasquez looked across at Bolz, who nodded. By now, Harvey Schlossberg, the police psychologist, had joined them on the front lines. Still, nobody even knew the gunman's name, much less why he had killed two persons, wounded a third, and was holding more than a dozen others on the bus. Maybe it was time for a slight holding action. If nothing else, it would give the city police sharpshooters and their counterparts from the FBI a chance to calculate their position. Already, Bolz had ordered a twin of the Vermont Bus Company model, so the assault team could gauge its exact interior, just in case there had to be a charge.

He had also begun to arrange with the FBI to have a plane readied at a satellite area in the extreme eastern section of the airport—a procedure the bureau had used before. The FBI man said he needed time to set up. Two years before, in the same area, bureau sharpshooters using telescopic sights had blown another gunman right off the stairway of a plane before the man could even think about squeezing the trigger of the revolver he held on a hostage, who walked away un-scratched.

"Listen," Julio announced finally to Bruce, "I'll get you word as soon as we have any movement on this side."

"Yes, okay," Bruce said, and then he could be heard more clearly now, relaying the message to his captor and draw-ing this unpromising retort:

"We do not want to talk anymore."

There was a delay of several minutes and, like fishermen flicking their lines, Bolz and Vasquez decided to try once more, this time in Spanish. If time was on their side, the dead silence could work against them, giving the gunman a chance to think, to calculate, to strike.

"*Que pasa, amigo? Que pasa? Que pasa?*" Vasquez said. He followed with a few sentences in Spanish, but the retort was familiar.

"He says when we want to say something, we'll say something," Bruce said, adding solemnly, "He says you have ten minutes left."

There was another pause and finally Bolz decided the immediate goal was to get everyone past 3:00 P.M., the gun-man's deadline, without incident. Once one deadline passes, others are easier to ignore. "Julio," Bolz said, "at five to, you have to get him talking so, comes the time, he'll ignore it." The men synchronized their watches, and Bolz, as if to rein-force his command, made a hand motion of jaws opening and closing.

It was Bruce who spoke next.

"Five minutes, he says," the young man announced.

"Five more minutes?" Vasquez parroted.

"Yes," Bruce said.

"Listen," Vasquez said. "I'm going to give you word as soon as I get it. All right? I hope it's the next few seconds I could get word back to you. We're trying very hard. Does he understand that we're trying and that he's putting us at a disadvantage?"

"He doesn't believe you," Bruce said.

"Well, we're not here to lie to him," Vasquez said, trying to sound annoyed. "We're doing everything possible."

"All right," Bruce said. "I'll tell him."

There was a pause, and then it was those on the bus who changed the subject: "We want to know," Bruce demanded, perhaps adding some of his own indignation to his captors', "what the hell you are going to do with a tank?"

"That tank is only a rescue vehicle," Vasquez explained. "It's not a tank, it's a rescue vehicle. He doesn't have to worry about it."

"He wants it out of here," Bruce said. "Outta here. Gone."

"I'm going to negotiate that right now," Vasquez said.

It was another basic technique: the I'm-on-your-side-it's-my-nasty-partners number. In a few moments he was back. "The reason that vehicle's here is so no one else gets hurt," Vasquez said. "We're missing one passenger. And we want to see if we can pick him up and bring him to some aid. That's what that vehicle's here for."

"Where is he?" Bruce asked in obvious disbelief.

"That's what we'd like to know," Vasquez fast-talked, "but we can't very well walk around without getting shot at, can we?"

"Well, he's not on the bus," Bruce said, understandably confused by now. For the next few minutes, with Bolz egging him on, Vasquez talked about missing tanks and passengers and whatever else he could think of, making very little sense but sounding sincere enough to make those on the bus wonder if they just weren't understanding the man.

Finally, after Vasquez promised that the armored vehicle would be moved, the gunman had another demand. "He wants all your SWAT people out of there," Bruce said.

Now it was the cop's turn to sound incredulous. "All our *what?*" Vasquez said.

"You know," Bruce replied, "the guys with the guns."

"He wants the guys with the guns outta here?" Vasquez said, and then he started in again, talking about cops and guns and almost anything that came into his head but the time of day—which was, of course, the one thing he did not want to discuss at that precise moment. In feigned exasperation, after again appealing for the gunman to speak directly, Julio declared: "Tell us just what he wants."

"He wants a plane," Bruce snapped.

Bolz, listening to the receiver, just shook his head. Damn, there was no fooling Bruce. Not even if his life depended on it.

"The plane is what we're trying to get cleared to him," Vasquez said. "That's what we're trying to get clear, a plane on the other end of that ramp so we could escort that bus—"

"What's taking so long!" Bruce interrupted.

"What's taking so long? Everything takes time. You think there's volunteers to get aboard a plane and fly it with a man with whatever weapon he's got? Let me talk to him. I'll tell him what the problem is. He's probably a better con man than I could ever be. I'm not giving him any bullshit. I'm moving that tank away from him."

"The tank's not the point," Bruce said. "He wants the plane."

"Listen, Bruce," Vasquez said, "if he could fly the plane, we'd give him the plane. We've got to get a crew. We haven't been able to get a crew together yet. A plane doesn't fly by itself or by remote control. Tell him that. And we're getting volunteers for this. Not everyone wants to go on that —"

"I told him that," Bruce said.

"If that's all he wants, I'll give anything he says to the press. If he wants the public to know, we will—"

"He wants them to know that time is running out," Bruce said.

Robinson had asked for a plane and $6 million.

The plane would be no problem. There were hundreds of planes at the airport, and most of them would do for the only use to which they could be put—as props. Because, whether he gave up his hostages or not, the gunman on the bus was not going to be allowed to take off in a plane this day. On the premise that, once airborne, a plane controlled by terrorists might crash into a populated area, killing hundreds, the FBI had formulated a firm policy: no terrorist would be allowed to take off from an American airport.

The money was something else again. The New York police have special liaison officers who work with banks in kidnapping cases, producing hundreds of thousands in cash, if necessary, on short notice. But such money is never handed over to police before somebody, usually the target of the ransom demands or some benefactor of his, signs a letter of authorization, in effect promising to repay the bank if the money is lost. But on the runway at Kennedy, no such signatory existed. No representative of the bus company, the only possible source of authorization, was even at the airport.

So while the police negotiators could stall Robinson on the plane, talking about how hard it would be to drum up a crew, for example, they knew that eventually they could show him a plane. When they talked about the money, lamenting the fact that it was a national holiday and there was trouble making contact with the banks, the bluff was purer. There was no money to show the gunman and there never would be. And it was such a concern to Bolz that at one point he talked to the bosses about taking up a collection, having all the cops and agents in the area empty their wallets, so they could show Robinson at least a couple of grand in front money. After some discussion this thought, too, was abandoned. The negotiators were on their own.

At 5:05, they heard the crackle of gunfire.

"Bruce!" Vasquez blurted into the phone. "Bruce, has he shot anyone? Did anyone get hurt? Bruce? Bruce? Do you hear me? Bruce, can I talk to you?"

For the next five minutes, the police could hear Robinson ranting in the background. Vasquez, a desperate tinge to his voice at times, was shouting into the phone in Spanish, trying to raise someone.

A woman picked up the phone and said, "He's going to

shoot someone if you don't do what he says. He's going to kill someone, and he said to tell you the boy doing the negotiating will be the first to die. He's not going to give you any more time."

And then, a minute later, Bruce was back on the line.

Vasquez asked whether the gunman planned to take any hostages onto the plane after the police pulled the plane alongside the bus.

"He said he'll tell you when the time comes," Bruce said. "He really doesn't believe you're going to bring him a plane."

Vasquez said that the police still had only a single volunteer pilot in its search for a crew and that the pilot too wanted to talk to the captor once he arrived from Manhattan, to get personal reassurance that there would be no trouble once the plane was airborne. "He wants a guarantee that he's not going to be injured," Vasquez said, "because he says it's not going to do any good up in the air if he shoots the pilot up there. It's not going to be good for him or anybody else."

Robinson said yes, he would talk to the pilot.

Then Vasquez said that the authorities also needed to know how far the captor planned to go, so they could provide the correct plane and enough fuel. "The type of plane that is coming is a short-range plane, you see?" he said, trying to sound logistical. "Now, does he have intentions of going very far with this plane? If he does, we may have to make other arrangements."

"Three thousand miles," Bruce responded. "Tell the pilot it's three thousand miles. And he says that as far as the money is concerned, have as much as possible. The rest he will have you send to him. He says the only thing he wants to do right now is get off this bus. And he's getting impatient."

Vasquez continued to talk, reviewing what had been said, but Bruce interrupted him.

"That's it," he said. "There will be no more talk."

The police could hear some sort of commotion on the bus. Two young girls had started to scream, complaining to their parents that they weren't feeling well and wanted to go home. The more they screamed, the more edgy Robinson seemed to get. He had been battling for control—of himself, first, and now of this situation. The pressure was almost unbearable, and the whining and screaming had become a distraction he simply could not tolerate.

"Okay," he told the girls' mother. "They can get off." He went forward and opened the door. The girls looked at their mother and she nodded and bent down to hug them and whisper something to them. Then they clambered down the aisle of the bus and out the door and raced into the arms of the police.

"Thanks very much for letting the kids out and we're going to do whatever you say," Vasquez said. "Tell him that was very nice of him, what he just did. Can we bring you anything? Something to drink? Bruce? Tell him that we're very grateful for what he did, that it was real nice of him to do that."

But Robinson wasn't buying. If anything, he had become further infuriated by the notion that the police had interpreted his latest action as a friendly gesture.

"The only reason the kids are out there is because they're sick," Bruce reported. "He's not trying to be a nice guy."

With all the equipment on the runway, there would be a problem taxiing the plane close to the bus, Vasquez told Bruce. It would be easier if the bus could be driven to the plane. Was there anybody on board who could drive the bus?

Bruce said he would try. He was back a few minutes later to say that he had been unable to get the diesel engine started. Bolz nodded. From the manner in which the bus had lurched to its final halt on the runway, police who said they were familiar with diesel engines had told him, it was obvious that the bus could not be restarted without mechanical adjustments. The engine had flooded and would have to be drained.

That had been a reassuring opinion, and Bruce's failure seemed to corroborate it. As long as the bus could not go anywhere on its own, the police could at least be certain of containing the situation.

There was a long period of silence after that and then the

voice of a woman screaming, "Look, we're human beings! It don't matter what kind of people we are. We just want to get off safe, do you understand?"

"Yes, dear," Vasquez told her, "I understand. But we're trying to do that for you. Don't get excited."

"Well," she said in a considerably calmer tone, "we're rather excited now. He keeps getting very anxious."

Vasquez said he understood Robinson's anger. "We don't want to fool him in any way," he said. "The only reason is the plane, I explained that to Bruce. The plane cannot be brought into this area. It has to be put in a satellite area where he can then board and take off. I wanted to know, since Bruce cannot drive the bus, is there another man capable?"

"No," the woman said, "there isn't anyone here who can drive the bus."

"So we'll have to make arrangements for that, too. These are all problems we have to help—"

"He says you should have been doing this a long time ago!"

"Well, he doesn't want to talk to us, so—"

"Well," she said, "he doesn't want to."

"I understand that, dear," Vasquez said. "We're only trying to have him help us so that we can help him too. We're not trying to fool him like he thinks. We're trying to do what he wants. We understand. And we think he's a good human being for letting those sick children off. We understand his problems and we're trying to get him off this airport. I don't want him on that bus and I don't want to jeopardize any of your lives. What we're trying to do—if he'd only tell us himself. All right, he's asked for three thousand miles. We have to have a plane that goes that far, we have to have a pilot who wants to—"

"As soon as possible," the woman implored.

"I understand that," Vasquez said. "We want to get the plane as close as possible, but we only have one volunteer. Would you believe that? A pilot who's on his way here right now from Manhattan to fly the plane. We haven't had anyone else, and we've been trying to recruit three other people in order to get the plane off the ground. The pilot himself isn't going to be able to do it alone. He's one lone pilot. He's on his way. It's the Fourth of July. The traffic is terrible coming into this airport. As soon as he gets here, I'm going to put the pilot on so that he can talk—''

"Hold on a minute," the woman interrupted.

It was obvious that Robinson had another message. They were all there now—Wally LaPrade from the FBI, Jack Stone of the Port Authority Police, Jim Hannon, Neil Behan, and John Keenan, three chiefs of the NYPD, and Frank Bolz, who was running the show—watching the radio transmitter and waiting.

For ten, then twenty seconds, all was quiet at this center of the maelstrom of activity at the airport. And then there was the crackle of another transmission from onboard the bus.

"He said one thing," the woman told them. "He said if you don't get him off the ground, you are going to remember this Fourth of July."

CHAPTER NINE

Aboard
the Bus

With the air conditioning off and all but a single window closed, the climate aboard the bus on the runway was nothing short of stifling. For a long while, however, only the children would notice the discomfort of the heat and the stuffiness. Their parents and the other adults had to contend with a more obvious sensory perception: terror.

In many hostage situations, the dangers can be sublimated to some degree by the captives. There may be a captor or captors, weapons, threats, deadlines—but until a shot is actually fired or someone is hurt, the fear is relatively abstract. On the bus to White River Junction, that was never the case.

By design, the disgruntled sailor named Luis Rogelio Robinson had caused an optimum amount of fear in his captives from the outset. After his initial rantings failed to attract serious attention, he had walked up to librarian John McGavern and shot the man in the head, point blank. And while the shooting of the driver, Norman Bozick, could be laid to survival and self-defense—Bozick had tried to push Robinson out the door—most of the passengers believed that the shooting of the old woman, Nettie Blassberg, was a virtual execution.

Thus, by the time the bus came to a halt in the middle of Runway 13 at 2:30, the young man who had hijacked it had twice walked up to a defenseless hostage and fired. In the ensuing nine hours, he would point the same gun at many people, and, every time he did, each could hardly forget what he or she had seen Robinson do to John McGavern and Nettie Blassberg.

Also, while the shooting of Bozick was a more explainable act, it had taken a different kind of psychological toll. This was not a ship or a plane, of course, but it was a passenger vehicle and it did have a commander in the form of the driver. Stripped of its driver, the bus was not only immobilized, it was without an authority figure who might have offered assurance to the hostages.

To the police negotiators, this situation presented strategic advantages to be seized upon and exploited. But onboard it merely added to the Alamo-like atmosphere of siege and the sense of helpless desperation. The ever-increasing mobilization of armament and manpower outside on the runway was an impressive display to the police, Port Authority, and FBI commanders in charge, but it hardly reassured those afforded the most panoramic view of the situation—the hostages. Onboard there was one mad gunman with a single weapon and a bag of bullets. Outside, there were dozens of police riflemen who just might kill them in an assault if he didn't do it first.

Robinson made countless speeches about his plight as a maligned black and Hispanic sailor, but he would not talk directly to the police for a long time, and he never revealed his name to the fellow passengers he had taken hostage. In their eyes he was as much a chaotic, unfathomable force tearing up their lives this Fourth of July afternoon as if a tornado had struck the bus in which they were confined.

When Robinson agreed to send a female passenger out to retrieve the field phone, the terrible vacuum was slightly lessened. The phone, however, had no external speaker, only the sort of standard armature found on a home telephone, with an earpiece at one end and a mouthpiece at the other. Thus only the person operating it could hear what was being said by the police. And although the gun certainly represented the ultimate source of power on the enclosed island of terror surrounded by the police on Runway 13, the man who held the gun had ceded the power of communication to another. Like control of the message-sending conch in William Golding's

Lord of the Flies, control of the phone would grant its handler a power of his own.

The power, and the added responsibility and terror it entailed, fell almost immediately into the hands of Bruce DeBoar, a twenty-year-old restaurant manager from East Hartford who really did not look even that old.

Only weeks before, Bruce had passed his own post-adolescent crossroads, quitting college in New York and moving in with his mother and stepfather. He had been a film major at New York University, one of the most expensive colleges in the country—even more so for film majors who must invest heavily in supplies. Bruce's father, a landscaper now located in Florida, had supplied enough cash for the first two years' tuition, with Bruce earning the remainder of the money he needed from an assortment of part-time jobs. Business turned bad that spring, and Mr. DeBoar sent word that the tuition money was not there. He invited his son down to Florida to live and work with him until things turned around, but Bruce declined. He decided to go to Connecticut instead, on the theory that, whatever happened, his fate would no longer be dependent on someone else's fortunes.

East Hartford was only a two-hour bus ride from Manhattan, where Bruce had a girlfriend named Lynn and all his other contacts from the past two years. He had come down to visit Lynn for the long weekend, after assuring his mother that he would return to East Hartford in time to turn the hamburgers at a Fourth of July picnic she had planned.

Before he had shot Nettie Blassberg and Norman Bozick, Robinson had ordered the black and Hispanic passengers to the rear and had kept the remaining whites and a Chinese man up front. Bruce DeBoar and Jackie Rostom, the young woman on her way to visit her sister in New England, were the only whites who remained. If the minority passengers were not exactly allies, Robinson certainly did not consider them as dangerous as the whites. *I'm it,* Bruce thought to himself. *I'm the next one he shoots.*

Bruce was suddenly transfixed by something he saw on the inside wall of the bus. It was a fire axe. Robinson was moving up and down the aisle regularly. It would not take

Bruce more than a few seconds to move for the axe, pull it from its mooring, and bring it down on the gunman's head.

But doubts raced through him. I've never hit anybody with anything, he thought. Can I do it? Can I cross that line? When I bring it up over my head, am I really going to be able to bring it down on *his* head? Or is there going to be that moment of hesitation?

And what about the others? What if it worked—if Robinson started to walk the other way and Bruce grabbed the axe, slammed it over his head, and, as he went down, Robinson fired, killing one of the other hostages. That, Bruce thought, is something I could never live with. He decided to forget the axe and play it cool. Bozick had tried to be a hero and so had Susan Bruso, and where had it gotten them? No, he thought, that was not the order of the day. He would bide his time and try to identify with this obviously disturbed gunman, to convince him that even a white man might be his friend.

Initially, a Spanish-speaking woman passenger had pulled the phone aboard and started to speak, but she had not been calm enough. Bruce had decided to remain silent, trying to be almost invisible. But now he decided that his best hope was to become useful to the gunman. He volunteered to take the phone. Robinson looked at him suspiciously, instinctively pointing the pistol at Bruce's head. But then he nodded. In the tortured world of racial mistrust and bitterness that had exploded for him this afternoon, Bruce was the ideal conduit for his message to the outside world. "No tricks, you understand?" the captor instructed. "Just tell them what I want."

"I'll tell you what he says," Bruce said. "Honest. Get a pencil from somebody and I'll write it all down for you."

"Tell them they've got fifteen minutes," Robinson ordered, after glancing down at the wristwatch he had taken from Israel Maldonado, the young Hispanic soldier with the duffel bag. And Bruce dutifully repeated the message with the stark drama of a movie actor: "You have fifteen minutes left."

The cop had alternately spoken Spanish and English to the woman, trying to find the most productive tongue in which to communicate. Now, of course, he was speaking in English, pleading with Bruce to ask Robinson to take the phone and negotiate for himself. Bruce knew enough from the previous exchanges to realize it was a futile request. "They want to talk to you," he told the gunman, as meekly as he could.

"How many times do I have to tell them no!" Robinson raged in return. "Tell them not to worry about talking to me. They know what I want and they better get it or more people are going to die! Tell them that!"

All that elicited from the cop was a request that Bruce ask Robinson if he would talk directly to a Spanish-speaking officer. My God, Bruce thought to himself, what the hell are they doing? He knew, of course. They were stalling. But if *he* knew, certainly the hijacker knew too. When Bruce relayed the message this time, Robinson just shook his head.

"Can you at least get the plane?" Bruce decided to ask, trying to move onto something substantive. After all, this was one of the largest airports in the world. Maybe $6 million was a lot of money, but how hard could it be for the cops to furnish a plane?

It was a "bad day," Bruce was told, a holiday. The executive offices of airlines and banks were closed. The cops needed more time. It was becoming clear to the young man from Connecticut that at some stage most of the exchanges reached a point that gave him two choices. First, he could try to reason with Robinson, explain the police position, and perhaps suggest a response. But the cops were giving him so little to work with. If they asked to speak to Robinson directly one more time, he thought he would scream. Or perhaps he could in fact scream—at the cops.

A combative position on behalf of Robinson and the hostages would certainly increase Bruce's credibility with the man pointing the gun at him. On the other hand, it would also add to the dangerous perception that both the captor and the hostages were beginning to share—that there would be no plane, no money, no way out except death or surrender. Bruce thought about the TV cop, Baretta, who would extricate himself from these situations by identifying with the street people he encountered. If I say the wrong thing, I'm going to get shot, he thought. I've really got to sound as angry as he is, to try to establish some kind of rapport. He had seen the others shot and he knew that he had to try something to gain the gunman's confidence.

"They say it's a bad day," Bruce told Robinson. "It's July Fourth and nobody's around to give them a plane. They're trying to reach some airline executives."

Robinson spat and gestured disgustedly at Bruce and the telephone with his left hand, cutting the air with a backhanded swipe of his knife. "No more," he said. For ninety seconds there was not a sound on the bus and then the cop was talking again, in Spanish. Bruce handed the earphones to Robinson, who listened for a few sentences and handed them back.

"When I want to say something," he declared, "I will."

"He says when we want to say something, we will," Bruce said, interrupting the Spanish appeal and hoping Robinson had noticed his change of pronoun. But the captor was not reserving his thoughts for such subtleties at the moment. "Tell them they have ten minutes," he said.

Robinson had been crouching in the aisle. In front of him were Bruce, Jackie, and the Hong Kong businessman named Jimmy Lo. Beyond, in the left rear of the bus, were women giving hushed commands to their children and literally praying. Almost from the beginning, an older woman had clutched a rosary and recited in barely audible Spanish. Now, Robinson was up and walking to the rear; something caught his eye: a radio.

"Turn it on!" he commanded to one of the young men on the right side of the bus. There was a crackle and then some rock music. "You want the news, don't you?" Bruce called out from the front, and Robinson nodded and ordered, "The news!" The young man nodded and spun the dial until he found one of the city's two all-news radio stations.

". . . temperature is eighty-eight degrees at two fifty-five," a voice said, "and here is the hour's top story. Police have closed off Kennedy Airport where a bus hijacked earlier today in the Bronx was taken. At least three passengers are reported shot, and police believe as many as three hijackers may be involved, one a woman . . ."

Bruce and Jackie glanced at each other. If police believed

as many as three hijackers were involved, were he and she potentially *targets* in the cops' eyes rather than victims? Or, if not them, would an assault team be poised to kill the young soldier serving as a lookout at the rear window and one of the Hispanic women?

"You see," Robinson shouted to his audience, using the aisle as a stage, "you don't think they lie? They lie. They always lie. They tell the people there are three with guns in here. You know why? So if they kill you, they can make the people think you were with me. You're Spanish, you're black, your life ain't worth shit to them. They'd just as soon kill you as anything."

He finished the soliloquy with a flourish, glancing at the wristwatch and pointing his gun at Bruce: "Tell them they have five minutes until somebody else dies."

Again, the cops pleaded for patience and a chance to talk to Robinson. But that only made him more furious. He bolted up from his crouch, knocking over the bag of bullets and sending some of them skittering like marbles in between the empty seats.

"Get them!" he snapped at Jackie and she complied, dutifully craning to be sure every last copper-colored bullet was off the floor. Robinson put the knife in his belt and, holding the edge of the bag in his gun hand, slowly counted each bullet. Did he really know exactly how many there were supposed to be? What if one were missing? Bruce remembered Captain Queeg's strawberry scene from *The Caine Mutiny* and began thinking a step ahead, trying to fathom what he would do if Robinson next launched an all-out hunt for the missing bullets.

In fact, Robinson had his mind on larger forms of armament. He was at the rear now, surveying the police on the runway. "What are they doing with that tank out there?" he called back to Bruce. "I want it out of there. And I want those SWAT guys with the rifles out also. And tell them I mean now!"

The cop assured Bruce that the "tank" was an armored "rescue vehicle" but it would be moved if necessary. And what "SWAT guys" did he have in mind?

"Oh, Jesus, those clowns with the guns!" Bruce shouted, protesting more for Bruce now than for Robinson. "Jesus, they're not making things any better."

Again, there were assurances. The riflemen were there for everyone's protection, including their own, but if it would help matters to have the men and vehicles on the runway redeployed at a safer distance then the cop on the phone would "negotiate" that with his superiors.

Robinson was growing more upset. "You know," he told Bruce, "the others that got shot, they couldn't help that. But the next person that dies, it's on them, man. Because they think I'm stupid. That I'm forgetting about the time. And I'm not." Bruce reported to the police that someone on the bus was likely to die any minute now unless they started showing signs of cooperation.

"Die? We're going to move these people out of there. It takes a few minutes. Tell him—"

"That's not the point," Bruce interrupted. "The time limit he gave you is running out . . ."

"We still have time with him," the cop insisted.

In fact the five-minute warning had come five minutes and thirty-five seconds before.

"He's ready to kill somebody," Bruce insisted almost matter-of-factly now.

But the police were nothing if not persistent in their obvious effort at trivializing matters. Where exactly, the cop asked, did Robinson want the trucks and troops redeployed?

"I don't care what they do with their fucking trucks!" Robinson shouted in the background loudly enough for the cop on the phone to hear him. "I want the plane! You understand that and they understand that. And you'd better tell them they're making a big mistake if they think I'm giving them all this extra time."

Bruce delivered the message.

"You're probably a better con man than I could ever be," the cop told Bruce in response. "I'm not giving him any bullshit. I'm moving that tank away from there." He said it would take time to assemble a crew for the plane. Nobody could be assigned to such a mission. But in the meantime, the police wanted to provide a sign of cooperation. It was not enough for Robinson.

"Tell them I want the public to know why someone will die!" he shouted, lifting his pistol and firing—into the ceiling.

The passengers were close to panic, believing that the shot had been harmless more by chance than design. Robinson had fired to punctuate a sentence and he had pointed up instead of out when the gun went off—that was the difference between a hole in the roof of the bus and one in somebody's face.

Now he grabbed Bruce by the collar, the gun only inches from his head, and started talking about the Navy again.

"They've got to beat you, man, unless you show them you mean it, and then they throw your ass in jail," he said. "But at least you've got your self-respect. You didn't play their game. Because if you play their game, they just use you for a while and throw you away anyway. You think they care if you live or die? They just showed you how much they care. They got all the money in the world and more planes than they know what to do with. I asked for six million dollars and an airplane and they'd rather have me kill you than give it to me. Do you understand that? Do you know what I mean? They're after me, man, but if you get in the way that's too bad. People gotta wise up, do you hear me? We gotta fight back. We can't just lay down and die!"

CHAPTER TEN

"The Next Will Be a Child"

The police had established a cone of security on Runway 13.

It began with the Port Authority's armored car, parked with one side facing the rear of the bus about fifty feet away. Given the width of the bus's rear window, the length of the armored car, and the principles of plane geometry, there was an ever-expanding cone of space that Robinson could not see behind the armored car. That was where the police reconnoitered and where they placed a variety of potential tools. Among them would be a Greyhound bus that was the exact model of the green Vermont Transit Company bus. Captain Daniel St. John and his Emergency Services Division assault teams would have to examine the duplicate bus so they could understand its exact layout—just in case they were called upon to make a rush.

For the moment, Bolz was more concerned with the possibility of a "Phase Two"—the moving of Robinson and some or all of the remaining fifteen hostages to the FBI's satellite area in the easternmost expanses of the airport. The armor-plated NYPD photo observation truck would escort Robinson to the site, and Bolz assigned four police cars the mission of following along. For the moment, Vasquez and Robinson's surrogate negotiators had agreed that the police would supply baggage mules, the open trucks that haul luggage to and from planes, to transport Robinson and the hostages to the waiting plane.

There were lingering problems for Bolz and his team.

The negotiators still were not speaking directly to Robinson and could not build up much intelligence about him because they did not even know his name. They had jumped on a small lead: the note which he sent out to demand the money and the plane was written on the back of a bank statement. But a great deal of rapid legwork on the Fourth of July led, many hours later, to the disappointing realization that the paper had been borrowed from a hostage.

And while Robinson had not shot anyone since the start of communication, he had fired into the bus and ranted, exhibiting a simmering volatility that direct talk with him might have had under control by now.

But things could have been worse, too. Time was on the cops' side in any such standoff. If the gunman wanted to shoot the rest of his captives, he had had the chance. What he really wanted, in all likelihood, was a way out. And the longer the police stalled him, the more obvious a solution surrender became. This was the way Bolz and Harvey Schlossberg analyzed almost all of these situations, but it was an abstract notion that often escaped even the most astute cops unfamiliar with their tactics. At one point, as Bolz moved within his security cone, plotting a possible move, Neil Behan approached him.

"Hey, Frank," he said, "why don't you give it a try? This guy doesn't seem to be getting anywhere."

It was as if Bolz were some magician who had the right formula for talking down hostages. The formula, of course, was psychology, restraint, and patience. "Chief," Bolz said, "he's doing about as well as I could do. I'm better off back here on the logistics end, putting things together."

Vasquez and Bruce were talking about the move.

"Tell him to let us know what his moves are," the cop said. "We don't want to block any of his moves. We want to communicate with him, so there's no misunderstanding. We want him to know that we don't want to upset him, that we're not out to hurt him."

Bruce conferred with Robinson and then reported that the mules were to be brought thirty feet forward of the bus, on the side away from the police. "He wants the driver to get out," Bruce said, "put his hands in the air, and walk five feet away from the mule, and stand there, with his hands in the air.

The driver should have the money with him and leave it where we're going to be sitting, in the mules. And leave a bullhorn for us to communicate with.''

That sounded fine, Vasquez said, except for the money. "I have to get verification on where the money's located," he said. "I understood that this money was going to be placed aboard the plane."

It was a verbal shell game—the mules are coming, the money's on board, the pilot's in traffic—now you see them, now you don't. But was Robinson buying? Not that anyone could tell. "He wants you to know," Bruce reported, "that if you wait until dark, he's going to shoot someone and throw them out and make you pay for waiting this long."

Vasquez sighed.

"Well, it isn't us that's making you wait," he said after a moment. "We'd like to get you off to wherever you'd like to go. We can't just jump a plane. We can't just boss a pilot. There's a lot of reason for this delay and it's not our choosing. Tell him that if he shoots someone it's not going to do any good for him or anyone else. It only delays the matter. We're trying to rush this for you. We ordered mules an hour ago, I would say, and they're not here yet. You know we're dealing with the Port Authority. We're not dealing with a specific airline, so one person has to relay the message to another and so forth. You've got to get executives to give permission. There are a million little details that are being hurried through for your convenience. We're not trying to pull anything on you. We even offered you soda before. You refused. All right. But we're trying to make your wait as comfortable as possible."

A minute went by and then another.

"He understands your problem," Bruce said finally. "He doesn't think you do. And that's why it may happen."

"I'm dying to talk to him personally," Vasquez said, "to come to an understanding. I want him to have faith in who he's dealing with. I can't hurt him. What can I say to him on the phone? I'm not here to aggravate him. I just want to talk to him. We could talk, rap, I mean I'm sitting here holding this phone to my ear and I've got an earache already."

"He says you'd better make a miracle," Bruce responded. He had decided, for the first time really, that it was likely he would be shot. He thought about the twenty years of his life, the recent decision to leave school, and how sorry he had felt for himself. "Maybe I didn't appreciate things enough," Bruce said to himself, as if he was already dead. "Maybe I took life for granted."

"Well, listen," Vasquez said, trying to summon some indignation, "if he doesn't want to talk to us, we don't want to talk to him either. It's getting to the point that this is ridiculous. We're trying to do everything that he wants us to do, and he's putting all the pressure in the world on us. Do you understand. I asked to talk to him. I wanted—"

"He thinks that I'm getting your point across just fine," Bruce said, "and he thinks that I'm getting his point across just fine, too."

Schlossberg called Bolz aside. They had pleaded for the gunman to respond and had established a very defensive posture. It might be time, the psychologist suggested, to take the offensive by saying nothing. When Bolz delivered the message to Vasquez, the negotiator seemed upset.

"You're doing all right, Julio," Bolz reassured him. "But we're not getting anywhere, and Harvey just thinks this might be the way to go."

Vasquez called into the phone and, after Bruce responded, he delivered the message. "If he wants anything from now on, he's to call us," Vasquez said. "We'll be listening for his call. We'll get everything else ready. But anything he wants, we're not going to acknowledge it if it's not from him, okay?"

"All right," Bruce said very quietly. There was more than a hint of despair in his voice.

On the bus, Robinson listened for Bruce's report and then exploded. He grabbed Bruce and threw him to the floor of the bus, putting the gun to his head.

He looked up at one of the women and ordered, "Throw that thing out the window!"

Bolz saw the phone come tumbling out, but he also noticed that it was still dangling from the bus by its line. "That's okay," he shouted to the assembled brass, trying to reassure them that this was all part of the game. "He may pick it up again. He's doing that to show a reaction because we said we would not talk through his negotiators anymore."

Then they heard the shot.

"I had beautiful communications," Vasquez said plaintively. "What the hell happened?" There were tears running down his face. He was certain Bruce had been shot.

"Keep everybody clear!" Bolz shouted along the front line. "He may throw a few shots out to prove a point!"

Inside the bus, Robinson suddenly left Bruce and walked toward Jimmy Lo. Earlier, Robinson had asked him if he had any connections in the Orient, knew anybody who could come up with a lot of cash. Lo had shaken his head. Now he was mumbling to himself in Chinese. There were tears in his eyes, Bruce noticed. "Shut up!" Robinson ordered, but instead Lo stood up, possibly because he had misunderstood.

There was no misunderstanding about what happened next. Robinson raised the gun and fired at point-blank range. Lo slumped forward, struck in the chest.

"Pick him up and throw him out the window," Robinson motioned to Bruce, "or else, you're next."

Bruce felt himself moving like a robot. He had never seen anyone shot before today and now this was the third person (not counting McGavern, whose shooting he had only heard). And I'm likely to be the fourth, he thought, his mind in a haze. He lifted the Chinese man up, carried him to the window, and tried to drop him gently toward the ground. Somehow, he succeeded. Lo wound up on his feet.

The cops shouted for him to run toward them, but instead he first went the other way, toward the front of the bus. Finally, he reoriented himself and staggered to safety. He was carried to a mobile hospital unit within the security cone. Blood was flowing from his chest and back, but that was a good sign. Robinson was firing jacketed bullets, which move through a man at high velocity, not pausing to tear up his insides en route.

The shot had come at 7:19.

Three minutes later, police could see the phone being pulled back through the open bus window.

"Was that proof enough?" Bruce asked. "I mean, what the hell are you doing!"

"What do you mean?" Vasquez asked. "Why did he throw the phone out? Why can't he speak to me?"

"He doesn't want to speak to you. He wants his demands met. He just shot a guy."

"I see that," Vasquez said.

"There it is in black and white," Bruce said, "What the hell is going on?"

Bolz joined Vasquez and Jack Fitzsimmons, the backup negotiator. "Tell him he's not giving us a chance to do what he wants," he told Vasquez.

But that just brought Bruce to a higher pitch. "What isn't he giving you a chance to do?" he asked. "What? What! What do you need to talk to him for?"

"Tell him what he did was very foolish," Vasquez said. "He's not accomplishing anything. We're trying to get his demands met. What the hell's the matter with him?"

"He doesn't believe you," Bruce said, sounding drained. The emotion had switched to Vasquez. "He's making it more difficult for any volunteers to even go near that stupid bus," the cop said. "That's what he's doing!"

Robinson told Bruce to tell the police that they were not cooperating.

"*We're* not cooperating?" Vasquez responded. "We're breaking our chops over here trying to get the things for him. And this is the way he's behaving? I told him before. Why doesn't he let the rest of the children off?"

"The man is losing his patience, that's all," Bruce said after a few more exchanges.

"So what is he going to do? Kill all of you? What's that going to get him?"

Again, Vasquez talked of the problems in getting volunteers to fly the plane and drive the mules to the plane and of the more basic problem, of communicating with the gunman through emissaries. And then there was another crackle.

Robinson had fired into the ceiling and then ordered everyone down in the bus. He had Bruce on the floor now. "Don't worry," he told him. "I just want them to think I shot you, that's all. Stay down and nothing will happen."

"He shot again," Vasquez stammered over the phone. There were tears in his eyes. "He shot again. Jesus Christ. Talk to me, Bruce. Bruce, talk to me . . ."

Now Vasquez turned to Bolz and Schlossberg. "Everyone's down in the bus," he said. "I can't see anyone in the bus. He was up by the open window and now he's not there. It's a matter of life and death. He's for real. You'll wait till he dies!"

Vasquez was back on the phone now. "Bruce!" he shouted. "Bruce! Speak to me, Bruce!"

Bolz had been preparing himself for this for some minutes. Julio Vasquez was a proven cop, a first-rate detective. There was no shame in what had happened to him on this runway. Bolz and Harvey had talked about the problem over and over through their training work. When the psychological transference occurred between negotiator and perpetrator, that was bad enough. But now there had been a transference between negotiator and hostage and that was far worse. Vasquez was lashing out now at the police. Why had they risked Bruce's life? Couldn't they have given the gunman some more of what he wanted? Why had Schlossberg demanded that he speak only to the gunman?

"Julio," Bolz said, as gently as possible, "trade places with Jack for a while, okay?"

For a moment, Vasquez looked at him, uncomprehending. Then he stepped aside and Jack Fitzsimmons picked up the phone and called, less emotionally, for Bruce.

"Hello."

"It was a woman's voice.

"Where's Bruce?" Fitzsimmons asked.

"Bruce is sitting down," Jackie Rostom said.

"Is he all right?"

"Yes."

No, Jackie said, in response to his question, nobody had been shot. She turned to Robinson and said, so that the police could hear: "What do you want me to tell him? He's just making small conversation."

"We want the safety of you people," Fitzsimmons said. "Tell *him* that."

"Will you listen to me?" Jackie said.

"I'm listening," Fitzsimmons said.

"We're *human beings* in here!" she said.

"We'll bring the mules in sight," Fitzsimmons said.

"Please!" she said. "He's going to shoot everybody!"

"We don't want him to do that," Fitzsimmons said. "We're bringing the mule in sight."

In fact, a Port Authority police officer had driven the baggage carriers just to the edge of the cone, out of the bus's sight line and no farther. He had seen too many hostages shot, and he was not going to provide Robinson with that easy a target. If the commanders wanted the mule closer to that bus, they would have to find another driver.

Bolz thought about choosing a driver and decided he could not send another man into the line of fire. "I drove one of those things in the Naval Reserve," he told Schlossberg. "I'm going to drive it."

Through Jackie, Robinson had ordered the photo observation truck to move back, out of sight. Vasquez was calmer now, and every few minutes, Fitzsimmons would ask about Bruce. Always, Jackie would say he was fine but that he could not come to the phone.

Bolz had donned a bulletproof vest hours before. Now he draped a second vest across the front windshield. He decided to do this in stages, to drive the mule just to a point where Robinson could see it from the rear of the bus and no farther. Then to drive it closer. "We do it in three pieces and he owes us for three favors," he explained to the bosses.

As Bolz drove to the edge of the security cone, peering from behind the covered windshield, he could see Danny St. John putting his crew through their paces on the duplicate bus. They were moving in the front door, the emergency exits, even through the luggage compartment, where a panel could be moved out, allowing access to the passenger area.

"Can he see it?" Bolz shouted to the negotiators.

"He wants it closer," they yelled back.

He went back to the mule and edged it farther along, close to where the chiefs were gathered, but outside the security cone and exposed to Robinson's line of fire. Holy shit, Bolz thought, glancing at the brass, I've only got three names ahead of me on the Captain's list. What the hell am I doing driving this thing?

He left the mule where it was and told Fitzsimmons to tell Robinson that the truck he wanted moved would be used to tow the mule to the airplane. That was killing two birds with one stone—accounting for the continued presence of the armored truck and also getting Bolz out of the line of fire.

As Bolz moved the mule almost alongside the armored car that the negotiators were behind, they could hear Jackie, sounding like a broadcaster, saying, "I can see it coming up now. Now it is coming up toward—No, we want it up *in front* of the bus, not behind it. In front of the bus and then the man is to get out away from it."

"We'll let the mule go up in front of the bus if he lets some of the people off the bus," Fitzsimmons told her. "Will he consider letting some of you off the bus?"

"No, he won't," Jackie said. "We're all getting on the mule with him. We will be unharmed once we get to the plane. Nobody will be let off this bus. We're all getting on the mule together. Please. Do as he says."

"All right," Fitzsimmons said. "We're getting a driver, a volunteer who's going to take it on up there. Not everybody's going to want to go up there."

"He's not going to hurt him," Jackie said. "Don't you think about *our* lives?"

"We *are* thinking of your lives."

"You are, huh! It doesn't seem like it."

Robinson had her tell Fitzsimmons that he had only let hostages off the bus as a matter of convenience, not through any bargaining. "He didn't do it out of mercy," she said. "He did it because there were too many."

Fitzsimmons tried to recapitulate.

"We're moving as fast as we can," he said. "We're trying to do as much as we can get done. We have the mules here. It took a long time to get them. Now we're getting things set up. This is the Fourth of July. It's not easy. He didn't pick a good day to do this."

"It may not be a particularly good day," Jackie said, "but it's a day for us to die if you don't do anything about it."

Each word had been enunciated as if she had intended to evoke as much dramatic emphasis as she could.

"We're trying to do the best we can. I mean we haven't fired any shots. We haven't done anything to him. We're trying to cooperate. He's not cooperating with us."

"What is there for him to cooperate about?" she asked.

"Just give us time; time to meet his demands. That's all we're asking."

"The mule is still back there," Jackie said. "Why isn't he coming forward with it?"

"Because they need a driver," Fitzsimmons explained.

"You *had* a driver," Jackie said impatiently. "How'd you get it that far without a driver?"

"The fellow who was driving it doesn't want—"

"Why can't you get the police to drive it. *I* can drive one of those things."

Bolz and the others smiled ruefully. There it was. Being a cop meant a lot of things to average citizens, including the idea that you were supposed to risk your life under any conditions to save theirs. Fitzsimmons pressed the idea, in return, that Robinson could demonstrate how sincere he was about providing safe conduct for a mule driver by letting some hostages go. "He's got to show some kind of good faith," Fitzsimmons told Jackie. "I mean, all he's done up to now is shoot people."

"He doesn't have to show you good faith," she said. "He showed you what he's going to do. That should be enough. We're in no position to negotiate. That man has told you what he wanted. He knows you're bullshitting. He's going to do something. People will be hurt. Do you understand?"

"I understand that," Fitzsimmons said calmly.

"Well, will you people do your job?" she shouted. "Do something! Do what he asks! He showed you he's not fooling around."

"Why doesn't he let somebody off the bus and show us that he's going to work with us?" Fitzsimmons asked.

"Why should he do that," Jackie shot back. "He showed you what he's going to do if you *don't* work with him!"

"Because we don't trust him."

"Do you want everybody hurt?"

"We don't want *any*body hurt."

"Well then, do what he says," Jackie pleaded. "We're telling you. Every passenger on this bus is telling you! *Please* do what he says. We believe he won't hurt us. He just wants you to do what he says . . ."

Jackie's voice evaporated into tears. But she picked up a moment later, sobbing as she spoke.

"It's getting dark," she said. "And as soon as it gets dark, somebody is going to get shot. Would you *please, please, do something!*"

"We *are*," Fitzsimmons responded without emotion.

"You're not doing anything!" Jackie said, more indignant than tearful now.

"We're doing more than you know," he responded.

Inside the bus, the volcano that was Luis Rogelio Robinson seemed ready for another eruption. He ordered one of the young black men to stand watch at the rear window, and when the man hesitated—fearing that an assault might be imminent—Robinson snapped, "Where's your mother? You sit right there. If you don't tell me something is coming through there, I'm going to shoot her first."

Then Robinson walked over to Jackie, took the phone from her, and, at 8:05, for the first time since he had triggered this siege more than six hours earlier, he spoke directly to the world outside the bus.

"Listen," Robinson said, "I'm getting tired of this shit. Now you guys are going to have to do everything I say or I'm going to shoot everybody in here—"

"We're—"

"Now, don't say nothin'! Don't say nothin'."

"We're trying to work with you," Fitzsimmons said, anyway.

"Now, you're not kidding me. First you had the money and now you don't know where it is. What do you think, I'm a kid?"

"As far as I know," Fitzsimmons said, "I've been told it's over by the plane."

"Well, you get it over here," Robinson ordered.

"They're supposed to have people running to and fro, handling this shit. Now, if you *don't* do it, I'm not afraid to die. I'll kill everyone on here. And you can shoot me down if you want to."

Fitzsimmons was just trying to keep him talking. "We don't want anybody else hurt," he assured Robinson.

"Well, then you're not cooperating."

"We *are* cooperating," Fitzsimmons insisted.

"No, you're not," Robinson said. "You've been playing games with me. Now just conning me has made the matter even worse."

"We're not trying to make the matters worse. We're trying to get the van and we're trying to work it out so we get everything you want."

"Why is it taking so long?"

"Because this is July Fourth," Fitzsimmons said, resorting to a now-familiar refrain. "We've got people to deal with. We've got private airplanes to get. We've got banks to open that are closed. This is July Fourth."

"So why did you lie to me?" Robinson asked. "Why did you tell them you had the money?"

"They said that the money was being counted and it *is* being counted," Fitzsimmons ad-libbed. "They're getting the people to the banks to get them opened. They just can't come up with a million or six million dollars at the drop of a hat. See, these are tough things to come by and we don't want anybody else hurt. We're trying to cooperate with you. We're trying our best. I mean we haven't fired any shots or anything."

"You haven't," Robinson conceded. "But you would try if you could."

"No, we wouldn't," Fitzsimmons said. "We really wouldn't. We understand where you're coming from. We know how serious things are. We don't want to see anybody else hurt. We're not going to shoot at you."

"Well," Robinson said, "the next person will be a child. And I mean it, because I want the public to see how silly you are if you don't cooperate with me. 'Cause, you know. You've seen me kill enough people to know that I mean business."

"I know you've done that," Fitzsimmons agreed.

"I tell you again," Robinson said. "I do not care if I get shot in the process. I am interested in getting out of here."

Yes, Fitzsimmons replied, the police understood that and were trying to arrange things. It was tough gathering a crew to fly a plane, he told Robinson, when those involved were aware they would be taking off with a gun to their backs.

"I'm not looking to hold a gun on them," Robinson said. "The only thing the pilot's got to do is stay in the room and do exactly what I tell him to do and he won't get hurt. Now I know that if I shoot in the airplane it will probably do some damage, but I will if I have to. But if he cooperates, I'll cooperate."

Robinson asked again about the money, and when Fitzsimmons answered only vaguely, he exploded. He reminded Fitzsimmons that earlier the police had reported amassing about $1,600,000 in cash. It had been an offhanded remark, but nonetheless too specific, and it was coming back to haunt them.

"Tell them to get that here!" he demanded. "Forget about counting it, just bring it over here. And I'll tell you one thing. I have a pair of glasses on. And when it gets dark according to that glass, my glasses, I'm going to start shooting. I'm going to get the hell out of here. And I'm going to make sure that everyone I leave on here's going to be dead. Do you understand that? And if anyone tries to rush this plane—I mean this bus—I'm going to shoot everyone in here first, and then I'm going to turn around and shoot everyone that's near me. And if there's anyone on that plane, aside from the people I will send on there to check it out, if there's anyone on the plane—I don't want a crew on the plane until I get on. I want them standing outside the plane. They will have my word that I will not shoot them. Everyone who died today or got shot today, with the exception of the old lady, that was your fault. I told you to stop following me. You kept following me around. The first man that I shot, he was shot because of your stupidity. He tried to jump me. The bus driver tried to be a hero, right? And he got shot. Now, if anybody rushes me—if anybody makes any crazy moves—I'm going to start firing."

It was a telling soliloquy, mixing fact and fantasy. Who

had been "following" Robinson when he shot John Mc-Gavern, the librarian? And poor Norman Bozick, the murdered driver? He had tried to be a hero, all right, but only after watching Robinson shoot the old woman, Mrs. Blassberg, in cold blood with her blind husband just a few feet away.

But that would be for the shrinks to ponder, if and when the police got Robinson out of that bus alive. Fitzsimmons had to press on. He asked where Robinson wanted to go in the plane. Flight plans had to be filed, he told the gunman.

"Well, listen, you're going to have enough fuel to get where I'm going and back," Robinson said. "So when we get in the air, then I will tell them where we're going, and you can just chart it out then and the pilot will zoom off in that direction. I've gone as far as I'm going to go with you. I've cooperated enough."

Fitzsimmons chatted with Bolz and came back at Robinson.

"The air people are alarmed that you have no destination," he said, "because the pilots are going to balk and they're not going to get on the plane."

"The destination," Robinson said suddenly, "is Cuba."

Could Robinson set some hostages loose?

"No," he said. "When I get on the plane, these people are all coming with me. When the plane lands and I've submitted myself to the people over where I'm going to, then I can release your hostages. And they can fly right back."

"Couldn't you just let some of the people go, to show us that you—"

"No," Robinson said firmly. "No. I already did that with the kids. I want to be emphatic. I have no intention of harming anyone. There was no emotion involved in killing those people. You guys forced me to do it. Now, I have no intention of killing them. But I will kill them if I have to."

"You can't let the rest of the children go?" Fitzsimmons asked.

"I already let enough children go," Robinson said.

"They don't have to die," Fitzsimmons said.

"No, no, no," Robinson said. "If they die, it will be because you charge me. Simple."

There was some quiet then and—perhaps this was a sign

that the tide had turned somewhat—Robinson was back on the phone without prompting, albeit to bait the cops.

"I want to make it clear that there are a couple of foreigners on this bus," he announced, "and I don't think their country's going to like it that they came to New York on July Fourth to celebrate whatever the hell they came to celebrate and they got shot."

With that, Robinson put the phone down and began his own limited reconnoitering, stationing various sentries at the windows (always using fellow blacks for that role, perhaps believing that, down deep, they would be on his side in a crunch). Then Jackie was back on, again asking for the mule to be brought to the front of the bus, beseeching Fitzsimmons to hurry.

He told her that the cops were having trouble hooking the mule up with the bulletproofed photo observation truck that would tow it to the plane under the latest plan. "We may have to go back to putting the driver in the dolly," he said.

"Well, hurry up and make up your mind," she said.

Matter-of-factly, Fitzsimmons asked, for the first time in a long while, whether Bruce was all right.

"He's not shot, is he?" Fitzsimmons asked her.

"No," Jackie replied. "But if you don't do it, Bruce will be shot next, so *pleeeese*."

Fitzsimmons asked if the gunman himself might want to drive the van.

No, Jackie said, he couldn't. But he *would* release one hostage after they arrived at the plane, providing the police supplied a driver to get them there. There was a further stipulation. The driver was to appear without a shirt.

"He's making it harder to get a volunteer," Fitzsimmons told her.

"It's not making it harder if you do your job," she said. "If you do your job, there'll be no problem."

The negotiators conferred. There was no way they would expose a cop to the line of fire without affording him protection, they decided, and that was reported to Jackie.

"Tell him I will not shoot him as long as you guys don't shoot at us or try to do anything other than to disperse the crowd," Robinson said, taking the phone. "I've already instructed these people on what to do and they will comply because they have seen enough people get shot. Now, all you have to do is keep your hands up. If you intend to get me, then you must be prepared to have all these people—or as many as I can shoot—dead. Now, I've said I have no intention of hurting the driver as long as you guys or the driver doesn't try to be James Bond or somebody.''

To Bolz and Schlossberg, it was not as paradoxical as it might otherwise have seemed to have the gunman threaten to kill fifteen people and, in the same breath, promise safe conduct to a cop. They had seen similar episodes in any number of prior hostage situations. The way sociologists explain the phenomenon is that the perpetrator and the negotiator have formed a new, minuscule society in the midst of the siege. That society has its own rules and mores, not unlike the rules of war agreed upon at Geneva. In both societies, the white flag has a sacred meaning that is held inviolate—and interestingly enough, never before had a perpetrator gone back on such a pledge.

Robinson had a new angle a minute later. ''I'm going to try to leave at least one person alive,'' he told Fitzsimmons, ''so he can tell the world exactly how you treated them.''

With the gunman himself on the phone, the symptoms were coming as fast as Schlossberg could analyze them now. He seemed to be a classic case. ''I'll leave one alive''—displacement of guilt, like the child who tells his mother, ''I'll show you. I'll kill myself and *then* you'll be sorry.''

It was that displacement reaction that is at the basis of virtually every suicide attempt. And the police had long since decided that hostage cases bore striking similarities to suicide attempts. It was this revelation that had allowed them to believe they could talk their way out of almost any siege, because just as every suicide attempt could be successful if the subject had really wanted death, every hostage-holder could have killed his captives before the police even arrived to negotiate. At least, that was the theory. Would Luis Robinson, who had shot four people, killing two of them, prove the exception to the rule?

''I don't know who the people are that you are relaying

this to," Robinson told Fitzsimmons a few minutes later, "but I can tell you that they have no feelings. I only wish that one of the people on this bus just happened to be one of their relatives. Then they would probably pay attention."

"We care about everybody," Fitzsimmons protested. "It's not a case of that. It's that we're trying to do the right thing. And in order to get a guy to volunteer—we got one guy, but he says he wants to wear a vest. He wants protection. All he's got is your word, you know? And the bosses over here, they're insistent that the guy has to wear a vest. At least let him wear a vest."

"Okay," Robinson said, "if he wears a vest then you're going to have to bring me a vest. I want a vest and protective gear for my head, and that guy can go ahead and do that, too. I don't want to see anything strapped to him. I just want him to be clean so that I don't have to worry about him, because I've got to pay attention to these people. I know that they're not going to panic as long as you don't do anything stupid."

It was 8:50. The sun would set in thirty minutes, but over the heads of the cops, in the direction in which Robinson was facing, streaks of darkness already appeared over the eastern horizon. Several miles eastward on this long airport, four FBI sharpshooters and four spotters were already in position, on specially constructed ramps designed for just this purpose. From one of them, five years before, Sal Naturelle had been killed at the end of what was to become known as Dog Day Afternoon. And he had just tried to rob a bank. Luis Robinson had killed two people and wounded two others and was now threatening to murder a child if his demands were not met by dusk.

The negotiating team had never lost a perpetrator, Bolz thought, and they certainly did not want to spoil that record here. But perhaps this unknown gunman aboard the one o'clock bus to White River Junction would leave the police no choice. And, if he really was intent on dying here on this airstrip, how many innocent people still on that bus would have to go down with him?

CHAPTER ELEVEN

Phase Two—
"It's Moving"

This was one of the busiest evenings of summer at JFK Airport, and the Port Authority had opened most of the field for normal takeoffs and landings in mid-afternoon, once it became clear that the bus on runway 13 was no longer mobile.

The Authority's next preoccupation had been with the press—dozens of reporters and television crew members were strung out behind the corrugated steel blast fence at the edge of the runway, standing atop car roofs for a peek at the activity a couple of hundred yards away on the runway. Once, shortly before 7:00 P.M., Robinson had fired a shot toward the reporters and it had ricocheted off the fence. That was about as close to the action as the press had come.

Unable to gauge much of what was happening by sight, reporters had tried to enter the Port Authority police station a half-mile back toward the main passenger terminals, adjacent to the wire fence gate that Robinson had ordered Norman Bozick to break open five hours before. But that building had been declared off limits to the reporters, who were directed to the Port Authority press office on the second floor of the International Arrivals Building. There, they were fed bits of information, some of it wrong, by officials who were themselves receiving third-hand accounts of the action on the runway. What the reporters knew for sure was that two persons were dead, two others were seriously wounded, and someone aboard that bus was holding off an army of police.

Out on the runway, with darkness approaching, Frank Bolz and his primary negotiator, Jack Fitzsimmons, were not learning much more either. They were still holding out the idea of hooking the baggage mule onto the photo observation truck —the "bread truck," police called it because it was a step-van (of the sort in which packaged baked goods are delivered) that had been converted into an armored vehicle in the NYPD's garage. The department had never been able to replace the cab windows with bulletproofed glass to withstand rifle fire and instead had rigged the truck so it could be driven from the rear, with an auxiliary accelerator, brake, and steering wheel, and a prismlike viewing system. They loved to test the truck on city streets because passers-by thought they were watching a scene from *Candid Camera*—a driverless van tooling down the block. But the bread truck had disadvantages, too, among them, limited peripheral vision from the rear driver's seat.

Julio Vasquez was backing up Fitzsimmons, and he reminded him that nobody had heard directly from Bruce De-Boar for more than an hour. With Robinson himself on the phone now, Fitzsimmons asked if Bruce was all right. Yes, the gunman said, and he allowed Bruce to come to the phone.

"Hello, Bruce?" Fitzsimmons said.

"Yes, sir," Bruce replied.

"Are you well?" Fitzsimmons asked. "You're not shot or anything?"

"Yes, sir," Bruce said, sounding very meek.

"All right," Fitzsimmons said, "we're working on getting the van ready. We're working on getting somebody to drive it. We told him that it's going to take time. And we understand how irritated you're getting. We're trying to do the best we can. We heard two shots before, and we thought you were shot. We wanted to know if you were shot."

"No," Bruce said. "He's not going to shoot me. He will stab me."

In fact, Robinson had his knife at Bruce's throat.

"I'm going to stab you and kill you," Robinson told him. "I want them to know that."

"They won't listen to me," Bruce told him.

Robinson took the phone again, and Fitzsimmons told him that once the armored truck was hooked to the baggage van, a lead car would move well in front of them to lead Robinson and the hostages to the plane.

"I don't want no cars in back of me," Robinson warned. "Do you understand that. I mean *none*. You know, I've been very lenient because I don't want to kill all these people and have no hostages left. But if I have to, I will."

"We understand that," Fitzsimmons said. "We understand that. But you need somebody in front of you."

"And listen," Robinson said, "when you pull the van in front, I want you to know that I'm also looking around. I don't want any of those 'I Spy' motherfuckers to be coming around me."

"Nobody's going to do anything foolish," Fitzsimmons assured him.

"You should have nothing to fear if you do what's right," Robinson said. "I want to see the money before I pull off. I'm going to send somebody out to get the money."

"Well, that's going to take time, you know—"

"Why's it going to take time?" Robinson said. "First you tell me the money's in the plane, then you tell me it's in the van. You were sure you had a million six hundred thousand. What happened? Somebody robbed it and ran off with it?"

"No, nobody's done anything like that," Fitzsimmons said. "We just don't have it here on the scene yet. I also told you that before."

"Let me tell *you* something," Robinson said. "I want you to know that I'll be able to tell if it's counterfeit or not. I don't care how big the bills are or anything. I'm just interested in the sum, the amount. If you fool me for one second, if I get out of this bus and I find that you've fooled me in any way, *in any way*, I'm going to start shooting people."

"Nobody's trying to fool anybody," Fitzsimmons insisted, talking very quickly now, playing the old shell game. "All I'm trying to do is relay the information that's being given to me. As far as the money's concerned, it was being collected and being delivered. According to the last message I got, it was being delivered to the plane. Now you want it on this thing and it's going to take time. That was the original instructions before, when you were talking through the other people, about it going over to the plane. At least that's the impression we got —that it was all right if it was over by the plane.''

It took Robinson a minute to mull that over. ''I want the money to be brought here,'' he said finally. ''I don't care about more time. I know it doesn't take much time to get from one place to another in this airport. You know, you can fool me all you want. In my mind, I'm analyzing where you're coming from. Now, you bring the money here. You tow it like you did the phone—whatever you choose to do to make you feel safe.'' He spit that last word out with contempt, mimicking the cops' preoccupation with their own safety in much the way Jackie had before.

The plane, Robinson repeated, could contain only those people he had personally allowed on board. ''They need a pilot and a navigator,'' he said. ''Just the bare necessities. I don't want no hostess with the mostest or nothing. If I find there's anybody on the plane aside from the people I count, then you're all going to be in big trouble because I'll just put a hole in the plane and have us all blow up. And I'm serious. You just have the people that are supposed to be on there. If you tell me that there are going to be three people on there, then there'd better be three people on there. I don't want no FBI, no CIA, no nobody.''

A half-minute later, Fitzsimmons reported that at least some money was at the plane.

''Tell them they bring it here,'' Robinson said. ''Tell them they've got helicopters that can fly up and fly down. Listen, I'm not silly; I'm not stupid.''

There were larger delays between transmissions now, and dusk was settling in, a fact that had not escaped the gunman. ''Tell them I'm going to get edgy as dark comes around,'' he warned, ''because I know that you're going to try your shit then.''

''We're already aware of that,'' Fitzsimmons said. ''We were told. You told us. The girl told us. We're fighting a time element. We're fighting a lot of things.''

Bolz drew Fitzsimmons, Vasquez, and Schlossberg aside. They were reaching a point of no return on the money.

Robinson had hinted, first through Bruce and Jackie and now directly, that he understood he would be given no money. If he really was going to retaliate for that by shooting one of the children, or anyone else, as night fell, maybe it was time for the police to take the initiative—force an issue and pray that a new turn of events, even a negative turn, would preoccupy him and keep him from carrying the threat to a horrendous conclusion.

They waited and heard no more from the bus. It was 9:00 P.M., and although the Weather Bureau had forecast a 9:20 sunset, it looked dark as a dungeon to Bolz, with the warm summer haze reducing visibility even more. If the alternative was to stand there and wait for another shot, this was worth a chance.

"Tell him," Bolz said to Fitzsimmons.

"Hello," he said over the phone.

"Yes."

It was Jackie's voice again.

"I'm told the money is going to be unavailable at this time. And that they can't get anybody to drive the van. We'll make the van available to him. If he wants the tow truck to take the van, we'll lead him over. Nobody wants to sit in that thing in front of him with a gun pointed at their head."

Jackie relayed the message and then asked: "Where is the money?"

"The money is not available," Fitzsimmons said. "He wants too much money. The banks are closed. I was told before that the money is going to be delivered over there, but I'm told that they don't have it yet and they would only—"

"I don't think he's going to like this much," Jackie interrupted.

"I know he's not going to like it," Fitzsimmons told her. "But we don't have it. He wants it right away and it's not available. Does he still want the plane to get out?"

"You lied to him, and he's not going to put any more trust in you," Jackie said. "You told him before that the money was here and—"

"I told him information that was given to me," Fitzsimmons said. "That's all I relayed to him was information."

Again, back to the basic negotiator's technique—*I* didn't lie, *they* lied.

"What were you saying about the plane?" Jackie asked with a sigh.

"He still wants the plane to get out, right?"

"Yes," she said incredulously. "Of course he wants the plane. What do you think this is all about?"

Jackie said that she would drive the van. There were several minutes of silence, and the police craned in the near-darkness to see if the young woman would alight from the bus to try to drive the baggage mule.

They could discern movement on the bus, but nobody was leaving. They could hear him barking orders like a drill sergeant. "Everybody move up!" Robinson was saying. "Get into these seats! Move. Move! Sit down here! You—in those two. You get right back there by that window. Watch it! Get in your seat right now. Right now! Now! Now!"

Someone was up in the driver's seat, but the bus lurched for a moment and failed to start. Then Jackie was back. Robinson had seen an airline baggage truck roll by in the distance. "That'll do just fine," she said.

"That's one of the trucks for the airlines," Fitzsimmons said. "As far as we know, it has nothing to do with what's going on here."

"They didn't know what that one was," Jackie reported to Robinson. "It had no radio or nothing."

"Tell him he's full of shit," Robinson spat.

"No, I'm not," Fitzsimmons said. "We have nothing to do with that van. There's no way we can contact it."

Suddenly, the bus's taillights went on.

"It's moving!" someone shouted.

"We are prepared to drive out of here," Jackie announced, almost triumphantly. Bruce DeBoar had started the bus. "We want an escort to the plane."

"All right," Fitzsimmons said.

Bolz could hardly believe his eyes. Dump the sump, my ass! he thought. All those guys with a little bit of knowledge who swore the bus would never start. But he was too busy to rue the false information for very long. Like it or not, this operation was about to go into Phase Two—the negotiation team's terminology for the movement of hostages. He had marked with masking tape X's the cars that he wanted to escort Robinson and the hostages to the satellite area. But there was little time to organize a motorcade.

"Pull up in front of us right now because we're ready to go," Jackie said.

"What do you want to do with the phone line?" Fitzsimmons asked.

"As soon as we start to go, we'll get rid of it," she said. "As soon as you see us, throw the phone out and turn around. That's when you give us the escort down there."

"All right," Fitzsimmons said.

Pat DiBenedetto, a Port Authority officer who had volunteered to drive the armored car as an escort vehicle, started it up. And behind the car, the runway looked like a Sebring racing start, with police officers running to vehicles that had been parked in the safety cone. Bolz, Fitzsimmons, and John Byron were throwing equipment into Bolz's car—vests, phones, a radio, a tape recorder—and then piling in on top of it. The armored car had pulled out, and behind it were at least twenty-five police vehicles.

Walter Lee, the Port Authority commander, suddenly pulled in front of DiBenedetto in the armored car and stopped. "Hold it," he said over the FBI's Blue Two radio frequency. "We have six cars marked for an escort. I want the other vehicles all pulled over to the side."

Bolz thanked Lee silently. He got out of his car and approached a Port Authority cop. "I want you to take the rest of us out there to the satellite area as fast as we can get there," he said. The bus, led by the armored car and the six other cars, with Walter Lee at the front, started lumbering off in one direction, and the other cars sped away in another.

It was 9:18. Lee knew what to do. A crooked city cab driver would have been proud of the long-way-around ride he was giving the hostage bus. Slowly, he drove the outermost extremity of one runway, then back and out another, creeping along the perimeter of the airport at fifteen to twenty miles an hour. Each stretch was three miles long.

By the time the bus reached the satellite area, at 9:55, the FBI and the police had been given plenty of time to establish position.

But the entire movement had taken too many of them by surprise, and not all had proceeded by the book. In theory, most of the forces should have gone to the satellite garage far across the way from the plane, a freight transport belonging to the Airlift International Company.

The satellite garage is an auxiliary crash-crew location, needed at JFK because the airfield is so long that no single garage could be positioned to enable the large, yellow emergency trucks to reach every possible crash site within the three-minute limit mandated by the Federal Aviation Administration. In the garage were two trunks containing an elaborate field communications system with a base telephone and six color-coded phones. The system had been delivered to the runway, but in the confusion of Robinson's surprising move, it sat there unused.

Almost everyone in the procession—police cars, private vehicles, ambulances—had gone right to the blast fence near the plane, where four FBI sharpshooters were poised on platforms, each with a communicator at his side—pre-positioned so that each rifleman could fire simultaneously at the target without getting in the line of fire.

Wally LaPrade, the FBI's special agent-in-charge of the New York office, arrived. It was really his show now, as it had been the FBI's show at the climax of Dog Day Afternoon four years before when Sal Naturelle went down with a well-placed bullet at this very spot.

Chiefs John Keenan and Neil Behan talked to LaPrade. It was unspoken bureau policy that no hijacked plane would be allowed to take off from an American airport. But it was also FBI policy to negotiate where practicable. Behan asked for another chance to talk it out. Yes, LaPrade said, that would be fine. "But you understand," he added, "that if he gets out of that bus without surrendering, we'll blow him away."

CHAPTER TWELVE

"I'm Luis!"

The airport was totally quiet again. All incoming traffic had been diverted from Kennedy and all outgoing flights ordered to stand in place with the initial movement of the bus at 9:18. Auxiliary lights, strung out like those on a Christmas tree, illuminated the satellite area near the Airlift International plane, outlining it and the bus, which had pulled to a halt a few yards away, its engine still running in the remote corner of the airport.

Perhaps a dozen law enforcement officers should have been in the immediate vicinity, with the rest in ready reserve. But the best-laid plans are often waylaid in the heat of battle. There were as many as ninety cops and agents at the scene, most hanging back near the blast fence less than a hundred yards from the plane.

Chief Neil Behan approached Bolz now. "Frank, the other guys haven't made much headway," he said. "I want you to try talking him out."

Bolz agreed. He took the bullhorn from his car and searched for a bulletproof vest. There was none. He scouted around and saw one lying on one of the blast-fence support beams. Somebody must have gotten too hot, he thought to himself. Well, I'll take it. Whoever left it, screw 'em. Then he saw the number inside the lining. It was D-10. Somebody had taken Bolz's own vest from the car and tossed it onto the fence.

It was truly a three-agency operation. Leo McGillicuddy, the FBI's negotiator, would go into the rear of the Port Authority's armored car, accompanied by a bureau sharpshooter. Pat DiBenedetto, the Port Authority cop, would drive, with Bolz in the passenger seat trying to talk to Robinson.

Slowly, DiBenedetto pulled the armored car close enough to the bus for Bolz to be heard on the bullhorn.

Onboard the bus, Robinson was devising his own plan for avoiding the fate that had befallen Sal Naturelle. He wanted the hostages to surround him when he departed, so nobody could get a clear shot at him. The idea was to tie them all to each other in a circle, with him in the middle. But there was no rope. "Everybody take off your shoes," he shouted to the passengers, "and undo the laces. I want all your shoe laces."

The armored car approached the bus. "Hello," Bolz said over the bullhorn. "Is everything all right?"

From an opened bus window, there were shouts that the four men in the car could not make out.

"Could you repeat that?" Bolz asked.

The police listened more intently now and understood. Robinson wanted a ladder to be brought up to the plane door so he and the hostages might embark.

"All right," Bolz said, "let me see what I can do. In the meantime can we get you something to eat or to drink?"

There were more shouts about the ladder. The police had purposely provided just the plane, tantalizing the gunman with its presence while leaving themselves plenty of room for negotiation. You never give anything away for free—that was one of the first lessons of bargaining. Here's the plane, we'll see about the ladder. Here's the ladder, we'll see about someone opening the door. The door's open, we'll see about providing a crew. All the time, you talked and dragged things out, hoping to wear the man down if you could not spot an opening to end the siege with more suddenness.

Bolz looked through the bulletproofed window and was shocked to see dozens of police who had come out from around the blast fence for a better view. If he could see them, so, certainly, could the gunman. He turned his bullhorn toward them and yelled, "Hey, you are all silhouetted! Get away from there."

They scurried back behind the fence, and Bolz told Di-Benedetto to move back to where the bosses were, to discuss the ladder.

Robinson was growing warier. Here they were, at the plane, and still there would be more delay. "It's too light here," he told Bruce. "I want you to back up a little, away from the plane."

Bruce struggled to find reverse on the gear shift, but he could not get the bus to move. Actually, he would learn later, he was in reverse but had failed to pull a lever that would disengage the rear axle. "I can't get it to go in reverse," he told Robinson.

"All right," the gunman said, "then turn around in a big circle and come in again, only farther away."

Bruce started to move forward—and there were shouts from the police. Immediately, the armored car moved toward the bus and so did a variety of other vehicles, including the NYPD's full-tracked armored personnel carrier—the "tank" Robinson had noticed so much earlier on Runway 13.

LaPrade ordered all police vehicles to back away. They were moving between the bus and his sharpshooters, who had been given orders to shoot at their discretion. But over the Special Operations frequency, a voice ordered: "Ram the bus!"

The armored personnel carrier moved up to the bus and struck it broadside. The bus tipped up in the air. Fearing that the bus would go over, the tank driver pulled back, and the bus bounced back down hard on the runway, on its wheels.

"Get down!" Robinson shouted to the hostages. "Everybody down!"

It was dark and hot, and the tension was heavy. On the floor of the bus, Bruce DeBoar could imagine himself being shot. He had seen it happen to the others, and all day, when he hadn't been otherwise preoccupied with Robinson's orders, he had asked himself: When it finally happens, when he shoots me, what will it feel like?

But Robinson was not ranting now. "If anyone wants to come with me," he said earnestly, "I mean with a share of the money and everything, I will take them."

Sitting on the floor beneath the driver's chair, Bruce DeBoar recognized the notion as pure fantasy, but when five seconds passed without a word, he decided he had to respond. From the outset, he had tried to play a role he associated with the television cop Baretta, to establish some sort of rapport. "Sure," he said, "I'll go with you. We'll get out of here. We don't need this. Look what they did to us. They rammed the bus!"

But Robinson shook his head. "Forget it," he said. "I've been a fool. They were never going to give me a plane. Never."

There was a moment of suspended animation. "Get us out of here," he told Bruce. "Let's go! Get this bus out of here or I'll shoot you!"

Bruce got back into the driver's seat and drove off. In a matter of moments, everything on wheels was in pursuit—the Port Authority armored car with Bolz in it (still clutching his bullhorn), the tank, the bread truck, and every NYPD, Port Authority, and FBI car in the area.

Bolz had brought two radios into the cab, one tuned to the FBI's frequency, the other to the NYPD Special Operations frequency. Since the car was already equipped with its own radio tuned to the Port Authority frequency, the cab became a cacophony of staticky transmissions—and more important, a mobile communications center. It was the only unit on the runway equipped to hear messages to and from members of every component of the militia that was forming behind the green bus. And in the confused chase that was to follow, this ability to communicate with everyone involved would be essential.

At first, when he had started the bus back on the other runway, Bruce had a strange feeling of satisfaction. After all those hours and all that impotence, something was happening. He was *doing* something. But now, as the bus sped off into the night, it was different. The gun was aimed at him, the police were chasing, and he was rocketing across the airfield, feeling no control whatsoever, knowing that he would crash or Robinson would shoot him or the police would blow them up.

But Bruce was still playing the percentages as best he

could. "Maybe I can get you out there by the water," he told Robinson. "I'll slow down and you jump off and then they'll follow us and you can take off."

Robinson listened, thought for a moment, and said nothing. Then they heard the shots, six altogether.

Chief John Keenan had ordered, "Shoot the tires out!"

Keenan was concerned that the bus would find an exit onto city streets. It was a valid concern, but the solution was too dangerous. At sixty or seventy miles an hour, a blown tire might have sent Robinson and the hostages to their doom. The Emergency Services men understood that, and they were the only cops in the chase with the firepower and training to comply with Keenan's order. Two other cops had pulled alongside and tried, to no avail, with their service revolvers.

It was real Hollywood stuff, except that in Hollywood they handled such scenes with special effects. On the runway at Kennedy, with their squad car doing sixty miles an hour, one cop was shooting left-handed (and he was a right-hander), and the other was shooting blindly over the roof. With all that, the pair managed, miraculously, to bounce five shots off the bus's tires. But the tires—heavy rubber and moving at the same sixty miles an hour—repelled the shells as if they had been designed to be bulletproof. It was probably just as well, because if one of the tires *had* blown, the bus could have flipped over, killing or injuring all aboard.

"Why are they shooting?" Robinson asked. "I want them to stop chasing us."

He called Jose Maldonado over. "I want you to go out there—we'll slow down and you go out there and tell them to stop chasing us or I'm going to kill all the hostages, you understand?"

"I don't have any shoes on," the young man reminded him.

Robinson reached down and pulled his sneakers off and handed them to Maldonado. He motioned to the young man's mother to open the door for him. "Slow down!" he yelled to Bruce. "Slow down and let him off."

The bus was doing about forty miles an hour when the woman opened the door. Her son went sprawling from the bus. He was wearing a blue tee-shirt, dungarees, and sneakers —the exact description police had of the gunman.

"There's the motherfucker!" an FBI agent shouted over the radio. "Run the motherfucker over!" someone else shouted over the police radio frequency.

"No. Hold it! Hold it! Hold it!" Bolz shouted into all three. DiBenedetto swerved to avoid hitting the young man, and another police vehicle stopped to pick him up and radioed that it was a hostage who had fallen or been thrown from the bus.

By then, Bruce DeBoar had turned down another runway and resumed top speed. From the JFK control tower, someone kept turning the purple-and-green runway lights off and on—trying to confuse the gunman but actually confusing the police who were in pursuit. There were too many vehicles in the chase as it was—even a couple of telephone company trucks had somehow wandered into the caravan—and with Bruce going up and down the runways, the police faced as much potential hazard from each other as from the bus itself.

In the dark, with so many different kinds of vehicles going in so many different directions, the chase seemed unreal, like something out of *It's a Mad, Mad World* or the old Mack Sennett comedies. Only in reality this was more like the chase scene from *The French Connection* multiplied tenfold—a life-and-death matter now not only for Luis Robinson and the hostages, but for scores of cops tearing across the darkened field as well.

"Get him into the sand!" someone ordered, and one of the squad cars moved alongside the bus and tried to edge it off the runway onto the soft, beachy Jamaica Bay waterfront terrain. When they succeeded, however, it was to no avail. The bus, going almost seventy miles an hour with plenty of weight for momentum, went right through the sand and turned back onto the runway—leaving a pair of police cars mired in its wake.

When that happened, DiBenedetto wheeled the armored car in an arc and picked up the chase, only to leave himself and Bolz staring at the NYPD tank lumbering straight at their front windshield. DiBenedetto, driving the armored car like a

Maseratti, veered around it and continued in pursuit of the bus, passing police cars on both sides trying to slow down and turn around.

They were heading back toward the taxiing area near the terminals now, where a number of planes had been halted in their tracks, full of passengers, waiting to take off. The bus made a bee-line for a TWA plane, and suddenly Bolz realized that nobody had ordered its crew to disengage the moving staircase or close the door.

"He's heading for the plane," Bolz told DiBenedetto. "If he takes the plane, he's got a planeload of hostages *and* a crew. Cut him off!"

DiBenedetto pulled alongside the bus and aimed for the staircase, trying to beat the bus there. At the last second, Bruce veered off and went around the plane, and DiBenedetto went the other way, narrowly avoiding contact.

He was heading for another plane now, and Bolz yelled, "He's going to crash!" But he didn't. Almost miraculously, the top of the bus cleared the bottom of a jet engine by inches.

Now the bus was heading back away from the terminals, toward the fuel farm, the area where tank trucks load up before filling the planes. Trucks were parked there, and the bus rolled through them on a slalom course, with the armored car in pursuit and the bread truck also close behind. The men driving that vehicle had abandoned their rear steering wheel, with its narrow prismatic view of the windshield, on one of the runways, and they were now in the front seat.

The bus snaked across the fueling area, leading Bolz and DiBenedetto into a near crash with one of the tank trucks before it rolled back onto clear tarmac again.

"He's heading east," DiBenedetto told Bolz. "If he knows where to go, he can clear the field and wind up on city streets."

That was all the police needed—a chase through the streets of New York. "We can't let him do it," Bolz said. "Stay with him! Keep on his tail!"

The bus swerved left and raced down a roadway. Hangars were at its left and a cyclone fence was at its right.

Dead ahead was a guard shack, a gate, and Rockaway Boulevard in Queens County, New York City.

Inside the shack, a Port Authority watchman saw the bus coming and ran. DiBenedetto had pulled alongside the bus at its left.

"Ram him, Patty!" Bolz shouted. "Ram him!"

DiBenedetto made a hard right turn, but the two vehicles were still moving at high speeds. By the time the armored car struck the bus, crunching it into the fence, the bus had moved slightly ahead of it and the car had impacted just behind the bus's front left wheels.

"It was like when one train passes another," Bolz would remember later. "I saw these windows fly by me and I was looking inside, trying to locate the perpetrator. All I saw were old women, crossing themselves and praying. Then I felt us start to tip over."

The bus had hit the fence and caromed off against the armored car, which was at a severe disadvantage in terms of leverage because of where it had struck the bus. The car had begun to roll on its side when Bolz, DiBenedetto, and the two men in the back felt a second jolt. The bread truck had crashed into the armored car on its left, unintentionally but quite successfully propping it up.

They could hear the crunch of metal against metal. There was smoke from the engine and, instantly, Bolz thought of a scene from a movie he had seen the night before, *The Great Waldo Pepper,* and envisioned an explosion. But after propping the car up, the bread truck, too, had halted, and it was forward enough of the car to allow DiBenedetto to force the door just enough for Bolz and himself to squeeze out. Bolz stopped long enough to pull his bullhorn behind him—and the door opening was so small he had to twist it several ways before it would fit. They ran around to the back and opened a floor hatch so McGillicuddy and the sharpshooter could get out of the back.

On the bus, Robinson was still thinking. "Crash through the fence!" he ordered.

"We can't go any farther," Bruce reported. "We're stuck."

All this had happened, like a highway crash, a lot faster than it can be written or read about. And to the rear of the three disabled cars, Captain Danny St. John's Emergency Service team had pulled up and raced into action.

"Pull the wires!" St. John ordered. Several cops, schooled on the duplicate bus Greyhound had sent, opened the hatch in the back of the bus and disabled the engine. Now, the bus was certainly going no further until the police wanted it to go somewhere.

St. John led his containment team around the bread truck and they crouched down against the hood, looking into the front of the bus. "Come on, Frank," he called to Bolz. "Come on out around here and talk to this son of a bitch."

Robinson had retreated to the center of the bus, again surrounding himself with hostages. Bruce remained near the front, still clutching the wheel, at the open driver's side window.

"Are you Bruce?" Bolz asked.

Bruce nodded.

"Where the hell did you ever learn to drive like that?" he asked.

"You'd drive like that, too," Bruce told him, "if you had a gun pointed at your balls."

Bolz laughed. "Well, what the hell were you doing out there in the first place? Here, I'm going out there trying to make everything happen, getting you a ladder and food and working for you. And you take off on me. Here I'm trying to negotiate for you, and you go embarrassing me in front of my boss like that."

"Well, why'd you try to ram us?"

"Well, why'd you start driving around the airplane?" Bolz asked.

"I couldn't find reverse," Bruce said, "and he wanted to get out of the light. So I was trying to circle back."

"Oh," Bolz said. He shook his head. The entire desperate chase had been sparked by a misunderstanding. Now the young woman, Jackie Rostom, was also at the window.

"Listen," Bolz said. "I'd like to talk to the man, to try to get this thing squared away, you know? Where is he?"

"He wants to talk to you," Bruce told Robinson.

The gunman shook his head.

"Tell him I've been trying to help him and he pulls all this shit," Bolz said. "I'd still like to work something out. He knows he's over here now and he's not going to get the airplane. But maybe we can still work something out."

"He wants to know why he should trust you after all you've done to him," Bruce said.

"After all I've done to him?" Bolz said. "Hey, listen, I didn't start that bus. But I still think we can straighten things out. Hey, he didn't hurt anybody from the time we started talking to him. We know that. We appreciate that. I'd like to try to help him. We don't count any of the stuff that happened before. We're only concerned about when we started talking to him."

It was a lie—the line about Robinson not hurting anyone. He had shot Jimmy Lo in cold blood. But Bolz was banking on thought displacement, that psychological phenomenon that makes men believe what they want to believe when the truth is intolerable.

"He says to pull some of those cops back," Bruce said.

There was more talk, with Bruce as the intermediary, and finally Bolz agreed to have most of the police back off if Robinson would talk to him.

"If those people hadn't tried to get him, he wouldn't have had to shoot them," Robinson said. They still could not see him inside the darkened bus.

"I told you," Bolz said. "Don't worry about that. That all happened before. Since Julio's been talking to you and Jack Fitz has been talking to him, you haven't done anything. I'll speak up for you, tell them you cooperated. But now's the time to start cooperating."

Robinson said nothing.

"Hey, man," Bolz said. "Let me tell you. You've really done some shit here today. I want to tell you, the whole world was watching you. This is going to be some book. And then it's going to be one hell of a movie. Boy, I'd like to be in your shoes; I'd like to have a piece of this movie. I want to tell you, you're something. What's your name, anyway?"

"My name is Luis [pronouncing it "Lou-is"] Robinson," he said.

"Luis like in Joe Louis?"

"Right."

"Robinson like in Jackie Robinson?"

"That's right," Robinson said.

"Well, let me tell you, Luis, you're something else," Bolz said. "You've really put us through something. But like I said, since we've been involved you haven't hurt anybody. I'd like to see you cooperate now. I don't know if you've heard of our operation. We're the hostage negotiators. We've been doing this shit for four years now, and we've had almost a hundred jobs and nobody's ever been hurt. Now, I'd like you to throw the gun out and then we can have you come out. You can come out first or you can let the hostages go and then come out, whatever way you want to play it, Luis. You're the boss."

Inside, Robinson looked around at his hostages. "I can't shoot anybody else," he said. "I like everybody on this bus."

He took the gun and broke it down, handing the clip to Jackie, who threw it out the window. He's still some piece of work to the end, Bolz remembered thinking at the time. He's not going to hand a loaded gun to any of them so one of them can shoot him.

A few seconds later, the gun came out the window.

"Okay, Luis," Bolz said. "We appreciate that. You're doing fine. Now, like I said, you can come out first or you can let the others out. We're not going to hurt you, either way."

There was silence. He's still got the knife, Bruce thought. He wondered to himself whether Robinson might get cold feet at the last second and put the knife to someone's throat.

But Robinson told Bolz, "Okay, I'll meet you by the front door." Bolz and the Emergency Service team walked around to the other side of the bus.

Bruce DeBoar never looked back. He was the first one out, his hands in the air. Three women followed him down the steps, all with hands raised. Each in turn was frisked by police —who could still not be 100 percent certain of who the bad guy was, or even if he had acted without some accomplice.

And then a slight, dark man in a blue athletic shirt and dungarees reached the doorway, with one hand over his head and the other pointing a finger at his chest and shouting, "I'm Luis! It's me! I'm Luis!"

"Well, okay," Bolz said, forcing a nervous laugh, trying to keep matters calm. "Come on. Come on."

Then Robinson was down the steps, frisked for his knife, handcuffed, and led away. It was 11:30. Bolz had waited almost nine hours to see Luis Robinson, and he would not see him again. His part was over.

Bolz went back to the Port Authority police station, where Police Commissioner Michael Codd, Port Authority Police Chief Walter Lee, and FBI Special Agent-in-Charge Wallace LaPrade were preparing for a mass press conference, each praising the work of the other two's forces and lauding the cooperative effort that had led to Robinson's surrender. Bolz, St. John, and McGillicuddy sat in another corner of the room, watching, and then answered questions in turn. Upstairs, detectives and prosecutors were interviewing the hostages. Bolz would not see any of them, either.

It had been a long, long day, and Bolz still had to pack his equipment. There would be no debriefing this night. Instead he went home to a Rob Roy and gave Ruthie a detailed explanation of why he had not been there to start the July Fourth barbecue. He went to bed at 4:00 A.M., exactly twenty-four hours after he had gotten up. For a man who was practicing a new police credo—talk before you shoot—it was all in a day's work.

CHAPTER THIRTEEN

Profile of a Terrorist

Luis Rogelio Robinson was brought to the 113th Precinct stationhouse, the city police station closest to Kennedy Airport, to begin the legal processing that would certainly send him, one day, to prison or a mental institution.

Robinson listened to his Miranda warning ("You have the right to remain silent. You have the right to have an attorney present . . .") and said it was all right, he would answer questions. But when their questions were asked and answered, the police and prosecutors in the interrogation room early on July 5th still could not be certain of exactly why Robinson had done what he had.

He had been having problems in the Navy, Robinson said, problems he could not return to face. That was why he had hijacked the bus. Everything else, including the two murders and two woundings, had followed from the single act of taking the bus. The police, anxious to ascribe motive and premeditation to each offense, were pleased to hear Robinson say the he had shot John McGavern and later killed Nettie Blassberg as an example, so that the other hostages and the police would take him seriously. Norman Bozick, he said, had died "trying to be a hero," and Jimmy Lo had been shot "because he made me feel uncomfortable." All but Lo's shooting seemed to them to be rational, if horrid, actions. This one, some of the cops in the 113th thought to themselves that morning, would not be lost to the shrinks.

The gun, Robinson said, had been purchased from a fellow sailor, for protection. The knife had been pilfered from his parents' home in New Jersey. He had dreamt about hijacking the bus the night before, he told police, and had taken it as a sign. He was confused, disoriented. He felt he had been mistreated and misunderstood in the Navy, both by fellow seamen and by officers, and he believed that he was heading for a term in the brig, or worse, for charges filed with civilian authorities that could lead to a five-year prison sentence.

For a long time, Luis Robinson's life had been going downhill.

He had been born in Panama in 1950, the second child of Ernesto and Pearl Oliver, who lived as man and wife at the time but were not married. Shortly after his birth, they separated. In 1955, Luis's father married a woman named Doris Thomas, and two years later, when he was seven, Luis and his ten-year-old sister, Angela, went to live with them. Three years after that, in 1960, they had a son, Terrence (who was to die of leukemia when he was nine). Doris Robinson recalls that the adjustment of her two stepchildren was hampered somewhat by their natural mother, who characterized Doris as the woman who had stolen their father from her (a notion Mrs. Robinson dismisses as absurd since, she says, her husband had left Pearl before they even met).

Ernesto and Doris Thomas came to the United States with Angela, Luis, and Terrence in 1963 and had three more children. They lived in the Bushwick section of Brooklyn; concerned with the rowdiness and permissiveness they discerned all around them, the Robinsons raised Luis and Angela with a firm hand. There were no parties unless Mrs. Robinson knew exactly who the party-thrower was, and approved. Other forms of entertainment were also severely limited.

Luis traveled across the borough to Fort Hamilton High School, a public school that was open to any black pupil who wanted to attend under a program designed to foster integration in predominantly white schools that were under-utilized. Luis did very well, winning honors in English and French, and a scholarship to Bowdoin College in Maine, where, in his own words, "I went wild."

Perhaps it had been the strict upbringing. His father and stepmother had given him stringent Baptist training and insisted that he stay home nights. Suddenly, on his own at a rather posh college, Luis could not handle the void in discipline. And perhaps there were other pressures. The year he went off to Bowdoin, his eldest stepbrother died and his parents moved to New Jersey. He was also one of the few blacks on a campus laden with northeastern preppies, and he was a grand social success. His inexperience, however, was showing up socially as well as academically. It was no small irony that the Panamanian black from Bushwick had to come to Brunswick, Maine, to learn about drugs. He had simply moved too far out of his environment too quickly. He lasted at Bowdoin a total of six months.

The Robinsons were shocked by Luis's failure, but when they tried to reinstitute their own sense of values to help him pick up the pieces, things seemed to get worse. He moved into their home in New Jersey, even got a job for a time and contributed to the household, but soon left. Over the next few years he would turn up sporadically. When he wasn't there, his father and stepmother rarely knew where he was (and they apparently never knew that in August, 1971, Luis fathered a child born to a young woman he had met at Bowdoin).

When he came back to live with them in 1973, he acted strangely, pacing the floor or sitting and staring at the wall for long periods of time.

Again he left, returning periodically. Once, three weeks after one of his returns in 1974, his stepmother was chauffeuring one of the youngsters home from school when Luis overtook the car and jumped inside.

"Now I'm safe," he told her. "The cops were after me, but now I'm safe."

"What did you do that they're after you?" she asked.

"Nothing," he said, "but they're after me anyway."

A few seconds later a squad car *did* drive by, but the police officers inside did not seem to be looking for anyone.

The Robinsons suspected Luis was taking drugs, but had trouble admitting it to each other, let alone confronting him with the accusation. They did urge him to visit the New Jersey State Mental Institution at Princeton, and he voluntarily entered the psychiatric center at Princeton, remaining there for ten days before he was released into an out-patient drug-abuse treatment program.

There, Robinson told the psychiatrists that he believed he was suffering from flashbacks of trips he had taken under the influence of the hallucinogen, LSD. He said that he had been using marijuana since 1969 and had taken LSD about ten times, but that he had taken no drugs in the past six months.

David Addison's phone rang at 2:30 A.M. Addison is one of the top young, black criminal lawyers in New York City. He had spent the previous afternoon enjoying the holiday sun in the backyard of his home in the Park Slope section of Brooklyn, one of the borough's brownstone revival neighborhoods. Addison had been only vaguely aware of the siege at Kennedy Airport.

"A friend of mine has been arrested in Queens," the caller said.

"What's your name?" Addison asked sleepily.

"My name's John Smith. My name's not important. My friend's name is Luis Robinson. He needs a lawyer."

That was truly all Addison knew when he arrived at the Queens County Criminal Court Building the following morning. He did notice the commotion outside the arraignment room. He went to the law clerk and asked, "Who's Robinson?"

The man looked at him as if he were a bit touched. "He's the hijacker," he told Addison.

He saw Robinson in a holding pen a few minutes later, and they spoke for several minutes. Finally, Luis looked up. "Your vibes are good," he said. "You can represent me."

There would be little money in the case for Addison—Robinson's father was well off enough to pay something but not much—and there would be little chance of victory.

The obvious defense was "not guilty by reason of insanity," but New York's criminal laws made that close to an impossible defense in Robinson's case. The prosecution would only have to prove that Robinson knew what he was doing when he killed Norman Bozick and Nettie Blassberg and that he was aware that it was wrong. In some states, a defendant can be acquitted if it is proved that he committed an apparently rational crime under an irrational, irresistible impulse—but New York is not one of them.

Even Addison's mobility for plea bargaining was virtually nil. The New York law says that a killer acting under emotional duress can be convicted of manslaughter rather than murder. But Robinson would be charged not only with murder but with *felony* murder—the killing of someone during the commission of a felony. Since the emotional duress statute did not apply to the underlying felony (kidnapping) even if duress was proved, the murder charge would stick.

After talking with his client, Addison decided that his best chance was to have Robinson declared mentally incompetent to stand trial and committed to a mental institution. Years later, if and when he was adjudged competent, the time he spent in the institution would be counted against whatever sentence he received. He moved to have Robinson examined by psychiatrists to evaluate his competence. But that, too, was a long shot, since the New York law says that a defendant is competent if he understands the charges against him and can assist in the preparation of his defense.

Robinson was sent to the jail ward at Kings County Hospital in Brooklyn, where he was interviewed by Drs. Daniel Schwartz and Richard Weidenbacher, the same team that would be called upon to examine the "Son of Sam," David Berkowitz, following his capture a month later.

The psychiatrists found Robinson to be depressed, yet coherent. He told them that at the time of his brief hospitalization in 1974 he had been fearful that he would be killed and was prone to periods of inner hysteria. He had gone to the hospital, he said, not for his parents' sake, but because he became concerned that he might become a danger to his younger brother and sisters. He had always had problems dealing with his stepmother, Robinson said, because he felt that she viewed him as a threat.

Luis Robinson told the psychiatrists that he remained in the drug program in New Jersey, attending group therapy sessions, until it was closed in 1975. He read extensively about the Black Power movement and attributed some of his adjustment problems to racism. He became a health food advocate and decided to turn to religion—not the Baptist faith of his youth, but something else, possibly Buddhism. But the answers did not come, and Robinson decided that he would have to find them in his past.

He felt that the United States had somehow poisoned him, forcing him to deny his own heritage in an effort to succeed. That, he decided, was what had happened to him at Bowdoin, where his turning to drugs was a form of inner rebellion. He had a good mind and the will to succeed, but he had to seek his roots. In September, 1975, Robinson returned to Panama to see his natural mother. He stayed there for nine months, he told the psychiatrists, but found little solace. She had begun to sound like his stepmother, berating him for his failure at school and wondering why, nearing his twenty-fifth birthday, he was not already a doctor or a lawyer.

He was back in the United States barely a week, in Dallas, when he decided to enlist in the Navy.

The United States Navy, both it and Luis Robinson would probably agree today, was the last thing he needed.

Robinson would tell police the morning of his arrest that his troubles began when the Navy refused to allow him to undergo flight training. But naval officials say they have records indicating that Robinson was informed the day he enlisted that his status as a resident alien would not allow him the security clearance necessary for such training. But as time passed and he grew disgruntled with Navy life, Robinson began to attribute his failure to qualify to racial bias—which, according to any number of authoritative reports on the treatment of blacks in the Navy, was an understandable error.

Aboard the U.S.S. *Detroit* in Bath, Maine, Robinson started to become obsessed with the idea that the other sailors were stealing from him, that one of his shipmates would attack him sexually (evidence of his latent homosexuality, the psychiatrists decided later) and with the notion that he had to do something constructive on behalf of his people. But after his capture, black sailors as well as white would tell authorities that Luis Robinson was a strange bird.

He had requested an interview with a Navy psychiatrist,

but it led nowhere. His application for a discharge was turned down. And he had begun to steal, to make up, he said, for the money being stolen from him. Eventually, Robinson was arrested for forging a money order; and, before his trip home for the July Fourth holiday, he said, Navy authorities had told him he might be dishonorably discharged and turned over to the local prosecutor in Bath.

On September 6, 1978, Luis Robinson changed his plea to guilty. He told Judge Kenneth Browne, "I had a feeling something was going to happen and I had to run away." The deaths of Mrs. Blassberg and Bozick had been accidental, he said, the result first of Susan Bruso's attack and then the bus driver's own efforts to shove him out. Other witnesses gave markedly different accounts, but there was no trial, and thus they were never heard in court. Justice Browne could have sentenced Robinson to a minimum of twenty-five years to life in prison, but on October 6, 1978, he handed out a somewhat more lenient sentence—fifteen years to life. Under the New York State felony statute, Robinson will be eligible for parole in July, 1992.

PART THREE

Lessons of
the Trade

CHAPTER FOURTEEN

The Failures of Attica

Attica and Munich.

These two places—one an obscure village in western New York and the other a major European city—will be remembered not so much for what they are as for what they became—code words for agony, violence, grief, and the politics of terror.

For the New York City Police Department, they will always have another meaning. They provided dramatic evidence of the necessity for the city to call on some sort of ongoing resource if and when such situations present themselves—whether as full-scale takeovers of a jail or an embassy or as isolated incidents centered on a psychopath or a cornered criminal. It was shortly after the Munich Massacre, which had come on the heels of a siege in Brooklyn later to be made famous by the film *Dog Day Afternoon*, when Simon Eisdorfer, then Chief of the New York Police Special Operations Division, first conceived the idea of a Hostage Negotiating Team.

The two sieges were etched into history a year apart. On September 8, 1971, a group of inmates at the Attica State Prison rioted, captured guards and civilian employees as hostages, barricaded themselves, and began to negotiate. A year later, in the pre-dawn hours of September 5, 1972, eight well-disciplined Palestinians sneaked into the Israeli dormitory at the Olympic Village in Munich, overwhelmed several athletes and coaches who resisted, took those who survived as hostages, and began to negotiate.

In retrospect, there were mistakes of omission and commission at both Attica and Munich—errors in judgment that cost lives. It is easy to see that now, just as it is easier for military historians to re-fight a battle than it was for the generals who had to do it during the war.

After years of confronting one case after another, Frank Bolz and the hostage negotiators would come to respect the immense problems encountered at Attica and Munich. They have spoken in great detail with many officials who were in each place—and have been through intensive training sessions with some of the very New York state troopers who were on the front lines at Attica. Both Attica and Munich were failures, but you learn from your mistakes. Bolz often cites the failures of Attica and Munich in his lectures to police agencies on the principles of hostage negotiation—not to stress the failure, but to provide dramatic examples from which all law enforcement agencies can learn.

Those in charge of trying to save lives at Attica and Munich had two large hurdles to overcome. First, they were operating in largely uncharted terrain for police. Second, the political repercussions of both situations were overwhelming.

In normal police work, politics often influence decisions. In politically motivated hostage cases, consideration of public policy and private influence is even more apparent. On one side, the captor may be motivated by real or imagined grievances. On the other side, a police official confronted with someone holding hostages to make a political point can readily appreciate that far more may be at stake than the life of the hostage, the terrorist, or himself.

Police have learned over the years that normally the best way to handle the expressed political beliefs of a terrorist is to treat his statements and wishes literally, even if they seem unusual, and to work them into the negotiations. The best way to handle the more subtle politics of law enforcement itself is to develop as professional a force as possible and to observe established procedures—which can be cited later when the officer in charge is called to account for any mashed toes.

The problems confronting the authorities at Attica and later Munich, however, defied such axiomatic solutions. To begin with, each situation was complicated by not one or two but a large assortment of distinct political angles.

At Attica, at least three elements came together—and each of *those* was multifaceted.

First there were the inmates who held the prison. They were a highly volatile and very disparate collection of separate groups, ostensibly seeking "prison reform" but really in search of many different things.

Second, there was Nelson Rockefeller, ever the middle-of-the-road Republican governor, caught in a crossfire between New York's large minority population on one side and vocal, well-organized groups of peace officers on the other.

And finally there were the twenty-nine quasi-negotiators who formed a citizens observer group. Almost all of them were civic or political leaders who would eventually be called upon to explain their roles to their own constituents—the readers of a middle-class black newspaper, the followers of a radical Hispanic action group, or the voters of a rural state legislative district.

At Munich, of course, politics was literally the name of the game. The Black September terrorists were operating with the military-political fervor of latter-day kamikazes. The German government, which had wanted so much to stage a peaceful Olympic pageant to exemplify the new postwar Germany, was desperately trying to salvage a piece of that dream amidst the horror of Jewish athletes facing death less than thirty kilometers from Dachau.

The Israeli government, as unbending in its way as the attackers, saw any compromise as an invitation to future attacks. And the aloof, anachronistic Olympic Committee, perhaps in its fashion the most unyielding of all, insisted to the end that it was the Games that mattered more than mere mortals.

Given those political cross-currents, law enforcement officers at Attica and Munich would have best served themselves if they had fallen back upon accepted procedures and had allowed the chips to fall. But the crimes were so huge, so utterly unthinkable—1,200 inmates seizing a prison; a band of terrorists stopping the Olympic Games—that there simply had been no contingency plans for such bizarre circumstances. And that, again in retrospect, was the biggest mistake of all.

Prisons are no picnic.

Even those penal institutions renowned for their levels of leniency and grace—such as the federal prison farm at Allenwood, Pennsylvania, that was home-away-from-home for so many of the Watergaters—do not receive such rave reviews from their inmates. And despite all the let's-get-tough talk among law-and-order advocates who claim today's prisons coddle the convict, very few inmates so enjoy prison life that they refuse a release or willfully return.

The most distressing aspect of incarceration to the average law-abider would probably be his loss of liberty. However trapped one might feel in his day-to-day economic and social sphere, the notion of mobility persists as a psychological safety valve. Never mind that we *don't* escape the confines of our existence, the fact that we *can* escape is reassuring. But for prison inmates, the scheme is reversed. Knowing there is nowhere to go but to the next locked gate for a year or ten, the inmate is reduced to an existential life that places an overriding importance on seemingly small day-to-day events that outsiders would consider insignificant. A seemingly incidental squabble between two inmates, or an inmate and a guard, can be magnified into an event of cosmic importance. And the everyday brutalities of life inside—far from becoming acceptable—seem all the more demeaning to the inmates.

This is not to suggest that very many prison inmates sit in their cells and rant about the injustices that have been contrived to place them behind bars. Almost every convict can second-guess the handling of his case, the way a losing football players knows the score could have been reversed if the game had been played differently. The police took short cuts. The defense attorney was not up to the task. The defendant allowed himself to be coerced into a guilty plea. But just as the astute player might tell you how his team *could have* won the game, rather than insisting that they *should have* won, the sophisticated convict usually will not tell you that he is innocent, but instead will insist that he could have beaten the rap—which is, after all, what they pay off on in criminal justice.

So when prison inmates speak of penal reform they are not lambs bleating against the ravages of the slaughterhouse. Many inmates, particularly blacks and Hispanics, do portray themselves as *political* prisoners in the sense that they perceive themselves as victims of societal oppression. They were born and raised in poverty. They received an inferior education. They had few job opportunities, except those that most of us have deemed illegal. And now they are being punished for going in the direction they were shoved by society. Prison is just another step in the chain.

Small wonder that inmates with such an attitude do not make ideal prisoners for those charged by society with administering Attica and the other correctional facilities of the State of New York. Even the term "correctional facility" is part of penology's latter-day groping with the new breed of unrepentant inmate. Prisons are called "correctional facilities" now, and wardens are called "superintendents." Changes that go deeper than the names at the top of the letterhead are somewhat harder to effect, in part because, as in every other institution of government, the built-in bureaucracy in the prison system perceives change as threat.

When Nelson Rockefeller named Russell Oswald as his Commissioner of Correctional Services in 1971, the appointment was viewed with hostility by many professionals in the prison system. Previously, leaders of the state's prisons had always come from within, so that every superintendent could recall starting as a lowly guard (or, in penal newspeak, a "correctional officer") many years and civil service examinations ago.

But during the Rockefeller administration, the prison and parole departments had been combined. Oswald was head of the parole division. To the guards—from those on the cell tiers in places like Dannemora and Attica to staff aides down the hall from his own office in downtown Albany—Oswald was viewed with suspicion, if not contempt. He was an outsider. Such an attitude is understandable, if regrettable. "Sometimes," Frank Bolz says, "I have felt the same kind of suspicion from cops when I start training them in our method of hostage negotiation. I can almost hear them telling each other, 'Here's another fag big-city cop who doesn't have the balls to blow that asshole away.' Happily, the attitude changes when it begins to dawn on them that we are most concerned with the procedure that will get the job down without having anyone, including cops, blown away.''

Nonetheless, despite the resentment, Russ Oswald's elevation from ''outside'' had not provoked much alarm within the New York State Corrections Department because traditionally, Albany directives notwithstanding, each superintendent had been allowed pretty much to run his own shop. Superintendents who lived baronial style in rolling mansions on state property down the road from the prisons they administered felt secure in the belief that they were as much the first and last word of law in their own prisons as a ship's captain is at sea.

Attica's Vince Mancusi was probably no better nor worse than the state's other superintendents were in 1971. His greatest sin was one of misperception. He understood that tensions were high at Attica, but he close to blame ''troublemakers'' among the inmates rather than to take a closer look at root causes. The inherent conflict at Attica was racial. The prison staff came from the town, a rural western New York village halfway between Buffalo and Rochester that had no blacks and Hispanics in its population. ''The Up South'' inmates called the neighborhood.

The inmate population itself was ''whiter'' than that at any other major penal institution in the state, owing to its remoteness. Still two of every three of its residents were black or Hispanic. Many were from New York City, which was 360 miles away but might as well have been on another planet. Of 2,200 Attica inmates in 1971, more than 1,400 were from minority groups. Of 500 employees, 498 were white, one was black, and another Hispanic. But the cultural disparity between the keepers and the kept transcended even the arithmetic. The two groups literally spoke different languages. In ''the Up South,'' city street slang, when it was understood at all, was often jarring enough to intrude on the sensibilities of the rawboned, six-foot-four sentries from up the road.

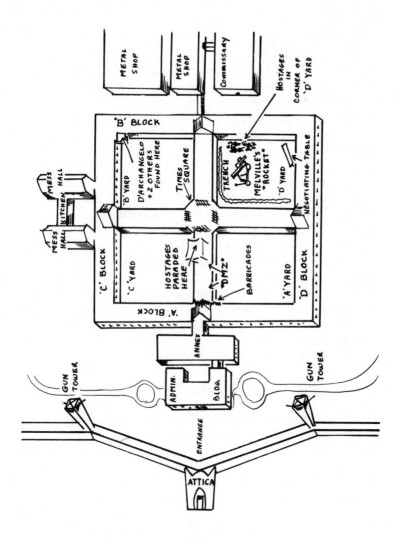

Beyond the culture gap were other conditions that even some guards understood to be intolerable. Sanitary supplies were limited. Each inmate received a bar of soap and a roll of toilet paper once a month and was allowed one group shower a week. Medical services were suspect, with a town physician attending at sick call and often presuming a diagnosis of malingering regardless of the inmate's complaint. Food was laden with starch, and what meat was served was usually pork—understandable when it is known that all of sixty-three cents per day per inmate had been budgeted for three meals, but a particular affront to the growing group of Muslim inmates who were forbidden to eat pork.

If minority inmates believed that racial bias had spurred them on the path to prison, once inside they were confronted with prejudice on a daily basis. There are no good jobs in prison—fifty cents a day was an outstanding wage in 1971—but some are better than others, and almost invariably these jobs went to white inmates. Censorship, designed as a security measure, was often Kafka-esque. The rural white guards routinely stopped any book or magazine geared for black readers. And anything written in Spanish—periodicals, books, or letters to and from Hispanic inmates—was held for weeks until one of the institution's two employees who could read Spanish found time to peruse it.

Discipline was often as arbitrary in its enforcement and degree as censorship. Standards differed from cellblock to cellblock and shift to shift—with an inmate's "jive" talk drawing a laugh from one guard at one time and three days later a "keep lock" from another. "Keep lock," which limited an inmate to his cell with meals brought to him, was a stronger form of punishment than loss of privileges, but milder than a term in segregation—the prison within a prison which was known at Attica as Housing Block Z.

But in a sense, every block was like segregation, in that inmates were routinely locked into their cells for sixteen to eighteen hours a day because of overcrowding. On the morning of September 8, 1971, the census board in Superintendent Vince Mancusi's office read "2,243," well over the 2,000-inmate capacity. Despite the fact that new concepts in court reform had actually diminished the state's prison population, places like Auburn, Attica, and Clinton were jammed—in part because no new prisons had been constructed in decades and in part because the prison system had never developed a very sophisticated classification system and thus doomed virtually every new inmate to a maximum security cell.

Attica was in no position to turn away customers, especially since it had cells enough for the extra inmates. The maximum inmate load had been devised not as a measure of billeting capacity, but rather as a guideline for program needs. Understandably, the paramount concern of prison administrators was security, and with more inmates to guard there were fewer guards available to secure areas for recreational, cultural, vocational, or educational programs. Without such activities, inmates not at work or eating or taking exercise in the yards were in their cells, getting bored for lack of distraction and, worse from the standpoint of the state, thinking.

Not that all the grievances of Attica belonged to the prisoners. The guards, too, had real problems.

Growing up in a prison town, young male Atticans routinely followed their fathers into the prison. They would start downstate at Green Haven Prison seventy miles above New York in Dutchess County. Green Haven served as a de facto on-the-job training facility for guards because there was no population center nearby. When somebody's uncle or cousin retired, one of the young guards would transfer to Attica. He would probably marry a local woman and buy a house, and they might well soon be working three jobs between them to pay the bills. The mayor of Attica was a prison guard, and so were a number of the shopkeepers on Main Street.

The prison had been viewed when it opened in the 1930s as a boon to the local economy, a necessary evil, the way a papermill might be looked upon in other towns. But the town's view changed considerably as Attica's inmate population changed. Atticans had always seen black faces among those relatives who visited, but now there were more of them and their attitude seemed harder and more defiant. The guards would come home with awful tales of the ruthless, foul-mouthed inmates, and the older ones would talk wistfully of the days "when we knew how to handle these guys." Such nostalgia may have been genuine, but it was myopic. The guards were just unable to understand that the outside world and not the inside world was the driving force behind their problems and that a return to corporal punishment and "doing what had to be done" would hardly have caused the new breed of inmate to "shape up."

At any rate, in 1971 a lot of men who worked at Attica were telling their families and neighbors that sooner or later there would be trouble inside. And the guards had begun to emulate a traditional inmate aspiration—the desire to escape. In the forty-year history of Attica, one inmate had escaped, a man named Sullivan, who hid in a laundry truck and was picked up in Greenwich Village some weeks later. The guards had a much better chance. All they needed was time and they could escape from contact with inmates to "safe" jobs at the front gate or in one of the twelve machine-gun towers that rose above Attica's outer wall.

The guards were not paid well—men with fifteen years' service were earning less than $12,000 a year in 1971—but in place of extravagant raises their union had won more and more concessions on job assignment over the years. Seniority ruled, severely limiting the prerogatives of commanders and establishing a system that could have come from Lewis Carroll or Joseph Heller. Just as men were getting experienced enough at their work to handle inmates, they reached an experience level that allowed them to choose "safe" jobs, leaving the inmates to less experienced officers who could look forward to a similar option at just about the time they were mastering the intricacies of dealing directly with the inmates.

And so on. But under the circumstances, individual guards could hardly be blamed for wanting out. "I've been in there for eight hours a day for twenty-four years," one officer would testify later, "so I figure I've done an eight-year stretch."

Inmates were routinely violent to each other, but rarely to a guard. That was a taboo, an offense that brought strong and immediate discipline. It was about as unthinkable for a prisoner to strike a guard as for a ballplayer to belt an umpire. But the guards knew that in 1929 there had been a violent uprising at Auburn Prison, where six buildings were burned and an assistant warden was slain. Again in 1970, Auburn had erupted briefly, with fifty employees held as hostages for eight hours, and several of them badly beaten. That autumn, down in New York City, guards at the famed Tombs Prison had been seized as well in a protest over conditions. The Attica guards knew, too, that "ringleaders" from the Auburn and Tombs takeovers were among the 2,243 inmates at Attica. They were also aware that inmates were organizing into ominous-sounding groups like the Muslims, the Young Lords, the Five Percenters, and the Black Panthers.

One of the great controversies within law enforcement in the aftermath of Attica centered on the issue of whether the riot should have been anticipated. After studying the hostage situations there, at Auburn, and in several New York City penal institutions, Bolz decided that when hostages are seized in prisons, the actual incident is almost always spontaneous, but that "the grapevine" in each case should have alerted authorities that pressure was building and their institution was ripe for an inmate takeover. And indeed at Attica they had much more than the grapevine to go on.

The letter reached Russ Oswald's desk in Albany in July. It called for such reforms as better food, more religious freedom, more extensive educational opportunities, a grievance procedure to iron out disputes, and better training for guards. It could have been written by a Ford Foundation study group on penology or a departmental task force. But it wasn't. It was written by inmates at Attica.

Actually, most of the demands were goals of Oswald's as well; and, while he was somewhat taken aback by the tone of the "manifesto," he sincerely believed there was common ground to be found. He had already embarked on a program of visiting various penal institutions in the state, and he decided to put Attica at the head of his list. On September 2, he and a chief aide, Walter Dunbar, went to Attica. They had hoped to talk with a cross-section of inmates, but soon after they arrived, word reached Oswald from Albany that his wife had taken ill and had been hospitalized.

Oswald and Dunbar met with Mancusi, who pressed an

earlier request that five "troublemakers" be transferred elsewhere. Oswald said no. He had observed the system in his old days at Parole—each superintendent discarding those inmates he did not like, creating a cadre of nomads within the system. If nothing else, the superintendents believed this approach at least kept such uncontrollable inmates from establishing a toehold anywhere, but Oswald suspected that they were more interested in taking the easy way out than serving the best interests of the system.

Before he left Attica, Oswald decided to record a message that could be played on the inmate radio channel that night. The Commissioner thought he was presenting a positive message, but his perspective failed him. He did not understand that, to deeply frustrated inmates, his arrival was viewed as little short of messianic. To offer a bland pep talk was in some ways more costly than to offer nothing. And Oswald offered the inmates little more than platitudes, urging patience. "I took my earphones off," one inmate listening that night later told a state commission, "and all I could hear was earphones hitting the walls and people yelling, 'That's a cop-out.' "

It was six days later, in A Yard on September 8, that the afternoon exercise period was interrupted by an extraordinary incident. A lieutenant broke up a bit of horseplay between two inmates, and one of them slugged him. Other inmates, realizing that the guard had mistaken the horseplay for a fight in the first instance, rushed to the inmate's defense and warned the guard not to spirit the inmate away. As if the situation was not unusual enough, two other elements made it seem positively bizarre. First, white and black inmates were jointly defending the miscreant, and, second, the guards backed off, allowing the inmate to remain in the yard.

That night, the inmate was dragged off to segregation in Housing Block Z, as was a second inmate who had come to his defense. Word of the removal spread up and down A Block, and with it went rumors of beatings and torture. "Wait until tomorrow!" one inmate was heard to shout above the din of clanging pans and epithets. "We gonna tear this joint up!"

And so they did.

It was, a special blue-ribbon investigatory commission concluded, a spontaneous uprising, although to this day almost every employee of the State Department of Correctional Services at the time, from Russ Oswald down, disagrees. But whether the inmates' takeover amounted to a planned ''rebellion'' or a spasmodic eruption of discontent is somewhat beside the point. The important things to consider are the end results: 1,200 inmates and fifty hostages in D Yard, and then, after four tense days, thirty-two inmates and eleven hostages dead or dying, dozens more wounded—numbers that lend dramatic representation to a string of failures by the authorities charged with running Attica Prison and those who took command once the takeover began.

Ostensibly, the insurrection began on the morning of September 9 when an officer escorting a ''company'' of inmates to breakfast ordered one of them to remain on his cellblock under ''keeplock.'' A few moments later, in an act of defiance even more extraordinary than those in the yard the preceding afternoon, another inmate reached over as he walked by the cellblock's electrical control panel and threw the switch to open the keeplocked inmate's cell. He scampered out and rejoined his blockmates on the way to breakfast. When word of this incident reached commanding officers, they ordered the company pulled back from breakfast and detained. A lieutenant rushed to take charge of the situation—and was attacked by several inmates and pummeled to the ground. The insurrection was on.

In the ensuing minutes, Murphy's Law prevailed. Everything that could have gone wrong for the prison administrators did.

Steel gates, presumed to be welded into the prison walls well enough to withstand any conceivable amount of force, buckled under a surge of humanity that, for the moment, was quite literally throwing off its bonds. As the surge spread, several guards were overwhelmed and beaten unconscious, while others were captured, stripped, and hustled away as prisoners of war. And even as the prison's administrators were getting their first inkling of how deep and widespread the trouble was, it was deepening and spreading further—out of the cellblock area toward the machine shop, where the inmates could find the raw materials for an arsenal of weaponry. Attica's communications system, about as outdated and decrepit as the prison's philosophy, was failing miserably; and the rampaging inmates reached a number of sections of the institution before word of their arrival had. Indeed, although the first officer had been battered to the concrete floor of A Tunnel at 8:40, the prison's powerhouse whistle, which doubled as a kind of quaint alarm system, was not sounded until 9:15.

A Tunnel was one of four enclosed walkways intersecting at the center of a square formed by the four major cellblocks. The tunnels, which were actually above the ground, served not only as viaducts between the cellblocks but divided the yard area inside the square into quarters. When inmates took their daily yard exercise, they were restricted to that quadrant used by the men imprisoned in their cellblock. One day a year, on July Fourth, the heavy steel gates at the intersection of the tunnels—the crossroads of Attica, which had been dubbed "Times Square" by the inmates—were opened, and inmates from one cellblock were free to visit with men from the other three. Now, on the morning of September 9, it was July Fourth all over again because the steel gates had been ripped from their moorings in a manner that would make locksmiths shake their heads in disbelief days later when they finally had the opportunity to examine the damage.

One of the reasons the McKay Commission concluded that the riot was spontaneous was because of the action of the inmates in the early hours of the takeover. Some inmates beat guards without reason. Others risked their own lives to protect such guards, even helping some of them to reach freedom. The commissary and the officers' mess were looted. While some inmates did reach the machine shop, other areas that would have provided lethal weaponry, such as the prison kitchens, were either ignored or reached only after they had been secured.

As the insurrection continued, many inmates gravitated inward. They could go only so far toward the prison's outer walls before coming within range of the officers stationed on the guntowers. The inmates, of course, had no guns. Their arsenal consisted of the homemade weapons common in every prison—shop equipment and baseball bats. With Attica's perimeter secure and the inmates moving erratically at the center, an early contingent of state police from the nearby Genesee barracks could have joined armed Attica guards and local sheriff's deputies in restoring order and liberating hostages, but they were never given the chance.

"If the failure to anticipate trouble was the first mistake at Attica," Frank Bolz tells his audiences, "then the failure to move quickly was the worst mistake. When we are dealing with a spontaneous group, we have found that it is mandatory that we project an immediate show of force—and it is the one time that we advocate the *use* of force if necessary. What we are trying to do is to break down the least adequate of the inadequate persons making up the rebellious group. When you isolate and overcome some members of such a group, the others tend to fall like dominos."

The prison and local state police commanders offered two explanations for not moving quickly to regain Attica. First, taken by surprise, the administrators were uncertain about whether or not they faced a carefully planned conspiracy and whether an outright attack might not meet with deadly resistance. Second, as astounding as this may seem considering all the local consternation over rebellious inmates, Attica did not really have a riot-response plan. From the moment the whistle sounded, Superintendent Mancusi and State Police Major John Monahan were operating on instinct.

Advance parties of state police were dispatched by Monahan with instructions to go as far into the institution as they could without encountering resistance. Certainly, the inmates had the numbers, and there was a great deal of legitimate concern about exposing firearms to capture. If a contingent of police was met by a horde of inmates, some inmates would be shot, but the contingent might well be overwhelmed in the process, giving the inmates the one element they still did not have—firepower.

Under these orders, A Block, the western side of the square of cellblocks facing the front gate, and C Block, the northern side, were immediately re-secured. A contingent of twenty troopers then advanced to B Block, overlooking D Yard from the rear. But when Monahan learned that the inmates had begun to mass in D Yard, he ordered the troops to withdraw from B Block, fearing they could be cut off and fall prey to an attack. In the days—and years—ahead, that decision, however well motivated, would haunt many people.

What Monahan probably should have done was to order his troops to remain in B Block while keeping the avenue for retreat open in case of an inmate offensive. The advantage of control of one of the two cellblocks overlooking D Yard would have lent immeasurable strength to the authorities tactically and psychologically. It also would have permitted the rescue of three guards who, unbeknownst to anyone at that point, had locked themselves into an outdoor toilet in the corner of B Yard where Cellblocks C and B intersected. When the police withdrew, leaving inmates in control of B and D Yards, the men had no avenue of escape. They were discovered hours later and became the forty-eighth, forty-ninth, and fiftieth Attica employees to be taken hostage. (Four days later, one of them, guard John D'Archangelo, was killed in the police assault.)

Many prison employees would ultimately blame Russ Oswald for prolonging the siege at Attica by deciding to negotiate with the inmates. But the decision to withdraw from B Block was far more crucial. It gave the 1,200 inmates who had gravitated to D Yard a chance to catch their breaths and organize.

Alerted to the insurrection, Oswald and several members of his staff had flown from Albany to nearby Batavia and arrived at Attica shortly before 2:00 P.M. The inmates controlled a major portion of their housing area and had shown an inclination to be somewhat reasonable, releasing nine badly battered hostages and allowing a medical team inside to treat those less seriously wounded. Mancusi told Oswald that he had already approached the forwardmost inmates stationed at the point where the state's control of the institution ended. He had been told: "We don't want to talk to you. We want Oswald or Rockefeller."

Such an assertion was predictable. Perpetrators of a hostage incident almost always want people other than those who are available to them to do the negotiating. "One of the first orders of business for any agency responding to such a situation is to decide who is to negotiate," Frank Bolz explains. "The taking of the hostages is done to gain an audience, not to harm the immediate victims. If murder was the intent, we would be handling a homicide instead."

Thus, Oswald's decision to handle the negotiations personally was crucial. He had no trained negotiator to do the talking for him and he wound up exposing himself—personally and strategically—when the proper move would have been to designate an intermediary who could pretend to be playing the inmates off against Oswald. "I had to balance emotion and reason," Oswald wrote later. "I had to live with myself and with my conscience in whatever I was about to do. The harsh choice would be to put down the rebellion on the spot, at whatever cost in lives and anguish, or to negotiate with the inmate leaders at the risk of demoralizing my own men . . . Our first responsibility as public officials and as human beings was to save as many lives as possible."

It was essential, with 1,200 men in D Yard, that there be a coterie of leadership with whom to negotiate. And, thus, an early irony: the prison administrators, who had worked for years to dissipate inmate leadership in the name of security, now desperately needed leaders to help convince the inmates to give up their hostages. There was a band of Muslims on duty at the demarkation point in A Tunnel, where police control of Attica gave way to inmate control. The first thing Oswald asked them as he strode through the tunnel was for a committee of "leaders" to meet him and other officials on neutral ground. That demand smacked of arrogance: right off, the system was telling the inmates how to run things on their own turf.

"We can't have a committee," an inmate responded. "There are no leaders. Everyone is the same. All the people have to decide this. You will have to come in on this ground and talk to the people."

In retrospect, Bolz believes that Oswald should have insisted on the creation of neutral turf. "That is a prerequisite for entrance into negotiations in a prison situation," he says.

"The physical and emotional dangers of walking into enemy-held territory at such a time are obvious. They want to negotiate as much as you do, if not more, and you have to negotiate from strength. Working out the ground rules for negotiations can be more important than the talks themselves, and giving ground so early on such an important question is foolhardy. You say to them, 'You don't want to come out to talk. We understand that. Well, we don't want to go in, and you should understand that, too. Let's find some place where we can both be comfortable.' "

If there was no leadership willing to leave the premises to discuss a settlement, a group of leaders—or at least spokesmen—had in fact begun to emerge in D Yard. Most of them were black and were either feared or respected or both by the others. And most were also intelligent and literate.

They included a New Yorker from the Virgin Islands named Herbert X. Blyden, who was still awaiting action for his role in the Tombs rebellion the year before; a well-spoken Muslim leader named Richard X. Clarke; a black "jailhouse lawyer" named Roger Champen, who had spent fully two thirds of his thirty-eight years in one institution or another; a tall, studious twenty-one-year-old black man named Elliot Barkley, a parole violator from Rochester nicknamed L.D., who had gained a remarkable degree of respect from the other convicts, considering his age and the fact that he had actually done nothing more heinous than forge his father's money order and drive his mother's car without permission.

Two whites who were at the inner circle of inmates leadership had already gained a measure of fame before September 9, 1971. One of them, Jerome (Jerry the Jew) Rosenberg, was considered by inmates and authorities alike the outstanding inmate legal authority, a lifer originally sentenced to the electric chair for killing two policemen in a bungled robbery in Brooklyn (a case on which a young detective named Frank Bolz had worked). He had studied law inside and now regularly left under guard to argue writs, motions, and appeals on behalf of other inmates who had won the right to his representation in a landmark federal court case. The other white leader was Sam Melville. Attica guards called him "The Mad Bomber." He had been the technical wizard of the Weather Underground's radical reign of terror in New York City in the 1960s.

As a practical matter, the state had begun to negotiate the moment Oswald and the Muslims exchanged their first conversation in A Tunnel. But Oswald was hesitant about going deeper into inmate territory for fear of being taken hostage himself. He decided instead to invite two men with strong inmate contacts—Arthur Eve, a black State Assemblyman from Buffalo, and Herman Schwartz, an inmate-rights attorney on the faculty of the State University Law School at Buffalo—to enter D Yard and open discussions. Acting on instinct after hearing radio reports of the takeover, each had driven to the prison and offered his services. Oswald felt fortunate to have them available. His employment of third parties would escalate through the next two days and so would the confusion. Were Schwartz and Eve merely conduits of information? Were they mediators? Were they empowered to negotiate for Oswald or the state? Nobody, least of all they, ever was quite sure. "One thing we *are* sure of as we look back," Bolz says. "Whenever you allow others who are third parties not under your command to negotiate, you are starting to lose control."

From Oswald's standpoint, the major advantages to sending in Eve and Schwartz were that they were not likely to be detained as hostages and they had enough rapport with the inmates to gauge the situation. In actuality, although many inmates were very friendly with the two initial visitors, for political reasons within the prison yard, the two were treated as rank outsiders. Barkley read them a series of six "immediate demands" over a bullhorn, to the cheers of many inmates, and they were presented with a copy that had been typed with a typewriter brought into the yard from one of the ransacked buildings.

Barkley said the inmates wanted (1) complete amnesty from "physical, mental, and legal reprisals"; (2) transportation "to a non-imperialistic country" for those who wished it; (3) federal intervention; (4) inmate supervision of the reconstruction of the portions of Attica they had just battered and burned''; (5) immediate negotiations on other demands, and (6) the conducting of all such talks in D Yard.

The two emissaries brought the list back to Oswald, along with the personal promise of the inmate leaders that he would be granted safe conduct if he entered the yard. Against the advice of his aides, Oswald decided to chance it, promising that he would stay for just twenty minutes. He went in with Eve and Schwartz, and they stayed for an hour, making no progress but promising to return later with members of the press after the leaders said the participation of such observers would be their only assurance that Oswald would keep whatever promises he made to them.

When he went back outside, Oswald was approached by Monahan. The state police major told him that a thousand troopers had reached Attica and that he was ready to direct an assault aimed at putting down the insurrection. It was 5:00 P.M.—at least four hours late. Oswald now knew firsthand that the inmates were well enough organized to respond in some manner, perhaps by killing the hostages. And as long as there was one hope in a hundred of talking the hostages out unharmed, then talking was preferable to the risks of an attack.

"I know we're hard on Russ Oswald at times," Bolz says, "but on this one, we're in his corner all the way. The immediate show of force must be just that—*immediate*. After twenty minutes to an hour, you must assume that the loose, spontaneous participants have become part of a structured and directed group of inadequate personalities with anxieties running rampant. Having failed to seize the moment for an effective use of force, the state had little choice but to attempt to relieve those anxieties through time and negotiation."

For the sake of manageability, Oswald decided that only five of the ever-growing press contingent would be invited inside—a two-man television crew and three "pool" reporters. The five men who went in were later described by Oswald as "courageous journalists who had volunteered to cover the meeting at the risk of being taken hostage."

Actually, the way the dozen reporters camped outside the front gate saw it, the biggest risk was *not* getting in. Little information had been available to them under the twin spires on Attica's outside wall, and, to make matters worse, the only bar in sight, a tiny roadside tap-house across the highway anomalously named the Tipperary Inn, had been shuttered by its proprietor moments after the arrival of a busload of blacks from a Buffalo community development group.

There was some heated discussion about how the three pool reporters should be chosen. Those from papers in Buffalo and Rochester—some of whom had covered many stories at Attica—claimed proprietary rights of turf. Those from the wire services, which send their copy all over the world, said they were obvious choices. And the man from *The New York Times,* Fred Ferretti, announced to general derision that he had to be included in the name of history.

Finally, Gerald Houlihan, the state prison's press relations director, said he would pick the choices out of a hat. He marked three X's on slips of paper and crumpled them up before tossing them into a bag with nine crumpled blank slips. Ferretti picked first and then walked off to the side to open his slip. "I've got one," he announced a moment later. Bob Buyer of the Buffalo *Evening News* soon chimed in, "Me, too." And when, a moment later, a Buffalo radio newsman picked a third X, Houlihan tossed the bag away and ushered the five men through the first of a series of steel doors into the prison.

Just as it clanged shut, they heard an angry shout from behind them, as a reporter from Rochester investigated the papers still in the discarded bag and found one marked "X."

But it was too late. Ferretti stifled a laugh. A lot of men have gotten into this place for forgery, he thought to himself, but not quite the way I'm doing it. He looked down at the piece of paper he had marked with his own pen and crumpled it into his pocket.

"The idea of bringing the media into a hostage incident has strengths and weaknesses," Bolz says. "We have permitted pool reporters to observe the negotiations in action, but never to become part of the incident, except once, by accident. The introduction of television cameras can sometimes spur antics by the perpetrators of the siege—endangering not only the progress of negotiations but the safety of the hostages as well."

Along with the media representatives, Oswald, Schwartz, and Eve, a second state legislator went inside this time—a conservative Republican from nearby Geneseo named James Emery. He was an insurance broker with no previously demonstrated interest in penology, but his presence could serve as a political counterbalance to Eve's, simultaneously demonstrating a serious intent to negotiate to the inmates while appeasing the guards and troopers who were positioned, weapons at the ready, still waiting for the command to retake the prison.

Most of the talk on this trip was still rhetorical, but some business seemed to be under discussion. Oswald left the yard briefly at 6:45, carrying a new list of fifteen "practical proposals." He returned a half-hour later, accompanied by Dunbar, and agreed to facilitate the signing of a federal court order restraining the authorities from taking physical reprisals. This, too, must have been viewed by many inmates as more symbolic than anything else. They knew from painful personal experiences the year before at Auburn and the Tombs and the Queens House of Detention that enraged guards could be counted upon to brutalize inmates following the retaking of a prison, whether their superiors had "guaranteed" their safety or not. Yet it was agreed that Schwartz would fly in a state plane from Batavia to a town in New Hampshire, where U.S. District Judge John Curtin of Buffalo was attending a judicial conference, and that Curtin would sign such an order.

That was it for negotiations that first night, but outside the purview of the inmates, others who would shape the state's ongoing response to the insurrection were arriving at the prison, among them Rockefeller's Director of State Operations, T. Norman Hurd; his Commissioner of General Service, Almerin T. (Buzz) O'Hara, his secretary, Robert Douglass, and his chief counsel, Michael Whiteman. The billionaire governor was in Washington, attending a White House conference on international spying, but clearly he had assigned the top guns of his government to handle the Attica problem.

These were Rockefeller's most trusted aides, but were they the right men to have at Attica?

Hurd was a seasoned professorial bureaucrat, a former budget director whose only seeming use would have been to evaluate the long-term consequences of possible commitments made to the inmates.

Douglass and Whiteman were well-heeled lawyers of the Wall Street–Park Avenue variety, political-button men in both the best and worst sense of the phrase, honed to evaluate every decision in state government in terms of its short-range and long-range political effect on Rockefeller.

Of the four, O'Hara held the least prestigious job. At sixty, his role in state government was to run the bureaucracy that oversaw state-owned buildings, and his most pressing duty was management of the yet-to-be-completed $2 billion South Mall across from the State Capitol in Albany. But O'Hara was sent to Attica for his military expertise, not his savvy in building management. He had been a decorated World War II officer and had risen, after the war, to command the New York National Guard. He was said to have enhanced his image in the Governor's eyes some years earlier when a ghetto riot in Rochester fizzled shortly after guardsmen rolled into town. Those on the scene, however, had credited the success to a variety of fortuitous circumstances, which did not necessarily include O'Hara's leadership.

And if ever strong leadership of military and quasi-military forces was needed, it was at Attica. To begin with, there were the disparate forces—guards, state troopers, sheriff's deputies, and, in reserve, guardsmen at armories in Buffalo and Rochester. "A mistake," Bolz says flatly. "Only one of the forces should have been deployed on the front line, with the others relegated to very specific reserve functions. These were forces that had never trained together and whose commanders would no doubt fall victim to interagency rivalry. In many of our situations, two or more agencies—often the NYPD and the FBI—respond. But we have gone to great lengths in our training to develop an understanding of each other, so that when we meet at a job, misunderstandings are kept to a minimum."

Aside from the problems each agency was having in adjusting to the others, there was concern that, aside from the grave situation in D Yard, inmate-sympathizers might roll into town, precipitating a riot *outside* the prison.

"Sometimes," Bolz says, "the people *outside* the situation can be as devastating and destructive as those holding the hostages. At the John and Al's Sporting Goods job in Brooklyn in January, 1973, for example, it is well known that Steve Gilroy was killed and two other officers were wounded by the perpetrators. What is not so universally remembered is that, as the three-day siege wore on, nine cops were injured on the outer perimeter—struck by bottles and rocks hurled by crowds who had gathered to watch in a carnival-like atmosphere. A year later, in Hollis, during the longest job the team itself has ever had, thirty-three hours, we were infuriated by neighborhood kids setting off cherry bombs, apparently hoping the explosions would provoke a gunfight.''

And, worst of all, the lawmen outside Attica were not standing by at a siege involving merely hostages, they were watching helplessly as convicts held their brother officers.

''When we started our program,'' Bolz says, ''I think the hardest point we had to make was that a negotiator wipes the slate clean, so to speak, and starts from scratch. Police could not grasp the idea that even if the perpetrator had already committed murder, we had to concern ourselves with the future—with preserving the lives of the remaining hostages and the police who might be killed or wounded attempting an apprehension. At Attica, of course, where all the perpetrators had already been convicted of a crime, this sort of rationale carried little weight with the officers outside. Nobody doubted that they were willing to risk lives in an effort to liberate their comrades. Hell, as far as I'm concerned, they demonstrate that element of courage the day they take their oath of office. The point that should have been made to them was that nobody should *have* to die if negotiations are concluded successfully.''

For Oswald, the crisis went beyond Attica. News of the insurrection had spread to prisons throughout the state, some with as much potential unrest as there was at Attica, and in at least two prisons, Elmira and Napanoch, the guards were threatening to walk off their jobs in sympathy with their perception that Oswald was selling out their Attica brothers by negotiating with their inmate captors.

To the credit of the state's higher authorities, they left

Oswald in charge. But with so many pressures on the sixty-three-year-old bureaucrat, it is easy to understand why some precautions were never taken and other decisions were drifted into. The most important, and potentially damaging move, was the state's decision to expand its list of community observers.

From the start, inmate leaders had demanded to speak to a variety of public figures, and the potential participation of some of them, such as radical attorney William Kunstler and Black Panther Party chairman Bobby Seale, was viewed with consternation by Oswald and Rockefeller's men. But the peril they believed went with the inclusion of such men was overshadowed by the danger of openly rebuking the inmates by shutting them out. Thus another solution—never stated per se, but obviously reached: neutralize the explosive effect of "dangerous" observers by packing the group with numbers. "It was a solution that merely piled one problem on top of another," Bolz says. "Kunstler and Seale could not negotiate for the authorities and they were too volatile to employ as pawns. They should have been excluded as irrelevant to the issues at stake."

By Friday night, an assemblage of nearly three dozen men, some of them minority politicians personally asked to come by Rockefeller, was ready to enter Attica.

Interestingly, three men who had flown up from New York on their own, members of a self-help ex-convict group called the Fortune Society, had urged Oswald to limit the actual D Yard contingent to no more than six observers—Eve, *New York Times* columnist Tom Wicker, New York *Amsterdam News* publisher Clarence Jones, State Senator John Dunne of Garden City, and (if he arrived) Bobby Seale. When Oswald told them he would not take it upon himself to impose such a limitation, the three left in disgust, predicting with some insight that the Attica insurrection would be turned into a circus followed by a bloodbath.

In truth, just about everyone who showed up at Attica and announced his intention to help was admitted. That would be the sole explanation for the admission of one Jaybarr Ali Kenyatta, a tall man with a turban who was apparently mistaken by officials for Charles 37X Kenyatta, a respected Black Muslim leader from Harlem. *This* Kenyatta was, in fact, a former mental patient and ex-convict from Buffalo. While the authorities cringed at the thought of a Seale or a Kunstler, they allowed such a man inside D Yard, where he ultimately made what experts later termed were two of the most vitriolic, damaging speeches uttered by anyone there—inmate, official, or observer.

"Such an astounding error," Bolz says, "is a testimonial for the necessity to reconfirm intelligence. Police are human. Sometimes we hear what we want to hear, and the stakes are too high for avoidable mistakes that can have the effect of pouring water on an oil fire. Somebody shows up and says, 'I'm that guy's brother and I know I can talk him out of there.' Let him in? Maybe. But first find out from the guy's wife if maybe he hates his brother."

While the twenty-nine observers gathered, things were not going well for Oswald. After Schwartz returned, looking haggard from his all-night journey to New Hampshire to obtain the federal court order, the document was ridiculed by the inmates and denounced as a ploy. Rosenberg, the trusted legal mind, perused the order, then took the megaphone to announce: "This injunction is garbage. It doesn't give us criminal amnesty, it's limited to only one day, and it doesn't have a seal." With that, he melodramatically tore it in two.

The tension was mounting, and, more and more, Oswald became its focus. If some of their "practical proposals" were now viewed as negotiable, the inmates demanded, why hadn't they been seen that way before the takeover? And what real guarantees did the inmates have that Oswald would keep his word once order was restored and the reporters went on to other stories? The Commissioner proclaimed his sincerity, but that only seemed to incite more tension. And, finally, an inmate took the megaphone and demanded that Oswald himself be taken hostage. The inmate was shouted down by others cognizant that their safe-conduct guarantee had to be maintained to ensure the continuance of negotiations, but Oswald, fearful for his life, decided that he would not return to the yard.

While such a decision was understandable, it further robbed the talks of any chance of ultimate success.

"In terms of analysis, we have no quarrel with Oswald's refusal to risk his life in the yard," Bolz says, "although, as I have noted before, such a step backward was set up by Oswald's original decision to do the bargaining himself. If the perpetrators say they will not hurt you, our experience indicates that you can count on it. But if just one of them changes his mind, be assured that you may become a pawn in the dispute for power, and a hasty exit is the only reasonable alternative."

In all, thirty-three "observers" entered the yard briefly at 7:00 P.M. Friday and returned shortly before midnight to begin a session that would last until dawn. The committee, led at the outset by Kunstler—who viewed himself as the collective attorney for all 1,200 inmates—could reason with the inmates and synthesize their demands, like a mediator talking to one side and then the other in a dispute. But, with Oswald's departure, direct negotiations were gone from D Yard, and they would never return.

Despite all that, by Saturday afternoon, Oswald was optimistic. A local district attorney had agreed to grant amnesty for "property crimes" and to investigate crimes against individuals on a case-by-case basis rather than to hold the group collectively responsible. Oswald had agreed to enact by decree or to push for enabling legislation that would allow him to enact twenty-eight inmates' demands for reform—a veritable blueprint for penal reform that contained many of the same provisions the inmates had demanded from Oswald in their manifesto two months before.

Then, suddenly, the optimism was gone, rushing from the yard like air from a punctured balloon. Word had reached Attica that Officer William Quinn, battered when the inmates tore down the gates to Times Square Thursday morning, had died of his wounds. Oswald realized immediately that, with the murder of a guard to be accounted for, 2,800 reform provisions might not be enough if criminal amnesty was not among them. Now only Rockefeller could grant amnesty—and lawyers were at odds over whether even he had the power to do that. The state had granted its governor the power to pardon or to commute a sentence, but had it also provided him with the authority to forgive a crime in advance of prosecution? The question may have intrigued legal scholars, but it was moot: no governor of the State of New York was about to forgive rioting inmates for the death of a prison guard, and the inmates themselves were probably the first to realize as much.

"In an age of mass communication," Bolz says, "you cannot always maintain secrecy. But the report of Quinn's death at Attica underscores the importance of trying to keep certain information privileged in the name of the security of all concerned. I don't know if it was possible to prevent the news about Quinn from becoming public knowledge. But once it surfaced, many inmates began to believe they had nothing further to lose and that was a dangerous, destructive mood. To effect successful negotiations, we must keep the perpetrators in a problem-solving situation. They must always be made to believe that there may be a solution to their problems."

What was unknown outside D Yard (and probably to many inside) was that Quinn's death was really the fourth of the insurrection. Three inmates had been slain by then, their bodies secreted. But inmate murders regularly go unsolved, and even those responsible for executing the three prisoners must have understood that Quinn's death was the one that mattered. The fact that almost all those who emerged as inmate leaders were not serving lengthy sentences had been viewed earlier as a positive sign, an indication that reform rather than escape was really their primary motivation. Now, these men were exposed to prosecution for a capital crime, because in 1971 New York reserved the death penalty solely for those who killed a law officer in the line of duty. Now the inmates seemingly had nothing to lose—not even their lives.

When Bobby Seale finally arrived Saturday night, officials were still so shaky about admitting him that they elicited his promise not to incite further trouble. They needn't have worried. Perhaps Seale perceived that if Attica was bad politics for Nelson Rockefeller, who was stuck with it, it was equally bad politics for Seale, who was not. The rhetoric was there, but not the energy. Seale's lukewarm endorsement of the inmates' cause sounded to many in D Yard the way a political candidate's speech sounds to those at the fifth campaign rally of the day. Seale raised his fist skyward and then turned around, walked out the door, and went back to California.

Actually Seale's appearance was such a letdown that an off-with-their-heads tirade would have caused no more psychological damage. Quinn was dead, amnesty was impossible, and no state official was on hand to discuss the fine points of any further compromise. Shortly before midnight, the inmates voted to reject Oswald's acceptance of the twenty-eight demands for prison reform. Amnesty was their byword now, and they were prepared to ride it to oblivion if necessary, like a captain going down with the ship.

For most of Sunday, the drama was outside the walls, as Rockefeller, back in New York City now, mulled his options and determined that (1) under no circumstances would he go to Attica, and (2) a police attack had become inevitable.

From a tactical point of view, the Governor's direct intervention seemed unwise. In any negotiation, whether for the release of hostages, the settlement of a labor dispute, or an accord on corporate policy, there is an immediate advantage to the side that can send intermediaries to do the bargaining.

Employers, for instance, usually start with that advantage when they negotiate with labor unions. Both sides understand that company negotiators cannot make appreciable concessions without leaving the bargaining table to confer with corporate principals, while across the table the union delegates are already empowered to act as principals and can thus give ground more readily. In that sense, if the Attica "observers committee" truly had been empowered to negotiate for the state, or if Oswald had remained to negotiate on Rockefeller's behalf, the state would have enjoyed such a built-in edge, and any move at direct intervention by Rockefeller would have negated it.

The problem with all this tactical logic, of course, was that all meaningful negotiation already had ceased, and, although he cannot be faulted for refusing to talk directly to the inmates, perhaps a visit from Rockefeller might have spurred something constructive.

"Thus, Rockefeller's decision not to go to Attica was

debatable," Bolz says. "His presence at Attica might have provided valuable reinforcement for the guards as well as the inmates—indicating to the state's forces that he was backing them and to the inmates that he would personally react to their demands. Under no circumstances would we have advised him to negotiate. A negotiator becomes too emotionally involved, and, with such grave decisions at hand, the last person you want to expose to that sort of thing is the commander-in-chief."

Rockefeller's second decision—that forceful intervention was now unavoidable—can be faulted on many counts.

True, the situation in D Yard had deteriorated. The tension was so high that the Governor himself insisted that a contingent of nine observers and two reporters sign waivers of state responsibility before he would allow them to go back in Sunday afternoon. But the state's attitude, transmitted to the inmates by those visitors in mood as well as word, was one of intransigence. And there was still room for talk. There always is. Previous shipments of food were running low, for one thing, and how much time and goodwill would a fresh supply have bought?

Yet time—usually an ally of the authorities on such occasions—was now perceived as an enemy by the state. The massed troops were growing wearier and edgier. And inside D Yard, Kunstler, Eve, and the others who had gone back found themselves commiserating with the inmate leaders over what they considered a betrayal by the state—a note sent inside from Oswald earlier Sunday implying that the observers had endorsed his twenty-eight-point program as a basis for surrender.

Wicker, who had summoned great courage to return to the yard that afternoon as the one white man in the delegation, told a reporter later that he had desperately wanted to stand up, seize the loudspeaker, and beseech everyone to consider the realities, that total amnesty or political asylum (which was creeping back into the D Yard rhetoric) were impossible. *That* much courage, Wicker confessed, he could not summon. When the eleven men left D Yard at 5:30 Sunday evening, the lone message they carried back was a reiteration that Oswald's ultimatum was unacceptable.

Herman Badillo called Rockefeller personally and begged for more time. It was a hot Sunday night in New York, Rochester, and Buffalo, he reminded the Governor, and blacks and Hispanics were on the streets, their radios blaring music that would be interrupted with bulletins of a bloody attack on their brethren at Attica. Street violence was a real possibility, Badillo warned, and Rockefeller accepted his assessment and ordered the attack postponed until Monday.

In any hostage case, there is always the option of moving in. And while it is often a final alternative, the captors do not have to know that. There is no honor owed to anyone holding an innocent party against his will. Lull the perpetrator into a sense of security and, if there is a reasonable opportunity to liberate the hostage without injury, then go!

When elements of 1,200 convicts are holding thirty-nine hostages in the rear corner of a prison yard, the matter is lots more complex than it is when a spurned suitor has a knife to the throat of his erstwhile inamorata. But certain aspects remain constant. Timing is all-important. The element of surprise can counterbalance a lot of negatives.

One advantage held by the authorities during the four tortuous days of the siege was their knowledge of the prison layout, the location of the hostages, and the deployment of the hostile inmates and their homemade weaponry. Using that information properly, this much could have been done:

1. The assault could have come in the pre-dawn hours, when we are all at our psychological and physiological ebb. This approach has been used with success three times since, by the Dutch against South Molluccan terrorists.

2. It could have been effected with as much speed and finesse as possible.

3. The best-trained corps of troops could have been carefully briefed on its mission.

4. Finally, a minimum of force could have been employed.

What transpired in the early hours of Monday, September 13, was just about the opposite. And while no one can say what the toll might have been if the prison had been retaken properly, we do know the cost of the state's bungling of the assault—the death of twenty-eight inmates and eleven hostages and the wounding of dozens of others.

The sole drawback to a pre-dawn attack was the darkness. That left two obvious choices—waiting for the earliest streaks of daylight or employing some form of artificial light. But neither of those alternatives was seriously considered because the politics of the situation demanded (to Rockefeller's men at least) that Attica not be retaken in the dead of night.

Although Rockefeller believed that the political and judicial aspects of the amnesty demand had brought meaningful negotiation to an end, he also perceived political risk accompanying an attack that could result in the death of inmates, hostages, or members of the assault force. Before an assault, the public had to be convinced that every effort had been exhausted to find a peaceful resolution. And in Rockefeller's eyes that eliminated the viability of a surprise attack.

Skilled as they were in the illusory world of government and politics, Rockefeller and his aides approached the mission the way they encountered most hard decisions in the day-to-day running of the state. The fact that all avenues had not been pursued and that the state was attacking even though no hostage was in immediate danger was not important. The *appearance* of good intention was what counted, and part-and-parcel to the attack's planning was one last appeal to the inmates—a final, final ultimatum, to be delivered by Oswald to inmate leader Richard Clark at 7:00 A.M. Monday—in effect telling the inmates that if they did not surrender forthwith, the troops were coming in.

Actually, the note was not delivered until almost 8:00.

"For four days I have been using every resource available to me to settle peacefully that tragic situation here at Attica," it began. "We have met with you; we have granted your requests for food, clothing, bedding and water; for medical aid; for a federal court order against administrative reprisals. We have worked with the special citizens committee which you requested. We have acceded to twenty-eight major demands which you have made and which the citizens committee had recommended. In spite of these efforts, you continue to hold hostages.

I am anxious to achieve a *peaceful* resolution of the situation which now prevails here.

I urgently request you to seriously reconsider my earlier appeal that:

1. All hostages be released immediately unharmed and,

2. You join with me in restoring order to the facility.

I must have your reply to this urgent appeal within the hour."

An hour later, the inmates' response was issued with cruel, dramatic flair: eight hostages were marched, blindfolded, onto the catwalk above A Tunnel, an "executioner" behind each with a knife to his throat, ready to act when and if the attack came. Remember, this was a *response* by the convicts to the impending assault rather than an independent act. But it served to release the authorities from any of their lingering inhibitions.

According to Oswald's account, the plan for retaking the prison carried these provisions:

—Two National Guard helicopters would move in over D Yard, with a trooper exhorting the inmates to drop all weapons while he dropped large quantities of a highly toxic CS gas which was supposed to immobilize the inmates or at least render them "incapable of prolonged resistance."

—An absolute minimum number of troops would be sent into the prison with orders to fire only in protection of their own lives.

—State police, equipped with protective masks, standard-issue .38-caliber sidearms or .270 millimeter rifles would comprise the basic assault teams, backed up by National Guardsmen and sheriffs' deputies.

—Because of their obvious emotional involvement, Attica guards would play no part in the assault but would be massed and ready to reenter the prison after it had been secured.

The basic plan of attack involved moving into D Yard from two directions with eighty-man contingents after the gas dropped and then sending a twenty-seven-man force in after the hostages. Another 190 troopers would remain stationed at the perimeter of the yard as reinforcements with 146 more back at the main gate in case the inmate resistance was heavy or an escape attempt ensued.

Exactly what resistance did the state have reason to expect?

Ultimately, much of the inmate fortification, like most of their rhetoric, was more bravado than anything else. Tunnels leading to D Yard had been barricaded with heavy equipment, a crude, L-shaped trench had been shoveled in D Yard, and, thanks to the manufacturing utensils seized at the outset of the takeover, the convicts' personal homemade weapons were a cut more dangerous than their usual assortment of honed forks and spoons. An ominous-looking "rocket-launcher," fashioned by "Mad Bomber" Sam Melville, was stationed in the middle of D Yard, in front of Melville's own personal bunker. Presumably designed to hurl firebombs, the launcher would turn out to be totally useless, but, in fairness, the police had no way of knowing that. Homemade weapons, in fact, frequently pose greater danger because of the unpredictability involved. While an attack force might not like the idea that it is up against criminals holding guns, for instance, at least it knows the range of the guns. Nobody could be sure exactly what Melville's machine would do.

The troopers themselves were in a far meaner mood than those fellows in wire-rimmed sunglasses who flag you down for doing seventy miles an hour on the parkway. They had been growing more tired and bitter with each passing hour over four days of twelve-hour shifts—resentful of the inmates, of their superiors, of press accounts about the inadequacy of prison life, and of the idea that the hostages had been used as pawns (an opinion, incidentally, not shared by the surviving hostages who—to a man—said later they had prayed for a resumption of negotiations rather than an assault).

Burdened by such understandable emotions—fear and hatred—it was imperative that the attack force be well trained, well disciplined, and well commanded. And the key to all that became the greatest failure: communication. The commanders failed to direct, assure, and contain their troops.

The lack of communication began and ended with the decision to use gas. Many of those on the attack force were unfamiliar with the use of gas masks. They said later that they simply could not hear any commands and there had been no contingency for other forms of signaling. Once amid the confusion inside D Yard, they were left to their own resources, 160 individuals firing when they perceived any danger of hand-to-hand combat that could result in loss of a weapon.

The use of .270-millimeter weapons would come under scrutiny later, when investigators wondered why the state police, ostensibly charged with causing as little human injury as possible, would employ hunting rifles with soft-headed bullets designed to maim as they killed. For all their rhetoric about the brutality of the state, the inmate survivors later said the worst they thought they would encounter were rubber bullets. The authorities said rubber bullets were never considered because they believed the inmates themselves possessed deadly weapons.

According to the police, the first shots came after one of the executioners slashed the throat of a hostage, Officer Frank Kline, who in fact required fifty-two stitches to close the wound. Another hostage, civilian employee Ron Kozlowski, required thirty stitches. But Richard Fargo, another hostage who was held on the catwalk, later said that his inmate guard merely nicked him on the throat and whispered to him that it was "a sham" for appearances' sake. Then the inmate holding him fell over—dead of gunshot wounds.

With the opening of fire, confusion reigned. One of the state police commanders, Joseph Christian, moved toward a hostage held by an inmate—and was hit twice by fire from his own men. Other troopers attacked hostages, mistaking them for inmates. And, from above the yard came more fire—from a contingent of prison guards who had been equipped with weapons and allowed into the prison in contravention of orders directly from Rockefeller that they be held back.

When the gas cleared and the inmates were secured, National Guardsmen were allowed in to remove the dead and wounded. They later reported seeing Attica guards out of control, as others had been at Auburn, the Tombs, and the Queens House of Detention, attacking the recaptured inmates. Outside, officials began telling reporters that at least seven hostages had been slain, their throats slashed by inmate executioners, provoking the gunfire that had resulted in the killing of a number of inmates.

The shocker came two days later, from a coroner in Rochester, who revealed that every man who died in D Yard had been killed by the state's own assault force. Following a series of investigations, Governor Hugh Carey would try to "close the book" on Attica by granting clemency or pardoning all those inmates involved in the insurrection, including one man who had been convicted of bludgeoning Officer Quinn to death. Carey did that as an alternative to ordering criminal prosecution of any number of troopers and guards who may have been guilty of excessive force in their assault.

But the "book" is still open today, held there by a massive lawsuit filed by relatives of the eleven dead hostages as well as a number of others who survived their wounds. Rockefeller and Oswald have steadfastly maintained that the assault was their only choice and that critics of their handling of the insurrection are benefitting from hindsight. Regardless, the state's response at Attica serves as a virtual What-Not-to-Do guide.

"You look at Attica, at the death and the suffering, and you know," Captain Frank Bolz tells police in his training sessions, "that there had to be a better way." There was still room for negotiation. There always is. Some of the inmates may have been *willing* to die for their cause, but none of them *wanted* to die. The state could have preserved their lives, as well as the lives of the hostages, by pursuing new avenues of approach or by launching a sneak attack. By cutting off negotiations and openly attacking, the authorities created the worst possible environment for survival."

CHAPTER FIFTEEN

Twenty Miles from Dachau

Attitudes can change swiftly and decisively in this violent age. The odds are that if, not many years ago, someone stopped you as you approached the boarding gate at an airport and asked you to submit to a search, you would have been quite perturbed. Can't you hear the refrain? "What's going on here —this is America, not some fascist country!"

Today, the chances are that if you manage to stroll through an airport metal detector without your chainful of keys sounding the buzzer, you are likely to become concerned about what other metal objects in other passengers' pockets have also escaped detection.

Similarly, when the 21st Olympiad was staged in Montreal in 1976, few athletes or officials complained about the rigorous security measures that were enforced there. But in 1972, as West German officials prepared to stage the Olympic Games in Munich, they were concerned about keeping overt security arrangements to a *minimum*.

Neither German nor Olympic officials had to be reminded that thirty-two years earlier, Adolf Hitler had orchestrated the 1936 Olympics in Berlin as a paean to the Third Reich. Now their overriding thought was to project a more subtle political point—that less than three decades after the fall of Hitler and the onset of the Cold War, the Germans and the world community had progressed to the point that a joyous international extravaganza could be staged in Munich, barely twenty miles from the death camp at Dachau.

The last thing the Germans and the International Olympic

Committee wanted the world's participants, journalists, and spectators to find when they got to Munich was an armed camp. They had enclosed the Olympic Village—traditionally the most secure portion of the compound, where all athletes and officials are housed—with an innocuous wire-mesh fence (not even topped by barbed wire as many schoolyards are). A special police force patrolled the streets of the Village and nominally guarded its perimeter, but they had been instructed to stress friendliness and to avoid a confrontation that could lead someone to utter the dread epithet: "Gestapo!"

But if the Germans were basing their hopes for a smooth, incident-free two weeks of competition partly on optimism and partly on wishful thinking, then they were not very far from duplicating the spirit of the Olympiad itself. Indeed, the International Olympic Committee, a collection of wealthy sportsmen and government bureaucrats (and sometimes both) had operated the Games for years with one eye focused on the credo of the spirit of amateurism and the other eye tightly shut.

Politics, like professionalism, was simply not part of the Olympiad as these gentlemen saw the Games. More than half those scheduled to compete at Munich had been carefully chosen and trained for international competition by government sports agencies, which had weeded out the lesser performers and given the standouts such rewards as living expenses, university educations, military commissions, and high-salaried career positions that did not necessarily require the athlete to appear at his ostensible place of employment. No matter. As long as these men and women did not cash a paycheck rewarding them specifically for an athletic performance, they would remain amateurs in the eyes of the I.O.C.

This piece of myopia was accompanied by a second pretension—that athletes competed for personal satisfaction and not nationalistic hubris. In fact, by the I.O.C.'s own rules, no one could enter an Olympic competition unless sanctioned by his or her national amateur sports federation, and the news agencies covering the Games dispatched hourly tabulations of each country's total of gold, silver, and bronze medals the way they chart each bloc's total on key votes at the United Nations. But this was officially ignored by the Olympic Committee, as was the occasional glaring partiality shown toward competitors by judges from ideologically allied nations in events such as gymnastics and boxing.

Beyond the professed ignorance of such long-standing evidence of phony amateurism, the Committee's hypocrisy had extended by 1972 into a failure to recognize the broader political implications of the Games, including occasional defections of star athletes from totalitarian states, protest demonstrations, and the refusal of some nations to allow their athletes to compete against representatives of certain other nations.

Indeed, Avery Brundage, the octogenarian president of the I.O.C. who was overseeing his last Olympiad in 1972, had personally overridden efforts by certain American groups to boycott the 1936 Games as a protest against Nazism. And it was an old tradition (eschewed by the United States) that the flag-bearer of each nation dip his flag as he marched past the five-circled Olympic banner during the opening parade.

But, still, international politics continued to pervade the Games, and, at Mexico City in 1968, a new, intranational form of protest was seen for the first time. Two American sprinters, Tommie Smith and John Carlos, donned black gloves, and as they approached the victory stand to receive their gold and bronze medals for the two-hundred-meter run, they raised black-gloved fists skyward as the "Star-Spangled Banner" was played in honor of Smith's victory. Embarrassed United States' officials ordered the two young black runners expelled from the Olympic Village and moved to strip them of their medals. That reaction, however, merely served to underscore the point made by Smith and Carlos in their dramatic protest —that America's black youth was applauded at home as long as it could speed for two hundred meters or dunk a basketball, but any serious effort at societal advancement or expression would be met with hostility.

Such specifics aside, the I.O.C. should have learned at least this much from the Smith–Carlos affair: in an age of satellite communication, the chance to reach a billion or more people in a single act of protest would be very tempting for anyone with a message for the world.

There were any number of potential protests likely to surface at the 1972 Games, especially considering Munich's accessibility. The Croats and Serbs and South Moluccans had to be considered, and, of course, no group posed as obvious a threat as the assortment of pro-Palestinian terrorist groups that had already demonstrated a predilection for violent, eye-catching stunts on behalf of their cause.

In Munich, a pro-Arab terrorist had the perfect location in terms of accessibility. The burgeoning postwar West German economy was dependent on the importation of tens of thousands of men from the Near and Middle East to perform menial labor, which was beneath the Germans but far superior to the work available to these migrants in places like Ankara, Damascus, and Beirut. It was only natural that many of these visitors would gain transitory employment during the Olympics, feeding and servicing the athletes, officials, and tourists attending the Games. With such a potential for "cover," the opportunity for Palestinian infiltration of the Israeli team should have seemed limitless.

But to whom? To the host Germans? They would have had to guard the Israelis round the clock to be certain of securing them and that was clearly counter to the Bonn government's goal of limiting overt police presence. The Israelis? It was expected that each nation would provide some security forces, usually traveling incognito, to accompany its team, and certainly no nation in this world is more aware of the threat of modern-day terrorism than Israel, which has confronted it at home literally every moment for a quarter-century. But the logistics of the Olympic Village and other facilities were under West German jurisdiction, limiting the number of Israeli agents who could be dispatched to Munich, as well as how they might be deployed.

Exactly what steps the Israelis did take in advance of the 20th Olympiad is still buried in secret government documents. But it is clear from the shake-up that followed the Munich Games that the government itself found the performance lacking.

This much seems clear: an Israeli official journeyed to Munich before the Games and did not like the setup as it was outlined for him by the Germans. He told them that the Israelis preferred a high location toward the interior of the Village rather than its assigned dormitory space on the first two floors of a lower building not far from the perimeter of the Village on Connollystrasse. But the official returned to Israel with the matter still unsettled and, according to the Germans, did not maintain contact with them.

According to the Germans, an Israeli consular attaché had been designated by his government to coordinate such matters, and although he was invited to all relevant meetings, the man never came. Eventually several nations were shifted from the area adjoining the Israeli dormitory, but the Israelis themselves stayed put on the lower floors of 31 Connolly-strasse. There, as it happened, they were sitting ducks for the sort of invasion that was accomplished by eight highly trained terrorists just before dawn on the eleventh day of competition, September 5, 1972.

The terrorists called themselves "Black September." At least two of them had worked in the Olympic Village before and during the Games, and one had managed to duplicate a key to the front door of the duplex quarters housing the twenty-one Israelis who were part of the nation's men's team.

Six young men, disguised as athletes with automatic weapons secreted in the kind of satchels runners carry with them, had sneaked into the Village from different points and joined the other two in front of 31 Connollystrasse. They apparently hoped to capture all twenty-one men without firing a single shot and then to begin negotiating with the Israeli government. They had a laundry list of previously imprisoned terrorists, many captured on similar missions, whom they would demand in exchange for the Israeli hostages.

As had been the case with the inmate leaders at Attica Prison, these were men with a cause that transcended rationality. But there were some important distinctions between the eight pro-Palestinian fedayeen who converged outside the Israeli quarters that September morning and the men who had seized control of D Yard at Attica 362 days before. Whereas the Attica insurrection had been largely spontaneous, the attack on the Israelis was painstakingly planned. While inmate

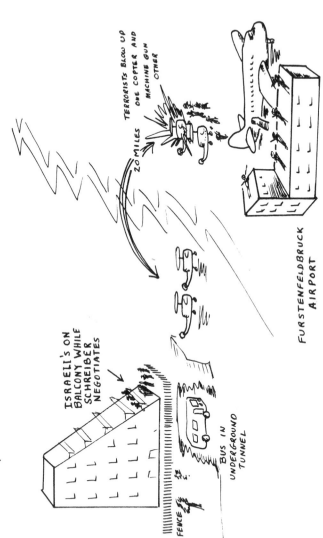

leaders at Attica were hard-pressed to control their motley forces, the Arab terrorists at Munich were highly disciplined. And while the inmates professed to be interested in reforming oppression in America, the fedayeen had a far less vague, far more immediate aspiration—the supplanting of Israel with a Palestinian nation.

In the aftermath of Attica, New York State officials could bathe in speculation over what, if any, steps might have eliminated the root causes of the inmate rebellion. In the aftermath of Munich, on the other hand, that was hardly worth considering. But the other three targets of second-guessing after Attica would be targets after Munich as well.

The first: Why was such a controlled environment so susceptible to attack despite all the forewarnings?

The second: Once the attack came, were all peaceful efforts exhausted before the authorities resorted to force?

The third, and perhaps most important in terms of the preservation of life: When the police moved in, were they adequately prepared?

If the terrorists were hoping for a bloodless takeover, they also prepared themselves for alternatives, armed as they were with Russian-made combat rifles and automatics.

Their first problem came not at the hands of their prey but at the front door of the Israeli quarters where the carefully crafted key failed to turn the bolt. Some men sleep more uneasily than others. The balky lock combined with the whispers of the intruders to awake a 275-pound wrestling judge named Yossef Gutfreund, who got out of bed and moved sleepily in the direction of the front door.

In his excellent account of the Munich massacre, *The Blood of Israel,* French journalist Serge Groussard theorizes that Gutfreund assumed the hand attached to the key at the other side of the door belonged to his friend, Moshe Weinberger, the popular, thirty-three-year-old Israeli wrestling coach; while most of the team attended a performance of *Fiddler on the Roof* the previous evening, Weinberger was off alone, and he was not back when the rest returned. It was a logical assumption. For one thing, locks were just one of many items that often failed to operate correctly in the hastily constructed Olympic Village. And, for another, after ten days of peaceful, heady competition even the wary Israelis had let down their guard.

Just as Gutfreund started to call out to the man he thought was Weinberger, the bolt clicked and the door opened just enough for him to ascertain the awful truth. Using every bit of speed, agility, and strength from his own wrestling days, the huge official threw his shoulder against the door and shouted a warning to his comrades. At least two of the intruders aimed their weapons at him, but the assault team's leader, Mohammed Mahmud Essafadi, ordered them to hold their fire. Gutfreund could have held the door against two, possibly three men, but there were eight of them, and after a valiant struggle of perhaps twenty seconds he gave way and was trampled, beaten with rifle butts, and bound.

Only minutes after the terrorists entered, Weinberger, the man Gutfreund had assumed was at the door, entered 31 Connollystrasse. Like Gutfreund, he sensed the trouble a moment too late. The alcove leading to the Israelis' duplex apartments at Numbers 1–4 was also used by athletes of other nations down the hall, and by the time Weinberger made out that the two strangers lurking near the doorway were Arabs and lunged at them, a third intruder, standing in the darkness a few feet away, shot him in the face. The invaders knew that between Gutfreund's shouts and the shooting of Weinberger, the others had probably been awakened, and they hustled the two men off, searching for the whereabouts of other potential hostages.

Some of the Israelis escaped, literally dodging gunfire. Others hid. And as the terrorists moved from room to room, they were able to capture thirteen men, reduced to twelve when a wrestler named Gad Tsobari made a successful death-defying bolt through the darkness to freedom. Others, summoning years of commando training, tried to counterattack. Weinberger, who had already lost almost enough blood to kill him, turned on two of his captors and was shot a half-dozen times more. A weight lifter, Yossef Romano, had secreted a kitchen knife during his capture, and when all sources of possible escape seemed blocked, he charged one of the Arabs. His knife pierced the bridge of the terrorist's nose, but it was no match for an automatic rifle and he fell to the floor, dead.

It was almost dawn. Those captured or killed were all billeted in Apartments 1 and 3. One of those in Number 2, a walking racer named Shaul Ladani, had been alerted by Gutfreund's shouts and escaped. But four others remained inside, apparently saved from detection by Weinberger. After his initial wounding, as the terrorists pushed him down the hall from Apartment 3, one had asked him if there were Israelis in Number 2. "No," he had answered without hesitation. "Uruguayans."

The four men in Number 2 split into pairs, positioning themselves on both levels of their duplex, trying to gauge their chance of escape. They were puzzled that, a half-hour after the disturbance had started, no police officers were yet stationed outside. Could the outside world remain unaware of the attack despite all the shooting?

They communicated in whispers, waiting for a sign. From their vantage point, they could see the exterior of Number 3 and, shortly after 6:00 A.M., they noticed in the light of sunrise that the curtains of the apartment had been drawn closed. If the apartment was not liberated, had it at least been abandoned? It was a risk, but one worth taking under the circumstances. In fact, all the terrorists and their hostages had moved down the hall to Apartment 1, leaving the four men an avenue of escape. Half-crouched, single-file, they scurried to safety.

Thus, the Arab invaders had suffered two strategic setbacks in the first ninety minutes of their siege. Hoping to capture the entire Israeli team, they had settled for barely half of it. And hoping to announce their feat to the world and begin negotiations without having had to fire a single shot, they had been forced to shoot down two of their prey, presenting instead a bloody testimony to the inherent brutality of their brand of political persuasion. And, unbeknownst to the invaders, two more Israelis, team physicians Mattityahu Kranz and Kurt Weigel, were only a few yards away in Apartment 4, unaware that the terrorists had taken their captives in another direction.

The Munich police were informed of the disturbance at 31 Connollystrasse at 4:47 A.M., alerted by a cleaning woman on her way to work at the nearby East German dormitory tower. Within minutes, they knew the nature of the problem because two of the Israeli escapees had called, one each from rooms inhabited by South Koreans and Italians. By 4:55 a responding officer reported by hand radio that he had spotted an armed man in the building.

Shortly after 5:00, Manfred Schreiber, Police Commissioner of Munich and commander of the Olympic security forces, was awakened with news of the invasion. He ordered all roads leading to the building sealed. A few minutes later, one of the terrorists passed a note to an officer through a ground-floor window, demanding that the State of Israel release 234 prisoners and that the West Germans free Andreas Baader and Ulrike Meinhof, imprisoned founders of the notorious gang of left-wing terrorists then plaguing the country.

After they had a few moments to study the note, German officials decided that the inclusion of those two names was merely a propagandistic afterthought because the names of other, less famed Baader-Meinhof prisoners were nowhere to be found on the otherwise-extensive catalogue of captured terrorists. Thus, from the outset, the Germans understood that essentially they were to be intermediaries in the negotiations, which were really between Israel and this group of pre-dawn invaders who signed themselves "Black September." The Germans had to be aware, as well, that as a matter of policy, Prime Minister Golda Meir and her government had steadfastly refused to bargain with any group of Palestinians, let alone a band of murderous night-riders.

Schreiber, respected then and now as one of the premier law enforcement administrators in all Europe, realized immediately that this was more than a simple police matter. Even as he moved to learn the extent of the Palestinian attack, Schreiber took measures to involve the proper diplomatic authorities. He was informed that only those sleeping in the Israeli quarters seemed in danger, that no parallel attack was underway against any of the 1,500 or so Israeli tourists who had journeyed to Munich to view the Games. Nor was there any indication that Jewish athletes from other nations, such as swimmer Mark Spitz of the United States, who had just won an unprecedented six gold medals, were in any danger. He imparted that information to his boss, Bavarian Interior Minister Bruno Merk, who was himself on the line with Bonn officials, trying to establish contact with Mrs. Meir.

As negotiations commenced, the terrorists' position seemed as firm as their hold on the Israeli quarters. Through a policewoman who spoke Arabic, their leader, Essafadi, issued an ultimatum: unless the government of Israel gave a firm indication that it intended to release the 234 prisoners the terrorists sought by 9:00 A.M., one of the surviving hostages would be executed.

At 8:45, Walter Troger, head of the German Olympic Committee and "mayor" of the Olympic Village, A. D. Touny, Egyptian delegate on the International Olympic Committee, and Schreiber approached the captured building and extended this offer to Essafadi: Troger, Merk, Genscher, and former Munich Mayor Hans Jochen Vogel would trade places with the Israelis inside. Several times in the ensuing hours, such an offer would be reiterated, and each time, as they did at 8:45 A.M., the terrorists would reject it summarily.

Touny, the first of several Arabs who voluntarily entered the negotiations, pleaded for more time. The Israeli government had barely received the list of prisoners whose freedom had been demanded as the price of the hostages' lives, he said, let alone discussed the demand. He asked for a six-hour extension of the 9:00 A.M. deadline. The terrorist leader, Essafadi, slender, impassive, and the only member of the group in view who did not wear heavy makeup or a mask, seemed to grow more confident as the conversation continued. He agreed to three hours, no more. By noon, he said, the Israelis would have to agree or watch a countryman sacrificed for their refusal.

Willy Brandt, the West German Prime Minister, personally apprised his Israeli counterpart, Golda Meir, of the deadline extension. Brandt suggested that Mrs. Meir and her government consider "a gesture" that would calm the terrorists and buy more time.

But she was stern. Brandt well knew, she said, that refusal to acquiesce to "terrorist blackmail" was an official, oft-stated policy of Israel. Brandt and Meir, both socialists, had in the preceding years helped their nations bridge the gap from the Nazi era and establish cordial diplomatic relations. But their transcontinental telephone conversation was strained. Brandt said that at noon he planned to personally announce that the West Germans would free Baader and Meinhof—a concession roughly equivalent in Germany at that moment to the United States releasing James Earl Ray and Sirhan Sirhan —and he again urged Mrs. Meir to prepare at least some offer. She told him that Israel's decision would be reached by her entire cabinet, but made it clear to him that her position in the cabinet meeting would remain firm. She wanted to offer the terrorists nothing.

At 9:10, the Arabs handed a handwritten note to the policewoman. It listed five demands and assertions—demanding that the Germans allow them to move the hostages to another location of their choosing within the Olympic Village; that three planes be readied for staggered takeoffs (each to leave an hour after its predecessor landed at an unnamed destination), asserting that any double-cross would lead to immediate "liquidation" of the hostages; that noon was an absolute deadline, and that other terrorists in other places (presumably outside Germany) were prepared to take action if the 234 prisoners were not released.

The policewoman returned at 9:15, ostensibly to inform the terrorists that the text of their note was being wired to Jerusalem. But she had an ulterior motive. The two Israeli team physicians, Kranz and Weigel, remained huddled in Apartment 4. And as she walked away from the terrorists, without a break in her stride, the policewoman signaled by hand for the men to run to safety.

Soon after, they moved, half-running, half-stumbling, to freedom in a few seconds that must have seemed like years to those observers close enough to see that one of the terrorists had spotted the escapees and had raised his rifle as if to fire. The two doctors did not look at all athletic as they stumbled up the street, and the onlookers could only surmise that the rifleman was never certain that they were Israelis. Unwilling, apparently, to risk the political price of shooting down a pair of uninvolved bystanders, he decided to hold his fire even after the two failed to heed his shouted command to halt. Throughout the siege, Essafadi and the others would converse freely with the Arab-speaking policewoman, never knowing that she had helped liberate two of their quarry.

A few minutes after the two men escaped, three of the terrorists walked out of the front door they had first entered five hours before and shouted to the German commanders to withdraw police officers they said were "spying from behind pillars." Again there was the threat of an execution in the event of noncompliance, and this time there was no mention of a noon deadline. Schreiber ordered six officers to retreat from forward positions. A second command from the terrorists elicited no further response, and, as if to demonstrate their seriousness, the three Arabs ducked back into the building and returned moments later parading four hostages, arms tied behind them and legs loosely bound at the ankles. They lined the Israelis up, faces against the building's wall, but made no further demands, and after a few minutes marched their captives back into the building.

German authorities and Olympic officials had some immediate decisions to make as they awaited the official Israeli government response. Among them was what to do about the Games themselves. The almost-universal immediate inclination was to cancel the day's events out of respect for the one hostage known to be dead, Weinberg, and the second believed to be dead, Romano. Even Avery Brundage, the old Olympic warhorse who often decided such issues first and then asked his fellow committeemen later, let it be known that he favored an immediate cessation pending resolution of the horrible siege on Connollystrasse.

But one man who urged, indeed insisted, that the Games proceed on schedule was Manfred Schreiber. By midmorning the Munich police chief had been given clear authority over the combined police and military forces, and he spoke with the air of a battlefield commander. The crush of reporters and curiosity-seekers would be a problem at any hostage scene, Schreiber maintained, but here in the Olympic Village it had the potential to be an utter disaster. Thousands of reporters from the world over now knew they were only a few hundred yards from the story of their lives, and tens of thousands of athletes and spectators were becoming aware, as news spread, that there was far more drama to be observed on Connolly-strasse than in any of the arenas of athletic combat. Already the siege dominated television coverage in Germany and was being beamed by satellite all over the world. And the last thing Schreiber felt the authorities needed was the postponement of the Games, virtually inviting perhaps 100,000 or more ticket-holders to queue up, craning for a personal view of history from behind whatever point he placed the barricades.

Schreiber's wishes did not go undebated. What would the world think, several officials asked, if news and pictures of this terrible ordeal were interspersed with news and pictures of volleyball games and sailing regattas? But the police chief was insistent. The preservation of human life had to take prec-edence over public relations considerations, and the better the Germans were in handling the immediate situation, the better they would appear in the long run. The Olympiad would con-tinue on this, the twelfth day of the 1972 Games, as if nothing else exceptional was taking place.

The Brandt government, in making the announcement, said the I.O.C. had decreed that the Games go forward (which it technically had, at the government's insistence). Later, after Elishiv Ben Horin, the Israeli Ambassador to West Germany, reported that the Israeli cabinet had voted to ask that the Games be stopped, Brundage had the final word. He issued a statement on behalf of the I.O.C., unilaterally ordered the Games halted, and announced that a memorial service would be held in the Olympic Stadium the next morning to honor the fallen Israelis.

Shortly before noon, with no word from Jerusalem, Schreiber, Touny, and three others—one a bodyguard—ap-proached 31 Connollystrasse and met outside the door with Essafadi to ask for more time. As he had three hours earlier, Touny again did most of the talking, but this time he was accompanied by a second Arab official, Mohammed Khadif, chief administrator of the Arab League office in Germany.

Touny told Essafadi that there had been some communi-cation problems with Israel and that matters had been further complicated by the Israeli government's decision to formulate its response as a cabinet, precipitating extensive debate. Essafadi, standing all the while with a grenade in each hand, motioned for the man who was apparently his second-in-command, a shadowy figure known as Tony, to join him in the discussion.

Khadif addressed the two of them next. The Black September group, he said, could have safe conduct out of Germany and could also negotiate with the Germans for a large ransom, a sum of money he noted might be put to excellent use in furthering the cause of all Palestinians. But in terms of their specific demands, he said, it was his opinion that Israel might be persuaded to part with perhaps ten prisoners, no more.

Essafadi said that he was not concerned with money now; that the Black September group (named in commemoration of the September, 1970, defeat of a militant wing of the Palestinian Liberation Organization by Jordan's King Hussein) had a singular goal—to free more than two hundred imprisoned comrades. He did agree to push the deadline back an hour to 1:00 P.M., but added that he was doubling the stakes: if no sign of compliance was received by 1:00, Essafadi said, not one, but two hostages would be killed.

Schreiber was a close observer of the noon meeting, trying to sense areas ripe for negotiation, points on which the terrorists were prepared to give ground. After it ended, he and Merk went to see Ben Horin, the Israeli Ambassador. Trying to be as diplomatic as he could, Schreiber told him Israel's continued refusal to negotiate would leave him little choice but to try to liberate the hostages by force. And it was his opinion, Schreiber said, that such an armed attack on the terrorists would doom many if not all of their captives.

The Israeli Ambassador was hardly in a position to make his nation's policy, let alone change it. He promised, however, to communicate both the substance and the tone of Schreiber's words to Mrs. Meir and the cabinet. Merk and Schreiber returned to another confrontation with Essafadi, a scant five minutes in advance of the latest deadline, and bought two more hours: 3:00 P.M. was the new deadline.

At that meeting, the German authorities noted, without

belaboring the point, that it had been many hours since the start of the ordeal and suggested they send food into the Israeli quarters. The wary terrorist leader said his men had prepared their own nourishment (indeed, one had worked as a cook in preparation for the attack), but said it was fine for the Germans to send supplies for the hostages' consumption. Actually, Schreiber had never given serious thought to drugging or poisoning the terrorists. But he did have three of his men outfit themselves as cooks in the hope that, once they had access to the building, they might gain valuable intelligence about the positioning of the terrorists or even, if the opportunity arose, attempt to liberate the hostages. He had stationed riflemen at key positions overlooking the captured building from every angle, ready to fire on command (although there was always the question of exactly how such a command might be relayed out of earshot of the terrorists since the government sharpshooters were not equipped with walkie-talkies).

Actually, if the underlying circumstances had not been so tragic, the effect of the efforts of the incognito cops to enter the building as cooks might have carried with it all the humor of a French movie farce—three men in white marching up to Number 31 with packages of food while hardly a soul looking on could have believed for a moment that they were anything but *politzei* in disguise.

How could so seasoned an officer as Schreiber have believed that the Arabs inside would fall for such a ploy? In truth, he said later, he believed no such thing but decided to allow its undertaking after a number of bureaucrats around him urged that it be tried. The terrorists halted the embarrassment of all concerned rather abruptly when they sent one of their number outside to meet the "cooks" and accept their food.

At 2:40, Schreiber and the two interior ministers, Merk and Genscher, were back in front of the building, again pleading with Essafadi and his sidekick, Tony, for more time. Merk said he could report that "nothing definite" had been relayed to German authorities by the Israelis. Mrs. Meir's government, he added, was having some difficulty amassing data on some of the 234 prisoners on the Black September group's list.

Whatever the ultimate Israeli response, Merk said then, trying to temper his statement with a touch of reality, it had become clear to the Germans that Israel would never consent to freeing very many of the prisoners on the list.

Waving his Russian submachine gun at Merk for emphasis, Essafadi embarked on a tirade that so concerned Schreiber that, almost instinctively, he moved his right hand toward his own sidearm. At that moment, Troger was ushering Khadif and still another Arab, Tunisian Ambassador H. E. Mahmoud Mestirim, toward the street meeting. They had remained a short distance away, ready to try to intercede if it appeared the terrorists were about to execute one of the hostages.

And, just as Khadif's sudden appearance had calmed matters earlier, so did Mestirim's entrance now. The Tunisian urged the terrorists to grant another two hours. With not another sound in the tense, midday heat of late summer, the conversation could be heard clearly in the building itself, where another of the group reacted in apparently spontaneous anger to the proposal of still more delay. "No!" he shouted in Arabic. "No more time!" But Essafadi knew better. He invited his comrade, later to be identified as Ibrahim Messaud Behran, down into the street to join in the discussion, and, within seconds, the man was back under his field commander's control.

Genscher chose that moment to play the small trump Brandt had placed at his disposal. The German government had authorized the release of Baader and Meinhof, he said. Essafadi said that it was primarily Arab fedayeen, not German radicals, that interested the Black September group, but the calculated effort at persuasion did score points with their leader. Essafadi granted the two more hours, warning that he expected "concrete proposals" before the end of the newest deadline. Khadif, for one, said later that as he walked away from that three o'clock session he was convinced that the terrorists would settle for a partial accommodation from the Israeli government, despite their rhetoric to the contrary. Whether the Israelis could ever offer even that much was something else entirely.

The next exchange came barely twenty minutes before

5:00 P.M. First the policewoman/interpreter and then Merk, Genscher, Troger, and Schreiber walked out to meet Essafadi. There had been a determination that this time no Arab spokesmen would be included in the entourage.

It was Merk who spoke. The German did not want to wait until "the last minute," he said, to acknowledge that "a final decision" from the Israelis would not be forthcoming in time to meet the latest deadline. Essafadi started to shout, and the German allowed him several moments to let off steam before Genscher started to speak. Germany was not altogether happy with the Israeli procrastination, he said, just as it was hardly thrilled by the fact that the Black September group had initiated this incident. But the country was trying its best to act as a mediator. Was there any other demand the terrorists could make upon the German's themselves, he asked.

Yes, Essafadi replied. The fedayeen wanted to fly to Egypt forthwith. They wanted to go in two airplanes, accompanied by their hostages, who would be liquidated if the 234 prisoners were not awaiting their arrival in Cairo.

Genscher was a seasoned politician, which is as good a credential as most for a hostage negotiator. He refused to be taken aback by the sudden demand and, instead, started to pick it apart. Two planes, the West German Federal Interior Minister said, would provide overwhelming logistical problems. He would be fortunate to outfit one plane under the circumstances. Essafadi almost immediately acknowledged that one plane would suffice after all. And in short order he agreed to another two-hour delay.

But now it was the Germans who had a demand. Merk said his government wanted proof that the hostages were still alive. On Essafadi's command, the Israeli fencing coach, Andrei Spitzer, was produced at a second-floor window, hands tied behind his back. In a conversation severely limited by the terrorists, Spitzer was allowed to acknowledge that all those Israelis who had survived the initial attack on their dormitory were still alive and that they appreciated the efforts of the German negotiators.

A moment later, following an exchange between one of the terrorists and Essafadi, a second Israeli, wrestler Eliezer

Halfin, was brought to the window in much rougher fashion than Spitzer had been, his hands and legs bound. "You're trying to trick us!" Essafadi shouted. "Your soldiers have surrounded the building and they're getting ready to attack us. Take a good look at that Jew! If you do not immediately order your men away, we will shoot him down where he is before your eyes and throw his corpse out to you. And in other five minutes, two more hostages will be shot right on the spot where you are standing!"

In the preceding hours, German sharpshooters had indeed edged into positions closer to the scene of the siege, preparing for a possible assault. Now Schreiber begrudgingly ordered them to pull back, uncertain of whether any of them really had been spotted, but unwilling to call the terrorists' bluff. It had now become clear why no Arab officials were included in this visit. The Germans, sensing that continued nonsubstantive efforts to assuage the terrorists had run their course, were trying a new tack, parrying with Essafadi and his band.

And now, the troops having been pulled back, it was time for another thrust. Genscher said that the conversation with Spitzer was not convincing enough proof to take back to Willy Brandt, who had come to Munich personally to involve himself in the crisis. The Germans wanted to see all the living hostages. Essafadi agreed that Genscher, alone, could go into 31 Connollystrasse to inspect the situation, and, almost immediately, he did.

Given what ultimately transpired, what the minister saw in Apartment 1 would no doubt stay with him for the rest of his life. The hostages were grouped in threes, bound together, with one trio on a bed, another on a second bed, and a third on three chairs lined up for the purpose. On the floor in the middle of the room was the bloodied body of Yossef Romano, where it had lain only a few feet from the nine Israelis who had survived all these hours.

Kehat Schoor, coach of the Israeli Olympic shooting team and, at fifty-three, senior man in the room, did all the talking for the Israelis, thanking Genscher for his efforts, responding that morale was high, and asserting that the hostages would have no personal objection to the Germans allowing them to take off with their captors for Egypt, provided that the Israeli government had given assurances that the freed Palestinian prisoners would be provided at the other end. Again, as at Attica, the hostages' own instinct for survival supplanted any ideological qualms they might have possessed barring co-operation with their captors. Under such circumstances even among men of proven courage the prospect of their senseless demise at the hands of zealots seems to promote the feeling that their own side ought to reevaluate its requirements as well.

The deadline was now 7:00 P.M., and it was Essafadi who summoned the Germans as it approached, to ask if the plane would be ready on time. No, Merk said, complications had arisen over the outfitting of such a plane with a competent, willing crew. No, he told the Black September leader, the German government could never agree to assigning air force pilots to the task, for such an order would be in violation of the treason laws prohibiting any official from willfully placing a component of the German armed forces under the command of an alien power. Merk, seconded by Genscher, asked for two more hours.

Essafadi said that radio stations monitored inside the building had been broadcasting news of the Israeli government's refusal to negotiate. Why didn't the Germans merely concede that Israel had rejected all negotiation?

No, Merk said, such broadcasts were mere speculation. Brandt personally had spoken by phone with Mrs. Meir only minutes before, he said, and had been informed that no decision had been reached. Essafadi extended the deadline until 9:00 P.M. and warned, in a somewhat more subdued manner this time, that the terrorists would abide no further delays.

To a man, the Germans standing in the street at 7:00 P.M. believed him. There had been little doubt among them, all along, that these Arabs were willing to die to prove their point and that in that event they were quite likely to take the Israeli hostages off the face of the earth with them. Whatever form it took, Schreiber knew that he had to plan his move now.

German Chancellor Willy Brandt called Egyptian Prime Minister Aziz Sedki to ask if the Egyptians would commit themselves to intervening on behalf of the Israeli hostages if a plane actually landed in Cairo later that night, and Sedki declined. The Egyptians wanted no part of the problem. That understood, if there was one element that the West Germans and the Israelis now agreed upon completely, it was that the Israeli hostages could not under any circumstances be allowed to take off with their captors. Thus, unless either the fedayeen or the Israeli government suddenly capitulated, a German assault was the only remaining option.

"We did not want to be responsible for one hostage after another being shot in the house in plain view of the thousand policemen who had surrounded the building," Schreiber would explain later to his friend, New York City hostage negotiator Frank Bolz.

Schreiber knew he had roughly four options—(1) to attack the terrorists in the building; (2) to attack them as they moved through an underground walkway to helicopters that would transport them to the airport; (3) to attack on the patch of grass that served as a helipad; or (4) to attack on the ground at the airport the Germans had chosen for the "departure" from Germany—the military base at Furstenfeldbruck, about fifteen miles from Munich.

The first and third options were discarded as too dangerous for the German attack forces and the hostages. The building that contained 31 Connollystrasse was designed like a fortress, and given the nature of the fedayeen weaponry, dozens of police might be picked off during an invasion—in addition to the prospect that the terrorists would have plenty of time to kill off their hostages as well. And the helipad location was just too close to potential bystanders to eliminate the likelihood that many would be struck in an exchange of gunfire.

Schreiber and Merk traced the proposed route from Connollystrasse to Furstenfeldbruck (down to riding to and from the field in a helicopter). They left it for Genscher, Troger, and Vogel to discuss the exact logistics of the presumed departure with the terrorists, informing Essafadi that, for the safety of all concerned, the military airport had been selected rather than the busy commercial airport he had initially demanded. The Munich police chief assigned his top security aide, Georg Wolf, to command a squad of five snipers who would wait in ambush for the terrorists, first at the tunnel. His great hope was to move soon after they left the building because such a point of attack promised to expose both the attacking forces and bystanders to the least danger.

At 9:00 P.M., Schreiber, Merk, and Troger met Essafadi and Tony and initially asked for a delay until the following morning. That was rejected out of hand. Schreiber, trying to be as cool as possible, then suggested the entourage of terrorists and hostages depart for Furstenfeldbruck almost immediately. No, Essafadi said, the fedayeen would move only after he had personally inspected the exact route of departure. At 9:12, after he had conferred with some of the others, Essafadi was escorted by the trio of German officials along a corridor of perhaps a quarter-mile to the two helicopters.

Back on Connollystrasse, the terrorist leader conferred again with the others and then informed the Germans that the long walk to the helicopters was not satisfactory to him. Instead, he demanded that a bus be pulled up to Number 31 to transport the entourage to the helicopters. That order effectively eliminated the planned ambush in the walkway.

Schreiber's options had disintegrated into a single plan of action—an assault at the airfield, where no civilians would be endangered and where the Germans could exercise most control, planting police in strategic positions on the field and even in the dummy airplane waiting there. (It should be noted that although Schreiber had been granted carte blanche to govern the ambush purely from a logistical standpoint, politics continued to color the various perspectives of what constituted the proper logistics. A Polish-born Israeli general dispatched to confer with the Germans, Zvi Zamar, urged an attack on the terrorists as they entered or left the busses—a plan of action that certainly seemed most likely to protect the hostages but simultaneously exposed the police and bystanders to severe danger, a trade-off that Schreiber simply refused to consider. His opinion having been rejected, General Zamar remained in the background, and his government, anxious to detach itself from any connection with the handling of the Munich Olympic

Massacre, would never acknowledge that he had even been consulted.)

The terrorists were so successful at their work (or perhaps the intelligence arm of the Munich police so deficient in theirs) that after seventeen hours of siege the authorities were still uncertain of so basic a fact as how many fedayeen they were aligned against. They knew of at least five. They were soon to learn that the actual number was eight—a piece of information that surely would have been helpful to Schreiber and Wolf as they discussed the specifics of the airport ambush.

The terrorists and their captives journeyed to Furstenfeldbruck in two helicopters—seventeen passengers in all—and Schreiber and the entourage of German officials, who had negotiated all day and night, rode in a third. Now, as they alighted from 31 Connollystrasse, Schreiber and the Germans could count eight fedayeen. There would have to be three additional police sharpshooters at the airport. But there never were. Serge Groussard reports in *The Blood of Israel* that when the officials landed at Furstenfeldbruck, the Munich police chief was shocked to learn that the aide he had placed in charge of the rescue attempt, George Wolf, was still unaware that the authorities back at the Village had counted eight terrorists.

It was hardly the last instance of the role poor communications would play in hampering efforts at the airport. Just minutes later, at 10:30, as the helicopters containing the terrorists and hostages approached, Schreiber and Wolf were confronted with another problem. As a last-gasp alternative, they had deployed eight police officers, dressed as flight attendants and crew, in the Lufthansa Boeing 727. But the cops on the plane grew mutinous as they sized up the situation. If the fedayeen made it as far as the dummy plane, the disguised crew reasoned, they would be captured, outdueled by far superior weaponry, or blown up. Without radio contact with his commanders, the lieutenant who had charge of the contingent could offer little reassurance. And finally, all eight—including the lieutenant—abandoned the plane. Now Schreiber knew that the fedayeen would have to be attacked before they placed any of the hostages on the 727.

Once on the tarmac, the fedayeen split up, with Essafadi, Tony, and two others leaving the helicopters and the remaining four to guard the hostages and the two two-man copter crews. Essafadi and a second man (possibly Tony, although there is dispute on that point) walked up to and into the plane and then alighted, their initial inspection complete. They had approached the plane about forty yards apart, but now they were somewhat closer to each other. Throughout the day as he moved about, Schreiber had noted that each terrorist had been careful to take two hostages with him. "It is a technique used in mountain climbing," he said later. "Three go up, two go back. It takes a long time, but it's very effective. The terrorist is always secured by the presence of one hostage."

Thus, as the two fedayeen walked away from the plane, Schreiber decided that the authorities' best ploy was to order them shot and to hope that the move would shock the others into submission. There were five sharpshooters to aim at two targets. Amazingly, their first round of fire missed.

"That the first shot aimed at the ringleaders did not cause their death can be explained by the psychological strain, by the law, and by past history," Schreiber said later. His major point was that under German law at the time it was illegal for a police officer to shoot to kill, and his five marksmen had been so trained. Now, as they were beseeched to violate that edict, they apparently had been trained too well.

Thus, the sharpshooters' barrage precipitated the last thing the Germans wanted—a gun battle. And their efforts were made still more difficult by the fact that the well-trained terrorists managed to shoot out all the lights near their helicopters within seconds. The terrorists were lighting the sky with automatic weapon fire, but the small army of Germans held their fire, fearful of blowing up the two helicopters and the hostages they contained. The four crewmen, unable to free the hostages because of the heavy fire, tried to escape. Two succeeded unharmed, a third was wounded, and a fourth, Lieutenant Paul Blankenhagel, became the lone German casualty of the Munich Massacre, shot dead on the runway.

The battle raged in fits and starts for more than two hours, and before it ended, all nine hostages were dead—four killed by terrorist gunfire, the others blown away by one of the grenades Essafadi had held at the ready during the entire twenty-hour ordeal.

Amazingly, three of the attackers survived and, even more amazingly, they were free men—and heroes to a major portion of the Arab world—less than two months later. Other terrorists had hijacked a Lufthansa jet and bartered for their freedom. It was the contention of the bitter Israelis that the Germans had been too quick to release them, relieved that their relations with the Arab world would not be further strained by a trial. In any event, such is the nature of the Middle East struggle that an escapade such as the Munich Massacre is not over when the final shot is fired. In January, 1979, Abu Hassan, the man credited with masterminding the Munich affair from his headquarters in Lebanon, was blown to pieces on a Beirut street in an explosion arranged by Israeli agents who had tracked him for more than six years.

What were the specific lessons of Munich?

"The mistakes, per se, were not as obvious as they had been at Attica," Frank Bolz tells his trainees when he reviews the massacre. "At Attica, those in command had the power to effect action. In Munich it was not that simple.

"I've known Manfred Schreiber since 1965 when he visited the United States and I was first vice-president of the then newly formed Steuben Association. I met him at the airport and drove him to his hotel and then gave him a cop's tour of the city. Since that day, we have been good friends, and in 1971, when I went to Munich, he reciprocated, giving me a complete tour of the area—including the Olympic Village, which was under construction at that time.

"We discussed security at the Games. It was something that preoccupied Schreiber, but he was as aware as anybody that there were limitations on him. The size of the Games and their political aspects would dictate what precautions could and could not be taken. And, of course, we had already seen examples in Europe and the Middle East of the sort of highly trained terrorist who was really more of a guerrilla than anything else. What precautions could ever keep up with such an operative hidden among hundreds of thousands of Olympic Games' visitors and employees?

"As the siege progressed, the pressure on Schreiber to take decisive action was mounting. It came from his own government, from the Israelis, and from the International Olympic Committee. It proved, I am afraid, to be more than a municipal police administrator could fend off for very long. Thus, the delaying—which should have been a positive factor from the police perspective—put as much pressure on Schreiber as it did on the fedayeen. Once they had put off the first deadline and then another and another, it had become apparent that their ultimatums were flexible. Only twice in my memory, in fact, have terrorists refused to allow deadlines to pass without resorting to force—on a BOAC plane that was blown up in Tunisia and on a train hijacked by South Moluccans in Belin, Holland. And yet, so many have died as a result of violence instigated by the authorities in hostage incidents.

"When he was left to his own devices, Schreiber seemed to be doing all right. The use of a female negotiator in a male-dominated siege is open to question because of the challenge it poses to the perpetrators. But Schreiber's resourceful woman cop seemed perfectly suited for her role. And the deployment of sharpshooters as well as crowd control personnel can hardly be faulted. With eight sets of well-trained eyes peering from the Israeli compound at all angles, the German police were still able to maintain strong positions. And, despite the fact that the drama was unfolding on a world stage, not a single extraneous outsider was allowed to pierce the perimeter once negotiations commenced.

"The pressure on Schreiber was intense and—although he is too proud and loyal a man to blame others after the fact —some of the moves attributed to him were dictated by others. I believe that if he had been left to his own resources, things might have ended differently. And, God knows, he tried. In a sense he tried too hard. Once it became obvious that what we call a Phase-Two operation—the movement of captors and captives—would be necessary, his methodical approach delayed the trip to the airport until past dark. And that proved to be tragic.

"Finally, there is the question of Israeli intransigence. The late Golda Meir was among the world's strongest and most resourceful leaders. But when she refused to make any meaningful movement, she was taking the ball right out of Manfred Schreiber's hands. Even the hostages—as diametrically opposed to the terrorists as one could imagine and having watched some of their comrades slaughtered—expressed a willingness to board a plane with the fedayeen. Upon analysis we believe that there was some transference involved in that expression, and that tells us that, regardless of the issues, there's a little bit of Stockholm Syndrome at work in every hostage situation if it lasts long enough. Remember, the idea at Munich was not to refight biblical wars, it was to save lives then and there. I do not buy the Israelis' theory that a hard-line approach would save other lives in the future. Judges and juries have plenty of time to weigh the idea of deterrence after the perpetrators are arrested. While they are still endangering lives, it is up to those of us involved to consider the question of a peaceful resolution far above anything else. And, at Munich, Dr. Schreiber and his men and women were not allowed to do that."

CHAPTER SIXTEEN

The Price
They Pay

Bruce DeBoar called his mother, then his girlfriend. Neither had been watching TV or listening to a radio all day. Each thought he was putting her on.

He went back to his girlfriend's apartment for the night, then left for East Hartford in the morning. The next day, a producer for the television show "Good Morning America" called to say that they wanted him for a segment the following morning. The producer said he would take care of the transportation to Bradley Airport and the plane to New York, and Bruce said that was fine.

Bruce had assumed a limousine would pick him up, but the transportation to the airport, midway between Hartford and Springfield, turned out to be a bus. He was fine until a business executive in the row behind him snapped an attaché case closed. Then Bruce almost jumped through the roof. He had nightmares for weeks, and when they had just about ceased, a pair of thugs staged an armed robbery at the restaurant he was managing and the nightmares started again.

While Luis Robinson was examined by more psychiatrists than most people meet in a lifetime, no agency of government thought to provide one for Bruce DeBoar or any of the other hostages. In Holland, officials have begun a program in victimology, providing free psychological and other supportive services for men, women, and children innocently drawn into the path of someone else's crime. But while it has become an accepted fact in this country that the criminal justice system ignores the victims of crime, little has been done to change things here.

Frank Bolz has a scrapbook of letters of gratitude from hostages his team has helped to liberate. But he says that even in those letters, he discerns a void, a sense that the system should have a program for those individuals who have been subjected to such trauma and who are then interviewed by a detective or a prosecutor and just sent home.

The father of the study of victimology is Dr. Richard Molders, a Dutch psychiatrist attached to the national health agency who is a veteran of negotiations with South Moluccan terrorists.

In New York, the idea of using psychiatrists as front-line negotiators was briefly considered and dismissed. Psychiatrists are used to one-on-one relationships with patients, who usually come to them voluntarily or are institutionalized and under the control of authorities. They may spend months with a patient, learning what he fears, what he welcomes, what in his background may have led to his instability. Their decisions are reached in an environment unencumbered by deadline pressures or fear of forceful retaliation that can threaten their own well-being.

Police, on the other hand, deal with personal crises on a day-to-day basis—from fender-benders to death notifications, from family arguments to interviews with sex crime victims. They can be trained and backed up by psychiatrists, sometimes at the scene of a situation when reinforcement and guidance are needed. Indeed, the control of the phenomenon of transference—the ability of one individual to relate to another's feelings—is the cornerstone of both psychiatry and constructive hostage negotiation. But it is the cop who can think like a shrink, not the shrink who can think like a cop, who is best equipped for all the possibilities of a siege.

Yet the utilization of Molders on the front lines in Holland led the Dutch to some major realizations that we in the United States would do well to share. Singular among them was the idea conceived by Molders (and advanced in this country by Dr. Frank Ochberg of the National Institute of Mental Health) that often a victim's tribulations don't end with the capture of his criminal tormentor. Rather, they start there. And while that is true with the victims of many crimes—the resident who cannot sleep for months after his home has been burglarized, for instance, or the senior citizen who refuses to go out of doors after being mugged—it is most true of the victim of a lengthy, highly personalized ordeal such as a sex attack or a hostage situation.

Immediately after they are liberated, some hostages laugh, others cry, and many do both. Later, there is often a pronounced sense of guilt, particularly if one or more of their fellow hostages have been killed. At the time of the murder, our best indications are that most of the surviving hostages feel little compassion for the victim, centering their emotions on their own plight, combining a heightened sense of fear and tension with the barest feeling of gratitude that someone else had been singled out by the terrorist. But that only hones the ultimate notion of guilt: "Could I have done something to save his life?" the hostage wonders. "Why was it him instead of me?"

There is also an almost perverse association with the fate of the captor: the Stockholm Syndrome. It is named for the reaction of the victims of a six-day siege in the vault of a Swedish bank. A lone gunman, trapped during a robbery attempt, herded a man and three women into the vault and then demanded and received the release of a former confederate who had been imprisoned. For almost a week, under the most intolerable conditions imaginable, the two men held off police. Without plumbing facilities, all hostages were required to relieve themselves into wastebaskets. One of the women went through her menstrual cycle without sanitary napkins. Hostages were paraded to the vault door with a loaded gun held under their chins. They were tied to safe deposit boxes with metal wire around their necks, so that if authorities bombarded the vault with tear gas the hostages would faint and collapse against the wire, choking to death. Finally, police drilled through the vault, shot gas into it, and forced everyone out. But at the end, the four hostages encircled their captors because, they said, they wanted to protect them from possible harm from the police. And later one of the women said she was in love with the bank robber and would wait for his release from prison to marry him.

Why?

Because, psychologically, the captor has had life-and-death control over the victim and has allowed the victim to survive, earning a sort of everlasting gratitude, the ultimate in transference. Cruelty, it appears, only served to heighten his emotional value for those susceptible to it. The pattern has been called survival identification. The Dutch, who equate most hostage cases with military actions, call it aggressor identification, and they note that it is hardly a new phenomenon. Europeans observed it extensively amid the horrors of Nazi concentration camps, where some victims earned places of honor with their captors by emulating them and often outdoing the Nazis themselves in their cruel treatment of fellow prisoners.

The Cat Olsen siege at the branch bank in Greenwich Village may well have been extended for several hours because the hostages declined an offer from Olsen to leave the bank. That was one form of transference. Then, after the liberation, one woman bank employee never returned to work—not even to pick up her final paycheck. And a second woman began losing large clumps of hair for no explicable physical reason.

But the New York City criminal justice system could do nothing for these women except to prosecute their captor.

The system, in fact, seems geared to react with contempt to the victim's plight. Bolz can remember a discussion between two high-level police officials during the Olsen siege, at a time when bank manager Larry Haber was on the radio, expressing the hostages' concern for Olsen himself. "You know," one said, "I think the guy's starting to milk this thing." The other agreed. Neither man seemed willing to understand that a police officer, let alone a layman like Larry Haber, could be reacting to the anxiety of facing a mentally unbalanced gunman for all those hours.

In another sense, though, the American criminal justice system is reflecting the wider attitude of the society it serves. Despite all their words to the contrary, Americans still stigmatize men and women who seek psychological help. It is quite likely, for instance, that if free psychiatric treatment were provided to victims of crime, few would accept it. Many would wonder, "What will happen to me ten years from now if I apply for a job and the personnel manager discovered I've been treated for mental problems?"

Thus, as Dr. Ochberg has pointed out, to ensure proper participation, a program geared to help victims overcome their post-crime anguish cannot consist merely of a free pass to the neighborhood shrink. It must be a total package, a team effort. Initially, victims should be debriefed by a law enforcement aide and a psychologist or psychiatrist. The victim can be made to understand that such interviews are the accepted routine. He or she can be given a number to call, twenty-four hours a day, if problems arise. And at the next interview, with the assistant district attorney in charge of prosecuting the case, the victim can again discuss matters with the psychiatrist as well.

Just the revelation that someone in the system is *trying* to understand their adjustment problems will go a long way toward aiding many victims. That is how Molders and the Dutch started—not so much with the idea of helping victims as with the announced goal of perceiving what long-range problems they are likely to confront in the aftermath of a terrorist siege. What they learned was enough to convince them of the necessity for such treatment. Now, it is virtually mandatory for such victims.

Two weeks after Luis Robinson's day in the limelight on the runway at Kennedy Airport, an unemployed accountant named Charles Hayes got into an argument with the managing agent of his cooperative building over Hayes's impending eviction for nonpayment of carrying charges. Hayes took a rifle from the trunk of his car and held the man hostage in his office for ninety minutes.

Negotiators learned Hayes had suffered business reversals (when a newly patented toothbrush holder had failed to find a market). They sent for two of his partners and commenced negotiations by phone. The partners were never needed. At about the same time that one Emergency Service officer observed through his field glasses that Hayes had deposited his rifle on a table and wandered off to the phone, another officer picked the lock on a rear door. When he learned what the man with the binoculars knew, it was short work to burst into the office and capture Hayes.

This one had been a classic wait-for-the-mistake-or-distraction job; and like those before it and those destined to come later, it was just a little bit different than any of the others. But there were almost always common elements as well. One of the most obvious was that, in attempting to use as little force as possible to defuse a lethal situation, the police were exposing themselves to potential risks. There were the very real physical dangers, naturally. And then there were the more deeply rooted psychological risks.

Physically the largest problem can be what Bolz calls ''the Superman complex.''

Put a cop on the job for a number of years, give him some success, and then put a bulletproofed vest on him, and he sometimes begins to think he cannot be hurt. And that can be a deadly misjudgment. When he is backing up other negotiators or coordinating a job, Bolz is forever alert against the exposure of police personnel, continually counseling that unnecessary risks are foolish and ill-conceived.

There was the day in November, 1977, when police were called to an apartment house on Staten Island to see about a man who had fired shots. It was almost noon. A short time later, there was a second call, from a woman, telling them that the man was locked in an apartment, had a gun, and was threatening suicide. That led police to think she, too, might be in the apartment and that they were confronting a hostage case.

They were not, they would later learn. Dewey Thomas, twenty-eight, was in the apartment alone. ''Get away from the door,'' he ordered when two officers from the 120th Precinct knocked. He had phoned his father earlier and said that someone was trying to shoot him. The Emergency Service Division opened the apartment door, using a small, powerful hydraulic wedge, and Bolz was able to begin talking to the barricaded man by field telephone, with negotiator Edward Zigo at the door.

The fact that there was no hostage did not make life much easier for the negotiators. Thomas told them that if they tried to remove him, he would precipitate a shootout. "If I'm going to go," he shouted to Zigo at one point, "I'll go like a man!"

Bolz was sitting in a rocking chair in the next apartment, looking into the hallway, the field phone in one ear and a listening device in the other. As the hours wore on, there was almost a casual air about the job. The police could see Bolz's rather unique perch as they moved on and off post. "Bolz has got himself a rocking chair," one of the cops on the Emergency Service assault team joked. "Now I know we'll be here forever."

As time passed, however, Bolz began to have an uneasy feeling. It wasn't even a hostage situation, but it was just the kind of dumb job that could lead to tragedy. Zigo was an aggressive, thorough investigator. He had gained wide acclaim the previous summer after he tracked down "the Son of Sam" from a parking ticket. He was one of the most dependable detectives on the negotiating team, but in the hostage business a man's aggressiveness could work against him unless it was carefully controlled.

Finally, shortly after 9:00 P.M., Thomas said he was ready to come out. He would slide the gun to Zigo and then meet him, unarmed, in the doorway. All along, Zigo had been using the door for cover. Now he moved into the opening to receive the gun. The apartment was in total darkness—and the cop was silhouetted by the background light in the hall.

"Move the hell out of there!" Bolz shouted to Zigo, and Zigo backed off behind the door.

A few minutes later, the gun came sliding out. Again Zigo edged into the line of fire, and again Bolz shouted. Dewey Thomas *said* he had just the one Saturday Night Special which he had just relinquished. Who knew?

Thomas did give himself up at 9:35, and it went into the books a ten-hour barricade case.

Someday, the negotiators understood, it would not end that neatly. Someday they might lose a hostage. Skill and patience notwithstanding, they were probably lucky to have gone this long with a perfect record. And, as Bolz and Schlossberg perceived it, the first slain hostage would present enormous psychological problems to the primary negotiator and the backup crew at the scene.

Nobody died that day, but Sergeant Robert Louden was emotionally overwrought, despite the fact that he had ended the situation successfully.

It had begun shortly after 8:00 A.M., when the eight- and ten-year-old sons of Arthur and Judy Schweiger raced out of their apartment and pulled a fire alarm. The boys told firemen that their father was holding a knife to their mother's throat and threatening to kill her. The firefighters called local police, who summoned the Emergency Service Division and the Hostage Negotiating Team.

Schweiger, a thirty-nine-year-old construction worker, seemed drunk. His wife was naked on their bed and he was straddling her, a seven-inch butcher knife in his right hand. "Don't come any closer," he told the first officers at the scene, "or I'll stick her." And as if to prove he meant it, Schweiger nicked his wife's arm with the blade, drawing blood.

Louden, who lives on Staten Island, was the primary negotiator. With him at the bedroom door were Sergeant Thomas Harley of Emergency Services and the Reverend Daniel Mercaldo, a minister who knew the Schweigers.

Schweiger was just seven feet away from the men in the doorway, but he could have been seven *thousand* feet away for all they could accomplish. They couldn't shoot him—they might hit his wife. They couldn't charge him—he could stab her before they made it halfway. And they knew that he had a criminal history, so there was no question he was capable of almost anything.

As Louden and the minister talked to Schweiger, he would occasionally laugh and nick another piece of his wife's skin with the knife, so that after an hour she was bleeding from cuts all over her body. Finally, at 10:10, the minister convinced Schweiger to surrender the knife, and it was over. He was led away under restraint, and his wife was released from the hospital after treatment for superficial cuts.

Bolz had been home in East Meadow when he was notified. He was en route as word came that the siege had ended. He told Louden to meet him in police headquarters.

It was nearly two hours later when Louden entered the office and began completing some routine paperwork. He gave no hint of any problems at first. "Tell me about the job, Bob," Bolz said, expecting a war story.

Instead, the thirty-six-year-old detective sergeant began to tremble. His hands shook, his eyes filled, and he seemed close to an emotional collapse. This was clearly no ordinary war story.

"Relax, Bob," Bolz said. "I've been through it."

He called John Byron and Kenny Bowen and told them to meet him for lunch at the Claddagh. He took Louden to the restaurant. Again, he asked about the job, and again Louden could barely speak. The three of them spent the next two hours gently getting Louden to explain the feelings he had had, watching little pieces of the woman being sliced away just a few feet in front of him and not being able to stop it.

They told him that he had done very well, and that, after all, it was part of the job. But, most important, they got him to vent his emotions. There were more hostage cases for Bob Louden, and while he would not forget the one in Arthur Schweiger's apartment, he would be strong enough to surmount it.

The Winfred Frocks dress shop at 2138 Broadway on Manhattan's Upper West Side was a cut-rate boutique. In late September, 1978, a thirty-year-old Bronx man named Joe Crespo got the best rate of all. He walked in, pulled a gun, and robbed the place. It must have seemed like an easy mark. Two weeks later, on Saturday, October 6, Crespo returned to do it again. This time, the cashier, a pregnant woman from Queens named Else Darbouze, spotted him and surreptitiously dialed police.

Officer John Duane was the first to arrive and enter, followed shortly by officers Steve Raina and Edward Goggin. A woman employee beckoned to the police. "There's trouble," she whispered, pointing to a side door leading downstairs. With their view of the rear of the store blocked by racks of dresses, Raina and Duane followed the employee and three customers down the side stairs. "There's a holdup," the employee told the police when they reached the basement.

The shop was on the ground floor of a large apartment house. Duane and Raina raced through a passageway and around to an exit on a side street. By then, Goggin had walked into the rear and had seen Crespo just as Crespo had spotted him. Each reached for a gun, but neither fired.

Crespo held Mrs. Darbouze as a shield—and a hostage.

"Drop the gun," Crespo told Goggin.

"You drop yours," Goggin said, positioning himself between the gunman and the eight customers.

Neither man complied. "It was a Mexican standoff," one cop said later. And that was the way it stayed until negotiator Conrad Mazza arrived. There was a telephone near the cash register, and Mazza was able to reach Crespo (although he would spend much of the next six hours competing for time with reporters).

Crespo talked of killing one hostage an hour unless he was provided with an escape vehicle. But he had been locked up three times previously for robbery, and he seemed to know the score. After ninety minutes, he agreed to release all but Mrs. Darbouze.

"You've got a rookie cop in there with you," Mazza had advised Crespo over the phone. "He's liable to do something stupid. You've got the cashier. Why don't you let the cop and the hostages go."

The eight women walked past the racks of dresses and out into the street, and so did Officer Goggin—still clutching his service revolver. By not giving up his gun, he had prevented an escalation in Crespo's firepower and helped contain the situation.

Mazza continued talking; he arranged to have a pastrami sandwich and a cigar sent to the gunman. Mrs. Darbouze, who had suffered a miscarriage not long before, was at times calm, near hysteria at other times. Finally, Crespo agreed to have a "physician" (he was really a cop) examine Mrs. Darbouze at the front of the store. First, he asked for another cigar, and, as the first one had been, it was left partway in the store by

Mazza, who backed off so that Crespo could pick it up and then retreat.

Crespo brought Mrs. Darbouze to the door, holding her by the arm. Mazza approached the doorway to arrange for the supposed doctor to enter. Then the woman felt the gunman loosen his grip, and she heard him whisper, "Pray for me." Mrs. Darbouze darted for safety. Mazza pulled her away from the door. Crespo had disappeared from sight.

"Stand clear!" Bolz shouted. "He may be coming out!"

He wanted to reestablish contact, hoping to talk the gunman into a surrender. About ten seconds later, there was the crackle of gunfire.

"He did it!" an Emergency Service officer shouted, almost in disbelief. "He did it!"

Joseph Crespo had put the .38-caliber derringer to his head and blown his brains out. When police examined the gun, they discovered an empty chamber. There were no bullets in the store, except for the one that had passed through Crespo's skull and lodged in the ceiling. He had come to rob the store with a single bullet.

Officially, it was a suicide. For Frank Bolz and the negotiators, Crespo had become the first perpetrator in the five years of the team's existence to die during a hostage situation. "That second cigar," Bolz said, shaking his head back at the Claddagh that afternoon. "It was a suicide ritual. We just didn't spot it."

APPENDIX

What to Do If You Are Taken Hostage

Though there are no guarantees that the New York Police Hostage Negotiating Team can give to anyone who might fall victim to a hostage situation, there are some actions and lines of conduct that have appeared to be successful in helping captives cope with their given circumstances, giving them an optimum chance to emerge safely and without bodily harm.

1. *Don't be a hero. Accept your situation, and be prepared to wait.*

Any drastic action on the part of the victim might bring immediate violent action from the captor. Do not feel that you cannot accept what is happening. We tend to think that these things happen only to other people, those we read about in the newspapers or watch on TV news clips. Accept your situation and be prepared to wait for rescue. Time is really an ally, not an enemy.

2. *The first fifteen to forty-five minutes are the most dangerous. Follow instructions.*

The beginning of the incident is the most dangerous for all concerned. The captor is going through a highly emotional state during his initial confrontation with the authorities, regardless of whether he is psychologically unbalanced or a criminal caught in an untenable situation. He is in a fight-or-flight reaction state and may strike out at this time. Follow the instructions of your captor; do not hesitate. It's not like a prisoner-of-war situation where you only give your name, rank, and serial number. You are trying to stay alive. After the initial shock of the confrontation subsides, the captor is better able to handle his own emotions and recognize his position. After a period of as little as ten minutes, the phenomenon of transference, or Stockholm Syndrome, can start to develop, and under the influence of this he is less likely to harm you. You will not be able to avoid it. It is natural, and it is what has kept many hostages alive.

3. *Don't speak unless spoken to and then only when necessary.*

The captor will undoubtedly be in an agitated state and may not want any additional stimuli or conversation. If and when he does start talking, try not to appear hostile, but don't be overly friendly or phony.

4. *Try to rest.*

As soon as things settle down, try to get as much rest as possible without turning your back on your captor. Sit down if permitted and even try to doze off, if you can. (As unlikely as it seems, the negotiators have had to wake up hostages to release them.) Many hostage incidents have ended when the perpetrator falls asleep and the hostages just walk out. Remember, his anxiety will be high and he will be very perceptive, maybe even prone to perceive more than what is there. He may be able to fend off sleep for a long period of time, but eventually he will become both physically and psychologically exhausted.

5. *Don't make suggestions.*

If you make any suggestion to the captor, and he uses it and it goes wrong, he may think that you planned it and are trying to trick him. You may cause him to start to develop negative transference—identifying you as his enemy instead of just a bystander caught in the middle—which we don't want.

6. *Escape: Should you or shouldn't you?*

Don't try to escape unless you are absolutely sure that you will be successful. And even then, rethink it. If you are recaptured, the captor might use violence to "teach others a lesson." It's not unlike broad-jumping across a twelve-foot chasm. If you can make eleven feet nine inches, that's a great jump, but you still didn't make it.

7. *Special medication or aid.*

If anyone, including you, needs any special medical attention, inform your captors. Chances are they do not want anyone to die on their hands or they would not have taken hostages in the first place. Be matter-of-fact about it and wait for the response, but don't pester him about it.

8. *Be observant. You may be released or escape and can help the police.*

Try to remember everything that you see and hear. Memorize things about the captors, their descriptions and conversations. What names do they use or how do they refer to one another? What kind of weapons and other equipment do they have? What precipitated the takeover? Where are the hostages being kept? Has a routine been established in terms of eating and/or sleeping? Try to recall the number and identities or descriptions of the other hostages as well.

9. *Be prepared to answer the police on the phone.*

You may be permitted to speak on the phone. Be prepared to answer questions with yes or no responses. If the perpetrator is listening, try to advise the police by saying something like "Don't lie to us, because he can hear what you're saying." If what you are made to tell the police is untrue, try to make reference to some relative or factual incident in an incorrect manner which will indicate the duress you are under. You can tip the police off by saying, "My brother will handle the bills" when actually you do not have a brother.

10. *Don't be argumentative.*

Don't create agitation with the captors or other hostages; noncooperative attitudes in the past have brought harm to some hostages. The captor may perceive this as aggression toward him. Get along with the others.

11. *Treat the captor like royalty.*

Don't turn your back on your captor unless ordered to do so. But don't stare at him either. A "down the nose" look may bring a violent reaction. A captor is less likely to harm someone with whom he has eye contact.

12. *Be patient.*

Even though the police may seem to be doing nothing, they are engaged in a complete program geared to save your life and the lives of all involved as soon as safely possible. Be patient and prepared to wait.

13. *If a rescue comes . . .*

If you believe a rescue attempt is taking place, or you hear a noise or shooting, hit the floor and stay down. Keep your hands on your head and don't make any fast moves. If and when you are ordered out, follow directions quickly—again with your hands in the open. Be prepared when greeted by the police to be frisked. Their intelligence may be incomplete or incorrect, and you don't want to bring about an erroneous reflex reaction if you balk. Remember, it's nothing personal.

Again, there are no guarantees, but after researching thousands of incidents throughout the world, following guidelines such as these has kept many, many people alive.

Index

317